AUSTRALIAN NATIVE TITLE ANTHROPOLOGY

STRATEGIC PRACTICE, THE LAW AND THE STATE

AUSTRALIAN NATIVE TITLE ANTHROPOLOGY

STRATEGIC PRACTICE, THE LAW AND THE STATE

KINGSLEY PALMER

Australian
National
University

PRESS

ANU PRESS

Published by ANU Press
The Australian National University
Acton ACT 2601, Australia
Email: anupress@anu.edu.au
This title is also available online at press.anu.edu.au

A catalogue record for this
book is available from the
National Library of Australia

ISBN(s): 9781760461874 (print)
9781760461881 (eBook)

Cover design and layout by ANU Press

Contents

Tables and figures

Acknowledgements

I am deeply indebted to all of those with whom I have worked in Aboriginal Australia since I commenced research and fieldwork in the early 1970s. While this is not an ethnography of any Indigenous Australian group, but a study of the application of anthropology to native title law in Australia, I could not have written as I have without the benefit of my research and study with Aboriginal people over many years. While there are too many individuals to mention by name, I am particularly grateful to the people of Yandeearra in the Pilbara region of Western Australia who were my first mentors and guides and who introduced me to the richness and complexity of Australian Indigenous cultures. In particular, I thank the late Peter Coffin, Clancy McKenna and Sam Coffin who taught me so much. In subsequent years I worked in the Maralinga Lands and Yalata (South Australia), over many parts of the Top End including the Victoria River District (VRD), Galiwinku, Numbulwar and Groote Eylandt. Later, as a consultant, I worked in many areas of rural and remote Australia on native title claims lodged over areas of the southwest, southeast, Goldfields, Pilbara and Kimberley regions of Western Australia. In South Australia, I worked with claimants in the far west and remote northeast of the state. In Queensland, I worked with Indigenous claimants who had lodged claims to central, north-western and eastern parts of the state and in the Torres Strait. In the Northern Territory, I worked on claims in the VRD. To all of the many hundreds of claimants with whom I have worked, I express my thanks and appreciation for their generosity, patience and forbearance as I sought to understand their culture.

Some colleagues have provided comments, suggestions, information or pointed out errors for correction. Others have discussed native title issues with me in the course of our work together and I have benefitted from their perspectives and expert knowledge. All have contributed in some way to what follows, and I thank them all for their assistance. Mindful that I may have inadvertently omitted some who should rightly be listed below, I apologise, but a book written over several years owes acknowledgement to many and this list may not be exhaustive. In particular, then, I thank Jon Altman, Wendy Asche, Robert Blowes, Lyn Coad, Ambrose Cummins, Julie Finlayson, Sturt Glacken, Vance Hughston, George Irving, Ian Irving, Tina Jowett, Sophie Kilpatrick, Jonathan Kneebone, Justin Lincoln, David Martin, Dante Mavec, Pam McGrath, John Morton, Olivia Norris, Sandra Pannell, David Parsons, Nic Peterson, Susan Phillips, Ophelia Rubinich, Lee Sackett, Basil Sansom, Sheree Sharma, Peter Sutton, Sarah Thomson, David Trigger, David Turnbull, Amy Usher, Daniel Vachon, James Weiner and Stephen Wright.

I thank Lea Gardam of the South Australian Museum for facilitating permissions for the reproduction of the Tindale genealogy, which is Figure 9.1 in this book. In particular, I thank Uncle Lewis Yerloburka O'Brien for generously giving permission for the use of this genealogy.

I also thank two anonymous reviewers who took the trouble to read an earlier draft of this book and provide many helpful comments and suggestions, all of which I was pleased to consider and mostly adopt.

I thank Emily Hazlewood and the ANU Press staff for their many editorial amendments and suggestions, and for delivering this book in its present form.

Finally, I thank Catherine Wohlan for urging me to finish this book, and for her encouragement, many helpful suggestions, critical comments and corrections.

Introduction

This is a book about the practice of anthropology in the context of Australian native title claims. The *Native Title Act 1993* (Cth) established a means whereby Indigenous Australians can make application to the Federal Court for the recognition of their rights to the continental landmass of Australia and its islands and seas. Such rights were identified in the legislation as 'native title rights'. The application is subject to legal process. Those who make the claim (the applicant) have to prove to the court that the native title rights have continued to exist substantially uninterrupted since the acquisition of sovereignty over Australia by the British Crown. They also have to show that the native title rights have not been extinguished by subsequent acts of the colonisers. In this, the onus of proof lies with the applicant. Even applications that seek determination by the consent of the participating parties have to satisfy the Federal Court of the justice of their claim according to the *Native Title Act* and subsequent case law. Consequently, applications for the recognition of native title require that the case be prepared and the pleadings developed. Lawyers must draft the application under instruction from those who make the claim, typically a group of Indigenous Australians who lay claim to a common area of land. Legal counsel must prosecute the application and, should the matter not be settled by the parties prior to trial, the application goes to a hearing. In these regards, an application made to the Federal Court for a determination of native title shares much common ground with other applications brought to that court. Like much else that depends upon a judicial process for its resolution, a significant factor in the prosecution of a native title claim is the evidence that supports the applicant's case.

Indigenous testimony was and remains the most significant component of the evidentiary process of a native title claim. However, others have also been recruited to the process. Principal amongst these are anthropologists. The involvement of anthropology and anthropologists in the native title process marked a continuance of their professional involvement in Indigenous relationships with the state – and in particular with legislation and related legal action that sought to recognise the rights of the original inhabitants of Australia. By the end of 1993, when the *Native Title Act* received royal assent, anthropologists had clocked up a substantial record of involvement in processes that sought to codify the recognition of Indigenous rights in Australia. Anthropologists had seen action in relation to legislation enacted by state governments, including the *Anangu Pitjantjatjara Yankunytjatjara Land Rights Act 1981* and the *Maralinga Tjarutja Land Rights Act 1984*. But it was in relation to the *Aboriginal Land Rights (Northern Territory) Act 1976* that anthropologists had found substantial scope for the application of their discipline. The late 1970s and much of the 1980s saw their frequent involvement in the preparation and adjudication of claims in the Northern Territory. The transition from this sustained involvement of some members of the profession in the Territory's *Land Rights Act* to the *Native Title Act* was not altogether smooth, particularly following amendments to the *Native Title Act* in 1998. Anthropologists who had undertaken research on an application and whose views, data and opinions were provided to the court were subsequently subject to a level of scrutiny, examination and cross-examination not previously encountered. The uses of anthropology in a native title claim consequently required a very exact application of the discipline and its methods.

A need for the expertise of an anthropologist in advancing applications for the recognition of native title is a response to legal process. The court recognised that the questions it had to consider in relation to an application were not likely to be illuminated solely by common or popular knowledge or even wholly by the lay evidence of the claimants. Comprehension of the claimants' society and its normative systems, beliefs, customs, land law and customary rights were all complex matters that required expert explanation and exegesis. A good anthropologist had the necessary training and expertise to explain to the court and the respondent parties how these Indigenous systems worked. This was usually done by presenting data collected during fieldwork along with anthropological commentary and archival research in a report, which also served to provide a helpful ethnographic guide to the parties to the application regarding the claimants, their beliefs and practices and therefore to key elements of the application itself. As a consequence, then, anthropologists were called to give evidence as expert witnesses both as a result of their contributing research, but also because they were recognised by the court as having specialist knowledge that might be of assistance in coming to an understanding of the perdurance of laws and customs – a key aspect of the proof of native title. Respondent parties also appreciated the importance of having an expert to comment on the application, on the reports provided by the claimants' anthropologist and any other matters judged relevant. Native title was then and remains a dynamic and active business ground for Australian anthropologists with a knowledge of and expertise in Indigenous cultures.

Native title activity has engendered numerous organisations. Claims are lodged and managed on behalf of the claimants by bodies created by the *Native Title Act* and known as Native Title Representative Bodies (or colloquially, 'Rep Bodies'). These organisations soon found that employing one or more anthropologists was helpful and indeed necessary. The National Native Title Tribunal (NNTT), also created by the *Native Title Act*, formerly employed a number of anthropologists, although this has decreased over recent years and is now reduced to one.[1] In the post-determination era, Prescribed Bodies Corporate, set up to administer land over which native title had been recognised, also had need of anthropologists, while existing land councils also employed anthropologists who were likely to become involved in native title claims one way or another. Respondent parties to claims – particularly the state departments with oversight of the assessment of claims made within their state – also employ anthropologists, as do mining companies and others with an interest in native title applications. Added to this list must be consultant anthropologists who work by commission for the various groups noted above and who have typically worked on researching claims and writing expert or connection reports used to further the application before the court.

Figures on the numbers of anthropologists directly involved in the native title business are found in a study undertaken by David Martin in 2004. Martin provided an analysis of anthropologists engaged in the native title business, based on a sample of those who responded to a questionnaire that returned 55 respondents (Martin 2004, 9). Martin considered this to represent 'between half and two-thirds of the field of current anthropological native title practitioners' (ibid.). Martin is uncertain as to what might be the total number of those employed directly in the

---

1   Pam McGrath, research director, NNTT, pers. comm. January 2017.

field of native title, but noted that government as well as non-government agencies also employed some anthropologists. A more recent study by McGrath and Acciaioli (2016a) surveyed 433 Australian anthropologists and found that there are at least 135 anthropologists currently working in Australia who have some level of expertise in native title and land rights.[2] The authors accept, however, that they do not know how representative the results of the survey are. The survey also provided an analysis of the age, sex and qualification levels of the respondents, and other data. These findings were presented by the authors at the 2016 Australian Anthropological Society conference, but are not at the time of writing available in published form.[3]

While the actual number of anthropologists directly engaged in native title may be quite small, the issues raised in this book will be of interest to others who do not engage directly with the native title process. As a part of the practice of anthropology, native title has attracted the attention of many academics as the subject of debate, particularly over the issue of the nature of applied anthropology and possible prejudices such direct application might have to the integrity of the discipline – a matter to which I return in the first chapter of this book. Despite this debate or perhaps in part because of it, native title anthropology has become the subject of specialised courses within universities. Native title features as a part of curricula, either with a view to educating those who might wish to take up a career in the native title arena or as a part of an understanding and appreciation of the practice of the discipline of anthropology in Australia.

That anthropology has become a significant factor in the preparation and adjudication of both applications for the recognition of native title, as well as post-recognition management, is evident. But native title is, as this book will demonstrate, principally about law. Members of the legal profession are more numerous than their anthropological colleagues and their involvement in native title business is significant. The role anthropology has to play is one of the many issues a good native title lawyer has to consider in his or her prosecution of a native title case. Present indications are that native title claims are set to continue for a while yet – a matter I discuss in greater detail in the following chapter. Along with outstanding claims and those yet to be lodged is the relatively

---

2   I thank Pam McGrath for drawing my attention to this survey and the survey results and accompanying references.
3   McGrath and Acciaioli 2016b.

new question of compensation claimable under the *Native Title Act* (see Chapter 10) and the post-determination management of native title, particularly disputes (see Chapter 8).

These considerations all speak to an anthropology that requires an understanding of the particular application of the discipline to the native title questions. This is something that lies outside of mainstream anthropological teaching and accompanying texts. It is a specialist craft of anthropology and one that has to be learnt, studied and explored by would-be practitioners. What I have attempted to do in the following pages is to provide some guidance as to 'how to do native title anthropology', and I have done so in the context of the broader issues of the *Native Title Act* and its associated social and public policy considerations. Above all else, I have contextualised native title anthropology within the framework of the legislation and the law that determines how it is prosecuted and how it might be practised.

There is a growing corpus of writings available about native title and I refer to these books and articles in what follows. The principal and still significant contribution to the practice of Australian anthropology in relation to native title claims is that by Peter Sutton who published in 2003 *Native title in Australia: an ethnographic perspective*. Sutton's scholarly work continues to provide an essential reference for all involved in any aspect of anthropological research in native title and I have relied on his findings and commentaries in what follows. However, much has developed in the native title field since Sutton published his work, and he did not cover some issues which I regard as now essential to any consideration of the anthropology required for a native title claim. Alternatively, Sutton has covered some topics that I have not addressed directly. It is my intention that this book will extend the account of the application of the discipline of anthropology to native title questions and provide materials relevant to the developing jurisprudence that so strongly informs and sometimes defines native title research.

This book has evolved through my own practice of native title anthropology and my observations over some decades of the often recurrent issues that appear to inform anthropological contributions – or, as the case may be, fail to inform them. Because of this, it is a book that is written with the practice of anthropology by anthropologists in mind. This should in no way be understood to be restricted to those who have been commissioned by the applicant in a particular native title claim.

Anthropologists who have been commissioned by respondents should also find what I present in the following pages of interest. Thus, while one reading of the following chapters could be that they provide an outline of what needs to be considered in a native title report, the text could also be used by a respondent to provide an indication of omissions in a native title report filed by the applicant. Given the necessarily close working relationship demanded by native title between lawyers and anthropologists, I also hope that members of the legal profession will find what I have to write in the following pages of assistance. It may also help to dispel some of the misapprehensions that some members of the legal profession, including judges, have of the work of anthropologists and help to explain in relatively straightforward terms some of the issues that agitate our interest. While I hope that what I have written here will be of interest and assistance to lawyers, I have endeavoured to steer well clear of points of legal interpretation. It will be evident to all who have had any involvement in the native title process that the case law and the underlying statutes are never far away. Thus, a book about native title anthropology cannot be written without some appreciation of the law that defines it. I have done my best to ensure that what I have written in this regard is correct but I write as an anthropologist, not as one who has any training or pretentions in matters pertaining to the law.

For those who study native title in universities or through dedicated courses, this work should provide a useful handbook of the practical application of anthropology to native title. It may also provide an appreciation of this branch of applied anthropology in the context of the continuing debate about the uses of anthropology in the twenty-first century. This debate is not unique to Australia and the involvement of anthropologists and anthropology in Australian native title claims will also be of interest to those involved in the application of the discipline to the recognition of the rights of indigenous peoples in many other countries as well. A more general readership may find the first and last chapters of particular interest since they seek to contextualise and then review native title in terms of the broader canvas of postcolonial Australia. Chapter 8 may be of interest to anyone who has an interest in mediating disputes and the relationship between objective 'truth' and resolution of the different versions of it found in many areas of social interaction, including native title.

Writing about native title does require a certain structure since some topics cannot be properly discussed until others have been set straight. The order of Chapters 2–5 reflects this requirement. Other ways might be devised in order to satisfy the demands of orderly discourse, but the arrangement suggested here has worked for me in the past. In Chapter 2 I examine the society question – identified in the Yorta Yorta case as a key concept in the proof of native title. My own observation is that courts are less concerned with the society question than they used to be. However, it remains a fundamental question for native title anthropology: how can the claimants be understood to comprise a society, whose members entertain laws, customs and share normative values that have endured since sovereignty?

In Chapters 3 and 4, I look at how anthropology can best understand rights and duties exercised in relation to country in Aboriginal Australia. In particular, I am interested to chart, in outline at least, the manner in which the customary system of rights to country has been understood by earlier ethnographies and anthropologists. Later studies subsequently developed a more ecumenical view of the system that is likely to have been in evidence over most of the Australian continent and islands, including the Torres Strait. Chapter 4 looks at how rights might be understood to be exercised in practice, according to the normative systems in evidence, along with some of the topics that frequently emerge from the ethnography and field data that may have relevance to a native title claim. Chapter 5 extends and builds upon the previous chapter and I examine some of the principal elements of Aboriginal religious belief and practice that might be relevant to a native title report. This can only be regarded as a very partial account of an enormously complex and sometimes arcane subject. I spend time discussing the difficulties of conducting research work in this context, particularly with respect to hidden or secret categories of knowledge that are gender and age restricted.

Chapters 6, 7 and 8 tackle what I have come to regard as some of the thornier problems encountered while undertaking native title research. While courts generally privilege the evidence of the claimants above all else, there is an all too evident problem about the reliability of such testimony in relation to issues of continuity, which I explore in Chapter 6. Assertions along the lines that 'we have always done it this way' may resound with conviction, but in an increasingly critical legal environment may not withstand close scrutiny of the sort offered up by respondent parties. This becomes particularly acute should authoritative assertions be made in contradictory form by opposing Indigenous groups. Oral testimony, particularly as it relates to continuity since sovereignty, is a matter that demands attention. In this context, the use of early texts (Chapter 7) has direct relevance as these may provide a means to demonstrate whether a particular law or custom was in evidence in earlier times. Use of the early texts and their interpretation is not, however, a straightforward matter. It is my aim in Chapter 7 to explore some of the difficulties attendant upon the use of early texts and how these might be obviated.

Chapter 8 is about inter-Indigenous disputes, a phenomenon I have witnessed increasing over the last few years of my practice. Such contests of truth and will place the anthropologist in a difficult position and such situations must be navigated with skill and caution. Native title has undoubtedly exacerbated disputes between Australia's Indigenous people. It is worth noting in this context, however, that when a group of people are recognised as having no rights to landed property, the scope for disputes over country is necessarily minimal. Native title affords recognition of rights to property and the (perhaps) inevitable disputes that follow are a consequence of that restoration. In this context, anthropologists have a particular role to play and I have set out what I have termed a practice guide to applied research undertaken in these often difficult and vexing circumstances.

Chapter 9 might be regarded as providing a guide for a must-have chapter in a native title report. Genealogies are becoming increasingly important in native title research as a result of the more or less universal acceptance that rights to country are gained from forebears. Thus, issues of the descent of rights through a bloodline may overshadow other means of gaining rights, while the necessary conditions for the realisation of rights through descent may get lost as time and intention denude filiation to render it a matter of genealogical reckoning through the provision of a pedigree.

Chapter 10 takes a brief look at a developing field of native title research: compensation. Based on a recent decision of the Federal Court in relation to an application for compensation for the loss of native title rights, I have set out some preliminary views on the sort of anthropology that might be conducted in relation to future claims. This is a topic that might be developed as the jurisprudence matures.

This book represents a compilation of materials I have slowly assembled over some years. All chapters have been expressly written for this book. They contain elements of my research and findings gathered over many years working in Aboriginal Australia, both in the native title era as well as prior to it. Chapter 1 contains the seeds of ideas developed for a seminar paper I delivered with Wendy Asche to the North Australian Research Unit in Darwin in 2011. Chapter 6 builds upon a paper I published in 2011 (Palmer 2011a). A draft portion of Chapter 8 was presented to a native title seminar held in Perth in 2017, convened by the Federal Court of Australia, the NNTT and the Centre for Native Title Anthropology (CNTA) at The Australian National University, Canberra. Likewise, a draft portion of Chapter 10 was first presented to the CNTA annual conference in Perth in 2017. Some of the material contained in the following pages has seen the light of day, in somewhat different forms, as prior publications. An earlier version of Chapter 2 was first published by the Australian Institute of Aboriginal and Torres Strait Islander Studies (AIATSIS) in 2009 and later reproduced as a chapter in Lisa Strelein's *Dialogue about land justice: papers from the National Native Title Conference* (2010*)*. I have substantially revised and updated it for this publication. Some of the ideas set out in Chapter 7 were first entertained in a paper I gave to the Australian Anthropological Society conference, Macquarie University, December 2009, and subsequently published in Toni Bauman's *Dilemmas in applied native title anthropology in Australia* (2010).

1

Certainty and uncertainty: Native title anthropology in Australia

The promise

Recognition of native title in Australia opened a new chapter in a legislated history that helped define relationships between the state and Australia's Indigenous minority. It was a complex mix of political will, postcolonial idealism and necessity. Its genesis was the High Court's recognition of a right in the famous Mabo case.[1] For some at least the Mabo decision was seen as a problem. It was understood to throw uncertainty in the way of development by acknowledging in law that there had been prior owners of the Australian continent. Moreover, the rights of these original owners of the Australian continent continued to be capable of recognition by the very jurisprudence that had alienated much of the land upon assertion of sovereignty by the British Crown. Prime minister Paul Keating, in his second reading speech for the Native Title Bill 1993, highlighted the problem, which he also embraced as an opportunity. In the context of the International Year for the World's Indigenous People, the formation of the Aboriginal and Torres Strait Islander Commission and a Labor policy sympathetic to Indigenous needs and aspirations, this was part of the longer-term legislated approach to remedy past wrongs. But there was a difference to previous attempts to afford protection to Indigenous attachment to land or restore rights to alienated country. The

---

1   *Mabo v Queensland* [No. 2] (1992) 175 CLR 1 (HCA: Mason CJ, Brennan, Deane, Dawson, Toohey, Gaudron and McHugh JJ).

Native Title Bill was demanded by many as a means to ensure certainty in the face of doubts as to the legal status of land – assumed since first European settlement to be the secure property of the state and foreign settlers. Keating promised certainty in this regard.

> Mr Speaker, some seem to see the High Court as having just handed Australia a problem. The fact is that the High Court has handed this nation an opportunity. When I spoke last December in Redfern at the Australian launch of the International Year for the World's Indigenous People, I said we could make the Mabo decision an historic turning point: the basis of a new relationship between indigenous and other Australians. For the 17 months since the High Court handed down its decision, the government has worked to meet this challenge. As well as clearing up the uncertainties of the past, this bill provides for the future – it delivers justice and certainty for Aboriginal and Torres Strait Islander people, industry, and the whole community. It provides for the determination of native title and for dealings over native title land.[2]

Sites and rights

In Australia, the late 1960s and early 1970s saw an addition to the legislated direction of Aboriginal affairs. As a result of campaigning by some leading academics at the time and a growing awareness of Australia's Indigenous minority and its members' close associations and deep spiritual relationships with country, attempts were made to protect land as isolated pockets of special significance that might be cordoned off and protected. With such 'sites' identified, development could go ahead without impediment and, so it was hoped, would avoid the difficulties that developed from an increasingly aware and vocal minority. Examples of such legislation that remain on the statute books are found in most states and territories,[3] sometimes preceded by attempts to vest land in an

---

2   Paul Keating, Native Title Bill 1993, second reading speech (1993).
3   Australian Capital Territory: *Heritage Act 2004, Heritage Objects Act 1991.* New South Wales: *Heritage Act 1977, National Parks and Wildlife Amendment (Aboriginal Ownership) Act 1996.* Northern Territory: *Aboriginal Sacred Sites Act 1989, Heritage Conservation Act 1991.* Queensland: *Aboriginal Cultural Heritage Act 2003, Torres Strait Islander Cultural Heritage Act 2003.* South Australia: *Aboriginal Heritage Act 1988.* Tasmania: *Aboriginal Relics Act 1975.* Victoria: *Aboriginal Heritage Act 2006, Heritage Act 1994.* Western Australia: *Aboriginal Heritage Act 1972.* Copies of these laws can be downloaded from www.austlii.edu.au. Source: www.environment.gov.au/topics/heritage/laws-and-notices/indigenous-heritage-laws/protection-under-state-and-territory-laws, accessed 4 January 2017. Many of these Acts amend or replace prior legislation of which the South Australian *Aboriginal and Historic Relics Preservation Act 1965* was the earliest.

Aboriginal Land Trust to ensure its safekeeping for future generations. While site protection legislation mostly placed the onus on the developer to ensure that no damage was done to sites in the path of the work proposed, the legislation was framed with the idea of providing protection for relatively small areas, effectively isolating significant places from their broader spiritual and social contexts. Thus, the 'sphere of influence' of a site, as it was termed in the famous Noonkanbah dispute,[4] was difficult to define and was often cynically regarded as employed by Indigenous interests in an attempt to stretch the site-based legislation to accomplish political ends.

Site-based legislation endures across the Australian states and territories but its usefulness is limited by its fundamental concept and, of course, by the political will (or lack of political will) to uphold it. For the most part (but not without exception[5]), prosecutions in relation to site destruction have been insignificant, unsuccessful or not forthcoming. Site protection legislation was, in its fundamentals, a liberal, beneficial act of the state to stem or mitigate damage or destruction of culturally significant sites while ensuring that the business of expansion and exploitation of the land and its resources continued relatively unimpeded. The legislation did not confer rights on Indigenous owners or recognise prior ownership – it protected certain things as being culturally important, like other heritage legislation or natural resource legislation, but generally at the discretion of the relevant state minister. It was a useful way forward but did not address the fundamental problem of the neglect of prior rights to country.

What became known in popular discourse as 'land rights' for Australia's Indigenous people also had a long history and provided a far more radical solution than site protection. The term was not always as commonplace as it

---

4   The Noonkanbah dispute developed as a result of a petroleum exploration company, supported by the WA state government, drilling on an area of cultural significance to the Noonkanbah people of the Fitzroy River valley in the central western Kimberley region of Western Australia. The community strenuously opposed the drilling and blockaded the access road to prevent the company's convoy from reaching the proposed drill site. Police, sent by the state government to accompany the convoy, broke up the blockade and arrested protestors. These dramatic events and those that followed received both national as well as international news coverage. A full account of the Noonkanbah dispute was given by Hawke and Gallagher (1989). These writers stated that I first used the term 'sphere of influence' in relation to the spiritual imbuement of the countryside extending from a focal point when giving evidence to the Mining Warden's Court in Broome in 1978 (ibid., 119). As far as I know, the transcripts of this hearing have not survived.
5   In 2013, OM Manganese was fined $150,000 for desecration and damage to an Aboriginal sacred site at their Bootu Creek manganese mine on Banka Banka Station, 120 km north of Tennant Creek in the Northern Territory. Aboriginal Area Protection Authority press release, 2 August 2013.

is today. I recall meeting Aboriginal people in the Pilbara in 1973 in relation to my work under the *Aboriginal Heritage Act* of Western Australia – the 1972 state legislation that sought to protect sites across the state. When I made mention of the phrase 'land rights', I found it to be an altogether new phrase for those with whom I worked. By the middle of the decade, however, it was seen as a promise of better things to come. But the realisation of 'land rights', that is, the recognition of Indigenous rights to land, was initially limited to the Northern Territory. Here it had its genesis in the failed attempt to gain recognition of customary rights to the Gove Peninsula.[6] Eventually, the federal government initiated legislation in conjunction with the Northern Territory to recognise large areas of Aboriginal Reserve land (so-called Schedule A land) as the property of its 'traditional owners', which was given over as fee simple title. Other land had to be won in 'land claims', a commissioner being appointed to hear claims, which were heard rather like a court case and adjudicated by the commissioner who made his recommendation to the federal minister responsible.

Some other states and territories also enacted their own land rights legislation. In 1981, the South Australian Government passed the *Anangu Pitjantjatjara Yankunytjatjara Land Rights Act* which afforded recognition of Indigenous rights to land of the Anangu Pitjantjatjara Yankunytjatjara people in South Australia, but did not allow others in the state to make claim for rights to country. The *Maralinga Tjarutja Land Rights Act* followed in 1984 and gave recognition of ownership to land that included land adjacent to the former atomic test sites in the Maralinga area of South Australia. In 1983, the New South Wales Government passed the *Aboriginal Land Rights Act* and there was also land rights legislation passed in Queensland (1985 and 1991), Tasmania (1995) and Victoria (1989, 1991 and 1992).

Like site legislation, however, these acts of state and territory parliaments were driven by liberal notions of justice and a desire to attempt to right past wrongs. There was no implicit or explicit acknowledgement of a prior right existing in Australian law that had survived colonisation. Rather, they were beneficial legislated enactments, acts of favour not of right, by seemingly fair-minded governments.

---

6   *Milirrpum v Nabalco Pty Ltd* (1971) 17 FLR 141 (NTSC: Blackburn J).

The paradigm shifts

All this was to change dramatically with the case brought by the people of Mer (Murray Island) in the Torres Strait for the recognition of what was termed 'native title' for those who claimed the island, its reefs and waters as their own since time immemorial. The idea that Australia was devoid of owners when the Europeans arrived and started to settle its eastern shores in 1788 was encapsulated in the convenient fiction of *terra nullius,* which means simply 'void country'. The British Crown assumed ownership of the Australian continent because, so it was argued, it belonged to no one else. The Mabo case showed that the title assumed by the Crown was, in fact, burdened by an existing title. The concept of *terra nullius* was wrong in fact and wrong in law. There were owners and they had been dispossessed, a process effected by force of arms, audacity and, eventually, weight of numbers, legitimated by the false assumption that the Indigenous inhabitants did not own land, but rather wandered aimlessly across it in search of food and water. Mabo changed all that. The rights of these owners, in accordance with their laws and customs, in their traditional lands, had in this case, so the High Court of Australia eventually found, endured through the decades of colonial settlement and were still effectual and recognisable in law. Acknowledgment of the reality of native title meant that Indigenous rights to country did not necessarily need to be legislated back into existence by beneficial acts of parliament because on Murray Island at least they had endured. And what obtained in the Torres Strait might equally apply over many other areas of Australia as well.

The Mabo case was brought under common law and potentially laid the way open for other similar actions. While outcomes in the court might be uncertain and might not yield the same result for applicants as it had in the Mabo case, the events relating to a small island in the Torres Strait and the High Court's ruling in that regard had set a precedent that might lock up land for years to come. The resultant uncertainty might only slowly dissolve with a complex, evolving and uncertain jurisprudence. There was an additional problem that developed from the application of the *Racial Discrimination Act* that had been passed into law in 1975. One provision of the Act was to make it an offence to discriminate against a person on the basis of their race. Mabo brought with it the possibility that any grant of an interest in land by the state might, in fact, be burdened by a prior native title right. Thus, the grant might be compromised or invalid. In order that the state might continue to effect its dealings with the land of

Australia over which it had previously exercised an unfettered and assumed sovereignty, there had to be some remedy to this possibility. A legislated framework would allow claims for the recognition of native title, subject to the criteria for proof of continuity of that title since sovereignty by the British Crown. Such an arrangement would allow for certainty in matters relating to grants of an interest in land and so alleviate potential ambiguities that developed from the Mabo decision.

At first some voiced what was to become briefly a popular hysteria: that the sacred Australian quarter acre block upon which the family home was built was now in danger of being appropriated. Miners, developers and pastoralists saw the Mabo decision as a serious impediment to progress and the federal government also no doubt saw this, as well as what prime minister Keating called 'an opportunity'. The 'problem' created by Mabo could be resolved through legislation that provided the framework for the recognition of native title which would provide 'certainty' as well as the basis for 'a new relationship between Indigenous and other Australians'. Unlike the sites protection and land rights legislation discussed above, the *Native Title Act* was an act of necessity, forced upon the government by the Mabo decision. The aspirations of the liberal postcolonial state were not absent from this equation, as the 'opportunity' was an idealised means to improve the lot of Indigenous Australians and the relationship between the state and the original owners of the continent. However, this opportunity would not have been manifest had it not been for the legal and political necessity to enact the native title legislation.

In this regard one legal commentator has remarked:

> Statutory land rights, though, do not represent 'native title' in a technical sense: the former is created by parliament while the latter refers to an inherent common law right, the recognition of something already there, with origins not in the authority of the settler state but in pre-existing systems of law and custom. It is the difference between a right and a favour. (Ritter 2009, 3)

Validation and recognition

Given this background it is hardly surprising that the *Native Title Act* was a complex and extremely bulky piece of legislation. The Preamble to the Act stated that the legislation would provide for certainty and for the 'validation of those acts' previously performed by the Commonwealth.

It would also rectify the 'consequences of past injustices' and 'ensure that Aboriginal peoples and Torres Strait Islanders receive the full recognition and status within the Australian nation to which history, their prior rights and interests, and their rich and diverse culture, fully entitle them to aspire'.[7] But bolting down the framework for a post-Mabo certainty while furthering a human rights agenda was never going to be a simple process. Running to well over 500 pages, the Act set out a whole range of procedural matters and organisations for the recognition of native title and its subsequent administration. These included issues of extinguishment, proposals to undertake work or development on land subject to claim (known as 'future acts'), agreements, compensation, corporate bodies that would administer native title if recognised, representative bodies that would progress applications for recognition of native title, the role of the Federal Court and the creation of the National Native Title Tribunal (NNTT).

There was at the beginning an idea that native title recognition could be accomplished through consensus and mediation. The NNTT, as established by the legislation, originally had a key role in this and its members were charged with mediating disputes without recourse to the Federal Court, which was seen as the last resort. The NNTT also served to provide an administrative function, undertook research and provided information and publications relating to native title. The NNTT was responsible for the registration of a claim which provided advantages for claimants in terms of negotiation over 'future acts'; that is, proposed developments on land subject to claim.

The role of the NNTT was subsequently eroded and, at the time of writing, applications for recognition of native title, while subject to the registration test by the NNTT, are now matters for the Federal Court. Inevitably, then, their progress to determination in favour of the applicant or dismissal is likely to be one of litigation and trial, unless there is agreement between the state or territory and the applicants paving the way for a consent determination.

Hidden in the labyrinthine edifice that was the *Native Title Act* was the definition of native title, which provided the basis in law for what applicants for the recognition of law might have to prove before the court or the NNTT:

---

7   *Native Title Act 1993*, Preamble.

223 Native title

Common law rights and interests

(1) The expression **native title** or **native title rights and interests** means the communal, group or individual rights and interests of Aboriginal peoples or Torres Strait Islanders in relation to land or waters, where:

(a) the rights and interests are possessed under the traditional laws acknowledged, and the traditional customs observed, by the Aboriginal peoples or Torres Strait Islanders; and

(b) the Aboriginal peoples or Torres Strait Islanders, by those laws and customs, have a connection with the land or waters; and

(c) the rights and interests are recognised by the common law of Australia.

Hunting, gathering and fishing covered

(2) Without limiting subsection (1), **rights and interests** in that subsection includes hunting, gathering, or fishing, rights and interests.[8]

A finding that native title exists (a 'determination of native title') is defined as:

whether or not native title exists in relation to a particular area (the **determination area**) of land or waters and, if it does exist, a determination of:

(a) who the persons, or each group of persons, holding the common or group rights comprising the native title are; and

(b) the nature and extent of the native title rights and interests in relation to the determination area; and

(c) the nature and extent of any other interests in relation to the determination area; and

(d) the relationship between the rights and interests in paragraphs (b) and (c) (taking into account the effect of this Act); and

(e) to the extent that the land or waters in the determination area are not covered by a non-exclusive agricultural lease or a non-exclusive pastoral lease—whether the native title rights and interests confer possession, occupation, use and enjoyment of that land or waters on the native title holders to the exclusion of all others.

8　*Native Title Act 1993*, section 223.

Note: The determination may deal with the matters in paragraphs (c) and (d) by referring to a particular kind or particular kinds of non-native title interests.[9]

It was, then, very much a lawyer's piece of legislation and, from the start, a business directed and controlled by the legal process. Unlike the federal government's Northern Territory *Aboriginal Land Rights Act*, the native title legislation did not benefit from close and informed advice from anthropologists. Nor was it a development made in close consultation with Aboriginal people. The popular phrase 'land rights' used in other legislation was replaced by the arcane 'native title rights and interests',[10] which were 'possessed under traditional laws acknowledged and traditional customs observed' by those with a connection to the land (or waters) that are recognised by the 'common law of Australia'. Moreover, only rights that are 'in relation to land and waters' can be native title rights. While 'native title rights and interests' specifically included those relating to 'hunting, gathering, or fishing', there was no attempt in the legislation to accommodate Indigenous systems and criteria of proprietary rights to country as had been the case in the *Aboriginal Land Rights Act*. The legal concept of native title rights and interests did not invite or readily identify issues or avenues for research that were obvious to the anthropological endeavour. There were no terms here that were common to anthropology or, indeed, that recommended themselves as the subject of our research. The critical anthropological issues were going to be ones that were to develop over the ensuing court cases that identified for potential litigants the matters that the courts held essential to the proof of native title. It would require a close working relationship between lawyers and researchers in order that their inquiry would be relevant to the legal processes and court requirements.

---

9   *Native Title Act 1993*, section 225.
10   The difference between a 'right' and an 'interest' is seldom, in my experience, brought to notice. A right is a legal concept, denoting an advantage or benefit conferred on a person by the rules of a particular legal system (Walker 1980, 1070). Interests, on the other hand, are 'those claims, wants, desires or demands which persons individually or in groups seek to satisfy and protect, and of which the ordering of human relations in a society must take into account. The legal system of a country does not create interests; these are created or extinguished by the social, moral, religious, political, economic, and other views of individuals, groups or whole communities. The legal system recognises or declines to recognise particular interests as worthy of legal protection …' (ibid., 629). According to this distinction, then, a right is the realisation in law of an interest: a benefit secured into the future of a present aspiration. 'Interest' is defined in section 253 of the *Native Title Act* self-referentially: 'a legal or equitable estate or interest', 'any other right' and a restriction, all in relation to land or water. The phrase 'rights and interests' is common in the native title literature, presumably because of its privileging in the Act. But the two terms are seldom differentiated in practice.

Interests, rights and the Federal Court

It soon became evident that progress for recognition of native title would be neither rapid nor expeditious. The original ideal that claims would be mediated by the NNTT met with limited success and amendments to the Act slowly diminished its role. While the Federal Court has always had a central role in the determination of native title claims under Parts 3 and 4 of the *Native Title Act*, the Federal Court became the principal focus of any applications and was also then responsible for the progress (or lack of progress) of the claims before it. Codifying and giving legal recognition to Indigenous interests in land by defining them as rights was inevitably a matter for the Australian judicial system. There is some irony in the fact that it is now the Federal Court that is responsible for the determination of rights that had previously been regarded by the colonial and more latterly the Australian legal systems as non-existent, consistent with the doctrine of *terra nullius.*

A judge of the Federal Court, Dowsett J, made comment on the centrality of the courts in the process of recognition of native title. He acknowledged that there was common law recognition that Australia's Indigenous inhabitants, in accordance with their laws or customs, were 'entitled as against the whole world to possession, occupation, use and enjoyment' of their lands, subject to prior extinguishment. That proposition, he wrote:

> set the course for the development of Native Title in this country … This led inevitably to the result that disputes concerning the existence and extent of Native Title would be the business of the courts. By virtue of Commonwealth legislation, those matters are now within the jurisdiction of the Federal Court. It is the primary Native Title court.

The judge continued:

> It is for the Court to supervise every aspect of each case so as to bring it to trial at the earliest practicable time and to resolve it according to law. That role, in no sense, excludes the possibility, or probability, of the parties reaching agreement. However the Court cannot properly leave the matter to the parties, or to anybody else, to resolve in their own time. The public, as well as the parties, have a clear interest in the speedy resolution of all litigation, including Native Title litigation. (Dowsett J 2009)

The declared fact that the 'court cannot properly leave the matter to the parties, or to anybody else, to resolve in their own time' asserts the status quo. Aboriginal Australians who seek recognition of native title are committed to be players in a legal process conducted according to alien rules and subject to uncertain outcomes in terms of gaining legal recognition of a native title right. It is true that native title law remains rooted in the recognition of prior right. However, the codification of that common law right into a legislative form, justified on the ground of providing 'certainty', has emasculated the ability of potential rights holders to gain recognition of those rights within the very system that was responsible for their first (and eventual) recognition under the common law of Australia.

The concept of native title in Australia brought with it the notion of continuity and discontinuity. Native title was capable of recognition only where there was a continuing system of laws or customs to support it. Moreover, native title had not survived the colonial settlement unscathed. Indeed, acts by the settlers and their legislators had emaciated the native title of Australia's Indigenous and original owners. Thus, native title was understood to exist where it had not been extinguished – that is, freehold and some leasehold and reservations for particular purposes rendered native title gone. Consequently, the family home was safe for the majority of Australians whose land was held as freehold, a fact that slowly cooled the initial hysteria over claims being made to people's backyards. Native title had survived on what was called 'Crown Land' that had not been granted by the state for any particular purpose and co-existed on most pastoral properties and some reserve land.

In time it became apparent that the *Native Title Act* did not confer land rights on Australia's Indigenous minority but rather set a relatively high bar for them to attempt to prove that their rights had not been extinguished or languished into oblivion. This had implications for how the claims, or applications for the recognition of native title, would be run. Apparent surrender of rights that had been assumed by parties who had since the time of sovereignty believed them to be unencumbered was not going to happen without a fight. Principal amongst the opponents of native title were those who considered they had most to lose from loss of rights to non-extinguished land – the states, the mining interests and the pastoralists. Under section 84(4) of the *Native Title Act* the states or territories were automatically a party to a proceeding, unless choosing not to join the matter. The Commonwealth was also entitled to intervene (section 84a). This meant that the role of the states and territories in court hearings was of fundamental importance and they took their role seriously, claiming they had a duty to challenge native title applications made with respect to land within their jurisdiction.

Most set up a review process to gauge 'connection' and so took the lead in evaluating claims, a role they have sustained. 'Connection Guidelines' were written with a view to providing guidance as to how connection materials should be presented. In this way, states and territories also became a *de facto* judiciary dictating the terms whereby a claim might be considered settled by 'consent', and if states or territories accepted 'connection' it was likely that other respondent parties would too. The object of this quasi-judicial evaluation was the evidence of the claimants, to the extent that it could be presented via affidavit or other 'connection' material as well. The views of the applicant's anthropologist were set out either as a connection report (to reflect the 'Connection Guidelines') or as an expert report, a manifestation of a court process relating to expert witnesses and forensic anthropology. This too was subject to scrutiny and evaluation. At least one Federal Court judge has been critical of this approach, finding that the states have at times assumed a judicial role that was never intended for them in the *Native Title Act*.[11] The assumed role might have the potential to prejudice the role of the Federal Court in the determination of native title, as set down in sections 87 and 87a of the Act. Anthropologists were not only operating in a highly contested field, but according to rules and conventions that lay far from their academic comfort zone.

Statistics on the numbers of outstanding claims are out of date almost before they have been garnered from the internet in a publication of this sort. However, the reader can check the statistics for him or herself at the time of reading this chapter at the NNTT website,[12] although web addresses seldom stay valid for long. By way of providing some idea of the situation, I have collected some data published by the Tribunal in November 2011 and compared it with similar figures published in June 2014 and again in January 2017. The table below shows these figures set alongside each other for comparative purposes.

---

11   'The power conferred by the Act on the Court to approve agreements is given in order to avoid lengthy hearings before the Court. The Act does not intend to substitute a trial, in effect, conducted by State parties for a trial before the Court. Thus, something significantly less than the material necessary to justify a judicial determination is sufficient to satisfy a State party of a credible basis for an application.' North J in *Lovett on behalf of the Gunditjmara People v State of Victoria* [2007] FCA 474 [37] to [38]. See also North J in *Hunter v State of Western Australia* [2009] FCA 654 [22] to [25].
12   The website current at the time of writing was www.nntt.gov.au/Pages/Home-Page.aspx, with a link to 'Statistics' on that page. However, the categories of the statistics provided by the Tribunal have changed over the years.

Table 1.1: Claims lost and won, 2011 to 2017

	November 2011	June 2014	March 2017[1]
Active native title applications	485	412	316
Finalised applications: native title determined in whole	66	92	315
Finalised applications: native title determined in part	65	142	
Finalised applications: no native title	41	59	63
Finalised applications: discontinued, struck out, dismissed, withdrawn, rejected or pre-combination	1295	1125	

[1] While the NNTT provides statistics available through its website, the categories for which data are provided are not consistent with past data sourced from the same site. Thus in January 2017 finalised applications for recognition of native title in whole are not disaggregated from finalised applications for recognition of native title in part. Data for applications discontinued, struck out, dismissed, withdrawn, rejected or pre-combination are not available.

Source: National Native Title Tribunal: www.nntt.gov.au.

In a period of just over two-and-a-half years between November 2011 and June 2014 the number of 'active' claims was reduced from 485 to 412, which is a reduction rate of approximately 30 claims per year. For the period of just over two-and-a-half years between June 2014 and January 2017 the number of 'active' claims was reduced from 412 to 316, which is a reduction rate of approximately 38 claims per year. Assuming that this increased rate of progress is sustained, it will be another eight or so years before all claims are finalised. Claims determined in whole or in part by January 2017 amount to 314, or a little over 14 a year for the 23-year period since the Act come into effect. The failure rate represented by the row 'Finalised applications: no native title' indicates only those applications that were not accepted by the court, indicating perhaps that should a claim go to court it has a reasonable chance of success. This is probably because lawyers are reluctant to expend the enormous funds required to bring a case to trial unless they consider they have at least a reasonable chance of success. The seemingly high figures of 'finalised applications' are variously described as 'discontinued, struck out, dismissed, withdrawn, rejected or pre-combination', being applications removed as a result of court decisions, technical problems or combining existing claims into a single new claim. Whatever the reason, these claims are not those that resulted in a positive determination of native title. This gives some indication of the complex web of the legal process and counter process that typifies much native title dealing in the court. This statistic is not available in the 2017 listing.

However these figure are read, it seems most likely that native title will exercise the attention of the Federal Court, the NNTT, Indigenous representative bodies and all the lawyers as well as the anthropologists who service them for some time to come yet.

The native title we had to have

In the initial essentialities that accompanied the decision of the High Court in Mabo, there was no necessary compassion or the conferral of the benefit of doubt. The finding of a native title right to Murray Island was a truth born of the common law and a matter settled according to the facts as the court had found them, subject to the rules that govern the Australian legal and judicial process. The consequential 'uncertainty' that accompanied this landmark decision drove the matter into the political domain. The ambiguities that faced the Keating government of 1992–96 gave them little choice. The fundamentals of British sovereignty and Australian dominion had been challenged by the Mabo decision. Prospective common law claims threatened the status quo while application of the *Racial Discrimination Act* meant that grants of land might be invalid or compromised. The final form of the *Native Title Act 1993* that passed through the parliament was a product of the political environment of the time. It was, as one legal commentator has it, a:

> product of petitioning, alliance-building, negotiation and compromise that in the end and for diverse reasons was supported by Labor, the minor parties in the Senate, most Aboriginal leadership, the Labor-held state governments and the National Farmer's Federation, but opposed by the Liberal and National parties, the Minerals Council of Australia, the states held by the centre-right and the government of the Northern Territory. (Ritter 2009, 5)

The legislation reflects the truth of Otto von Bismarck's reputed comment that 'laws are like sausages – it is best not to see them being made'. Like many terms of settlement, this was the last act of war rather than the first act of peace. Legislative amendments have continued that war of attrition. The state, territories and representatives of mining interests and primary industry are accepting of the legislation because it is now accommodating of their interests and, some would argue, loaded in their favour. This is why there is now but muted discussion of any further amendment and no political will on either side of the political divide to discuss native title law. Subsequent acquiescence to the state's demands for connection, substantial amendments, and the ever changing and seemingly compromised jurisprudence, now make this law that prescribes uncertain outcomes. For claimants, the way that involves least risk of failure is achieved through mediated agreements: deals done with the state as a result of their benefaction, indulgence and the granting of favours. This may also mean significant compromise and loss of rights, just as has been the case with many other acts of favour that have sought to protect, bestow advantage or right past wrongs.

Adding the anthropology

I have set out this brief potted history of the development of native title in Australia in the context of its legislative and political origins because it represents a field of inquiry that has significant keynotes. Native title is a perverse and conflicted field noted for its complexity and professional pitfalls. For anthropologists it brings immediate contact with much that is alien and the risk of damage and harm. This field of endeavour represents significant challenges for the practice of anthropology. After the initial and, with the benefit of hindsight, misplaced enthusiasm on the part of anthropologists for involvement in native title, the decisions of the Federal Court started to make their mark. I think it is fair to say that, for some of us involved in those early native title applications, we regarded the venture as being little different to claims made under the Northern Territory *Land Rights Act*. This was certainly true for aspects of the Miriuwung and Gajerrong[13] native title application as advanced in the Northern Territory portion of the claim. The court was not hostile to the aspirations of the Indigenous witnesses and the anthropology was fairly basic. However, the failure of the Yorta Yorta case, then Wongatha case,[14] and the later dismissal of the Jango compensation case[15] were sobering reminders of the complex nature of native title claims, their dangers, pitfalls and the vulnerability of anthropologists and claimants in the process. For anthropologists, to be involved in a native title proceeding is to be involved first and foremost in a legal context, boxed in by a legislated

---

13   *Ward v Western Australia* (WCD2006/002–Miriuwung Gajerrong #4), WAD124/2004. Determined 2006, FCA 1848.
14   *Members of the Yorta Yorta Aboriginal Community v Victoria* (2002) 214 CLR 422 (HCA); *Harrington-Smith on behalf of the Wongatha People v State of Western Australia* (No. 9) [2007] FCA 31.
15   *Jango v Northern Territory of Australia* (2006) 152 FCR 150 (FCA: Sackville J).

framework and subject to a judicial process. If an application ends up at trial, the anthropologist becomes a witness and subject to lengthy and at times disconcerting cross-examination. The *Native Title Act* and the developing jurisprudence that has emerged over the two decades since 1993 is one replete with non-anthropological concepts and definitions. It is as though there is now a whole new vocabulary that anthropologists must learn when researching and writing native title, which must then be accommodated within the theoretical and epistemological framework of the discipline. Thus, phrases like 'laws and customs', 'rights and interests', 'substantially uninterrupted', 'normative system' and words like 'society' and 'continuity' gained technical legal meanings that were not always amenable to anthropological analysis or even identification. To do native title anthropology was to attempt to straddle a divide between the law and the discipline – a divide that appeared to become bigger as the case law evolved (Glaskin 2017, 84–85).

Despite these difficulties, I think that it was never a realistic option to exclude anthropologists and anthropology from the native title process. At the heart of the proof of native title was the ability of the law to recognise an Indigenous system of law. The system whereby rights to country had been sustained and perpetuated in times past had been the subject of much anthropological analysis in Australia, particularly since the late 1950s. The academic contributions in this field, which I will discuss in later chapters of this book, were influential in both the Gove case and the drafting of the Northern Territory land rights legislation that followed. That stated, understanding how an Indigenous system of rights to land worked as both a religious process and a political undertaking was complex and likely not to have been uniform across the continent. Native title inquiry demanded a proper understanding of the particulars of this system relevant to the application area in question. Anthropology provided some insights that aided a gaining of this understanding. However, it was an understanding that had to accommodate the requirements of the *Native Title Act* and the constraints of the Australian legal system and the jurisprudential heritage from which they were descended. It was not and could not be simply a scholarly enterprise that sought to comprehend an Indigenous system that was part of another culture through the lens lent to it by the discipline of anthropology.

This disjunction was compounded by the sheer difficulty of the requirements of the burden of proof laid upon the applicants. For native title to have survived, it had to be demonstrated that the laws and customs of the relevant group or society had remained substantially intact since sovereignty. This back-dating of the evidence meant that anthropologists had to attempt to recover past systems and social formations. The only way to do this was to explore the diaries of early explorers, the journals of early European settlers and comb the later works of the early anthropologists. These, so it might be argued, recorded at least some aspects of the customary systems. Anthropologists generally work with the present and observe what goes on around them, rather than attempt to work out how things might have been in former times. The task, then, for anthropologists was challenging and was one for which the profession was largely unprepared. There was no obvious heuristic framework and little theoretical underpinning that would assist the manner in which these tasks might be accomplished. Yet, it became clear as native title progressed that the court would expect anthropologists to set out their views in this regard with authority and submit to rigorous testing through cross-examination in the witness box.

Native title as the recognition of a prior right is inevitably subject to dispute. Such contestation is not limited to debate between the state and Indigenous Australians, but extends to disputes between parties, including Indigenous groups, who are not in agreement as to who should be recognised as holding the native title right or being included in the group that is recognised ultimately by the court as doing so. This has led to overlapping claims and disputes between Indigenous parties that find their ultimate expression before a judge of the Federal Court. Being an anthropologist in the crossfire that typifies these disputes can never be expected to be a rewarding or welcoming experience. This contested environment is also one deeply informed by Indigenous values, systems and ways of holding rights to country that are subject to scrutiny by the court that seeks to determine whether they have endured, fundamentally unchanged, since the time of sovereignty.

Finally, and perhaps no new thing for the profession of anthropology, the development of native title opened up old wounds in the profession between the academy and those involved in the practical application of the discipline, often referred to as 'applied anthropology'. Practitioners in the native title field were accused[16] of prostituting their profession in

---

16   See Trigger 2011, 235–240 for a review of criticisms of applied anthropology advanced by a number of anthropologists including Bastin and Morris (2004), Cowlishaw (2003, 2010), Kapferer (2000), Lattas and Morris (2010a, 2010b) and Morris (2004).

favour of a legal system that determined outcomes, defined research practice and paradigms and narrowed the field of inquiry and, so the argument ran, the subsequent advancement of knowledge. Some said that applied anthropologists were complicit in imperial hegemonic process. While this is not a matter I tackle in any detail in this book, it is nonetheless an additional complexity in the anthropological endeavour and one which has coloured debate and no doubt influenced those considering a career in applied anthropology in native title work in Australia.

An ensuing defence in the literature characterised the involvement of anthropologists in the native title process – as well as in earlier times in the *Aboriginal Land Rights Act* – as legitimate applications of the discipline (Morphy 2006). Trigger (2011) provided a summary of the applied anthropology debate and refuted derogatory views about applied anthropology, particularly in native title contexts. He argued that rather than diminish anthropological clarity and focus, communicating findings to members of different professions and disciplines made for a better discourse and removed anthropologists from their 'intellectual comfort zone among colleagues' (ibid., 245). Sackett, an anthropologist with many decades of experience in the applied field, recognised in his native title work a requirement to base conclusions of facts transparently stated so that 'persuasion flows from opinions based on proof, not artful footwork' (2006, 7).

This is a book about the uses of anthropology in native title claims in Australia. The complexities and challenges I have outlined above raise issues for our practice and counsel the development of methodological and theoretical approaches to our inquiry. Some of these are novel while others may require a difference in emphasis and a reassessment of focus. The discipline needs a better tool kit to undertake complex research in difficult and overly fraught environments. The series of essays that follow examine some of the more important of the issues I have identified over the years of my practice as a native title anthropologist. Given the inherent complications, the seemingly alien operating environment and the potential to get burnt in the process, it is not a field for the faint-hearted. However, if anthropology is to be useful, then it also has to be relevant. It is my hope that what follows will contribute to some extent to the furthering of this need.

2

The society question[1]

Of proof and process

In native title cases an anthropologist is generally asked to bring data to bear on a legal proposition (though usually more than one) relevant to the points of claim and provide an expert opinion developed from field data, prior ethnography or perhaps the paradigms of the discipline more generally. This is not inimical to the orthodox practice of anthropology but it is both more narrowly defined and focused. Consequently, this is not the same as undertaking an anthropological study ('doing anthropology'), which is more open ended and may have an indeterminate destination, being variously a study of process or structure, change and meaning or a combination of two or more of these. Given that the understandings of a culture that develop from 'doing anthropology' are likely to be relevant to the opinions required by the lawyers, it is helpful to come to an understanding of the structural relationship between anthropology and the law. While the application of anthropology to the legal matter develops from the doing of anthropology, the two represent distinct fields of operation, with different parameters and theoretical underpinnings. In understanding this, we can come to an appreciation of the reasons why there may appear to be disjunction between 'doing anthropology' and the use of skills developed in that discipline to provide opinions to a court that will have status as expert testimony.

---

1   An earlier version of this paper appeared as Chapter 9 in Lisa Strelein's *Dialogue about land justice* (Aboriginal Studies Press, Canberra, 2010). It has here been revised, updated and expanded.

Getting involved with native title anthropology is, then, not simply about learning the process or developing an appreciation of the jurisprudence that defines the questions that we should address. It is also about understanding the nature of the interface between anthropology and the law and the ramifications that develop as a result of fundamental epistemological differences between the law and anthropology. The dissonance between anthropologists and the application of their science in native title inquiries develops from differences between the characteristics of the former and the demands of the latter. At the heart of this difference is the nature of the process whereby anthropologists seek to describe and understand social process (relationships, meanings) and a legal process that seeks evidence (testimony, statements, expert views) to support or deny that a particular criterion or requirement has been met. The former sees social process as occurring through time and defies absoluteness; the latter tests propositions at a point in time and requires a concluded view. The former stresses change and mutability, the latter stasis and immutability. It follows, then, that the gathering of data and comprehending them as social science, on the one hand, and meeting the requirements of the legal system with respect to the uses of anthropology as expert opinion in native title inquiries, on the other, are quite different activities.

The juxtaposition of law and anthropology is nowhere as immediate as when respective practitioners are required to develop an understanding of words that have attracted a special privilege, status and consequential meanings in both discourses. One example is the use of the terms 'society' and 'community'. These are both legal terms (derived, in this case, from native title law but not statute) that are fundamental to jurisprudential thinking. They are also terms of anthropology. The words and the ways whereby they come to have different meanings provide a point of departure for this chapter. I consider below how anthropologists might best accommodate terms that are words of law rather than of anthropology, while bringing their anthropology to bear on the subject at hand.

Native title society

In native title inquiries, the term 'society' has a meaning that is determined by jurisprudence rather than anthropology. The decision of the High Court with respect to the application made by members of the Yorta Yorta Aboriginal community provides the usual reference point for discussion of legal ideas about the centrality of a society to the concept of the perdurance of native title rights.[2] It also raises critical issues about the nature of the society, as required for native title law, at sovereignty, and a consideration of the relationship of the society at sovereignty to that of the claimants.

In the judgment of the High Court, the relationship between the continuity of laws and customs, and rights to land or water and the society, is set down:

> If that normative system has not existed throughout that period, the rights and interests which owe their existence to that system will have ceased to exist. And any later attempt to revive adherence to the tenets of that former system cannot and will not reconstitute the traditional laws and customs out of which rights and interests must spring if they are to fall within the definition of native title.[3]

The judgment then sets out how the relationship between laws and customs and the society is to be understood:

> To speak of rights and interests possessed under an identified body of laws and customs, is, therefore, to speak of rights and interests that are the creatures of the laws and customs of a particular society that exists as a group which acknowledges and observes those laws and customs. And if the society out of which the body of laws and customs arises ceases to exist as a group which acknowledges and observes those laws and customs, those laws and customs cease to have continued existence and vitality. Their content may be known but if there is no society which acknowledges and observes them, it ceases to be useful, even meaningful, to speak of them as a body of laws and customs acknowledged and observed, or productive of existing rights or interests, whether in relation to land or waters or otherwise.[4]

The judges of the High Court found as a consequence that in a native title proceeding:

> it will be necessary to inquire about the relationship between the laws and customs now acknowledged and observed, and those that were acknowledged and observed before sovereignty, and to do so by considering whether the laws and customs can be said to be the laws and customs of the society whose laws and customs are properly described as traditional laws and customs.[5]

---

2   *Members of the Yorta Yorta Aboriginal Community v Victoria* (2002) 214 CLR 422.
3   ibid., [47].
4   ibid., [50].
5   ibid., [56].

The 'society' provides the medium for the articulation of the relationship between the people and the laws and customs of that group. There is, then, a nexus between the 'society' and the laws and customs of its members.[6] An implication of this is that if the society ceases to exist then its laws and customs, while they might be recalled, are not meaningful.[7]

> Law and custom arise out of and, in important respects, go to define a particular society. In this context, 'society' is to be understood as a body of persons united in and by its acknowledgment and observance of a body of law and customs.[8]

In another native title decision (largely in favour of the applicants), Weinberg J quoted one of his colleagues as helpful in defining a society. He also went back to the Yorta Yorta case:

> The concept of a 'society' in existence since sovereignty as the repository of traditional laws and customs in existence since that time derives from the reasoning in Yorta Yorta. The relevant ordinary meaning of society is 'a body of people forming a community or living under the same government'–Shorter Oxford English Dictionary. It does not require arcane construction. It is not a word which appears in the NT Act [*Native Title Act*]. It is a conceptual tool for use in its application. It does not introduce, into the judgments required by the NT Act [*Native Title Act*], technical, jurisprudential or social scientific criteria for the classification of groups or aggregations of people as 'societies'.[9]

His Honour asserted that for the application of native title law the common English sense of the term 'community' is what is relevant. 'Arcane construction' (the likely province of an expert perhaps?) is not only unnecessary but would involve application of criteria 'foreign' to native title law.

His Honour Merkel J was less critical of potential experts but made it clear as to what was required. Merkel J wrote, in relation to the Rubibi claim, that the Yawuru applicants made claim for the recognition of native title as a community:

---

6   ibid., [49].
7   ibid., [50].
8   ibid., [49].
9   *Northern Territory v Alyawarr* [2005] 145 FCAFC135 [78], quoted in *Griffiths v Northern Territory of Australia* [2006] FCA 903 [513].

As stated above, the Yawuru claim is a claim for communal native title rights and interests as it is claimed to be made on behalf of a community of people, namely the Yawuru community as defined in the application. The Yawuru claimants, relying on *Members of the Yorta Yorta Aboriginal Community v State of Victoria* [2002] 214 CLR 422 ('*Yorta Yorta*') at 439 [29], 444-445 [47] and 445 [49], claim that the Yawuru community is a body of persons united in and by its acknowledgment and observance of a body of traditional laws and customs. Those traditional laws and customs are said to constitute the normative system under which the rights and interests claimed are created.[10]

In other judgments I have read, the term 'society' is used freely, but to convey the sense that it comprises those who share cultural commonalities and adhere to the same system of laws and customs. For example:

In 1838 there was an established Aboriginal society close to the western boundary of the claim area (Glenelg River). It was an organised society, the members of which built structures and adorned their environment with paintings including Wanjina paintings, made artefacts of wood, and used stone to crush and grind seeds and to shape into spearheads.[11]

In native title law, according to one authority, 'society' is chosen over 'community' because the former serves to emphasise 'this close relationship between the identification of the group and the identification of the laws and customs of that group'.[12] Presumably this differentiation is drawn from the ordinary English use of the terms, rather than from anthropology. Conversely, anthropologists might use the term 'society' for larger, complex groupings – I provide some general examples of this in the next section. The term 'community' is sometimes used for smaller groups characterised by closer social ties and interaction and the typical subject of anthropological inquiry.[13] The point is simple. Legal meanings and those of the social sciences show no automatic correlation.

In summary, there is a consistent legal view that a community has to be recognisable, because the laws and customs (the normative system) of its constituents unite members through joint or common observance. While

---

10   *Rubibi Community v State of Western Australia* (No. 5) [2005] FCA 1025 [18].
11   *Neowarra v State of Western Australia* [2003] FCA 1402 [61].
12   Strelein 2009, 101.
13   An example is a paper by S. Holcombe (2004, 163–184). The author shows that the term 'community' has a 'deep genealogy' in the social sciences.

it is not stated, it would be a reasonable assumption that those people who did not share these laws and customs, but observed others, would constitute a different society or community.

The identity of the pre-sovereignty claimant society is thus of fundamental importance to any consideration of the continuity of laws and customs, rights and interests. Getting to grips with the idea of a 'society' in a native title claim is then an essential first step in planning the way in which the case is to be presented and adjudicated. Strelein has commented:

> The need to establish a coherent and continuous society defined by a pre-sovereignty normative system creates enormous ambiguity in the requirements of proof. The nature of the group has emerged as a fundamental threshold question for native title claimants. The High Court's deference to the views of the trial judge in *Yorta Yorta* demonstrated the vagaries of an assessment based to a significant degree on a judge's perceptions of the group. ... Native title claimants must rely on the ability of a non-Indigenous judiciary to conceptualise the contemporary expressions of Indigenous identity, culture and law as consistent with the idea of a pre-sovereignty normative system. (Strelein 2009, 80)

In considering these matters, the court is also likely to have regard to the evidence of experts. Since no first-hand evidence can be adduced as to the nature of the society at sovereignty, the court must rely on experts to provide a view in this regard – though a court may draw inferences from the evidence of Indigenous witnesses as well. In determining the nature of the contemporary society the court is also likely to need the assistance of an expert, since the concept is a product of law not of Indigenous culture.

While the jurisprudence has moved toward a broader rather than a narrower understanding of how a society might be constituted and manifest, the native title society remains a starting point when defining the customary content of the claimants in any native title application. In this a good starting point is to consider a society for the purposes of a native title claim as being 'a body of persons united in and by its acknowledgment and observance of a body of law and customs'. While, as I noted above, the terms 'society' and 'community' are often used interchangeably, it is best to pick one and stick to it, examining the facts to see if the members of an applicant group can be shown, on the ethnographic evidence, to recognise the mutual observance of laws and customs and adhere to a common normative system. Members of a society should be shown to have an internal correlation of laws and customs such that its members can be understood, in the common sense of the word, to be members of a single 'society'. It is not necessary for a member of a society to know all other members of that society or to expect to interact with all others. Neither is it necessary for all members of a society to live in peace and harmony, since the sharing of laws and customs does not mandate concord. Constituent groups of a native title society may exhibit different cultural traits – including speaking a different language or dialect – and occupy or are customarily associated with distinct areas. This is a matter that has been subject to some debate by anthropologists (e.g. Palmer 2010b) and is a fundamental question for native title (Strelein 2009, 80, 98). In 2010, judges of the Federal Court[14] considered some of those aspects of 'law and culture' that had been held to provide grounds for concluding that the Bardi and Jawi constituted separate societies. These included such things as language (dialects),[15] self-referential terms,[16] country of association[17] and the circumstances of each native title application.[18] The judges concluded:

> Thus, in our judgment the linguistic evidence, the evidence of distinct territories or the existence of self-referents was not sufficient to displace the inference from the wealth of other evidence that the Bardi and Jawi people were a single society at sovereignty.[19]

The judges make reference to a number of other cases where this broader view of a society has been accommodated.[20]

In a more recent decision,[21] Finn J wrote that the evidence supported the conclusion that groups inhabiting the Torres Strait islands comprise a single society. His Honour likened the body of laws and customs (following the anthropologist Professor Beckett) to a quilt of united parts.[22] His Honour recognised there to be a relationship between the operation of the component island groups.

---

14 *Sampi on behalf of the Bardi and Jawi People v State of Western Australia* [2010] FCAFC 26.
15 ibid., [68].
16 ibid., [69].
17 ibid., [69].
18 ibid., [71].
19 ibid., [75].
20 ibid., [72] to [74].
21 *Akiba on behalf of the Torres Strait Islanders of the Regional Seas Claim Group v State of Queensland* (No. 2) [2010] FCA 643.
22 ibid., [490].

The laws and customs which regulate the internal (or 'domestic') workings, relationships, etc. of each island community largely replicate those of other communities though not entirely or in all respects. The communities themselves are linked each to the others not only by these largely common 'domestic' laws and customs, but also by common laws and customs which govern the relationship of one community's members to the members of another, both within and beyond the former's own land and waters.[23]

Societies are often made up of component subsets that may also need to be identified in native title anthropology and it is important not to conflate the parts with the sum of the parts. Thus, the term 'group' may serve to identify any component subset of the society.

Anthropological society

Social scientists in Australia have used the terms 'society' and 'community' without specialist sense to mean a set of people who can be grouped together because of shared cultural attributes. For example, the term has been used in the title of a few books and articles that examine Aboriginal topics. Ken Maddock had *A portrait of their society* as a subtitle to his 1974 book *The Australian Aborigines* (Maddock 1974). C.D. Rowley (1980) wrote a classic account of *The destruction of Aboriginal society*. More recently, Ian Keen (2004) has used the term 'society' in the title of his book *Aboriginal economy and society* as well as from time to time in the text without defining it. It is not included in his glossary of terms. However, the meaning is, to my mind, evident from the context (ibid., 2–5).

The term 'society' as used in the examples cited above provides, then, a useful concept rather than a specific one. It has the facility to convey a meaning that implies a group of people who together have things in common. This might include cultural practices, language and beliefs. However, it does not provide for a very tight or exact definition of what might be meant and therein lies its usefulness perhaps for those who have chosen to use it. Should this use be not understood for the shorthand it probably is, the use obfuscates important distinctions in the way anthropology understands the nature of social groups.

---

23   ibid., [490].

Generally, a 'society' for an anthropologist is not a 'thing' but comprises sets of relationships (Beattie 1964, 34–35). Beattie counselled that thinking of 'society' as a thing, like a frog or a jellyfish, was 'more embarrassing than useful' (ibid., 56). He argued that it was essential to jettison any analogy with an organism in order to focus on the relationships that exist between people who thereby recognise commonalities (ibid., 58–59).

Michael Herzfeld, in what he described as 'an overview of social and cultural anthropology', told us that at the beginning of the twenty-first century, 'one thing is for sure: the attempt to abolish uncertainty has failed' (2001, 133). He cited the 'most obvious victim' of this uncertainty as being 'the idea of the bounded human group – the "society" or "culture" of the classic anthropological imagination' (ibid.). Earlier, he cited Arturo Escobar who wrote, 'societies are not the organic wholes with structures and laws that we thought them to be until recently but fluid entities stretched on all sides by migrations, border crossings and economic forces' (ibid.).[24]

These views reflect a trend that typifies anthropology and its interest in understanding diachronic relationships and meaning, developed over time, through social process, rather than a science based on synchronic and structural classification. More recent anthropology has, according to Weiner (2007, 154), been 'dominated by social constructionism in its own "strong" voluntarist version – that, as agents, human beings make their own world consciously and deliberately'. This manner of understanding social process as construction and agency through time is in marked contrast to the idea of a society as a relatively stable and discretely modelled entity.

Based on some of the legal views cited above ('repository of traditional laws and customs'), it would appear that in law a society is indeed a thing. In anthropology, on the other hand, it is made up of sets of relationships, changing through time, defying reification and certainty. Herein, then, lies a fundamental point of difference.

---

24   Herzfeld provides no citation for this quotation, although he provides references to five of Escobar's works in the bibliography.

Aboriginal society

In Australian Aboriginal studies, terms like 'nation', 'community' and 'tribe' abounded, particularly in the early literature as early ethnographers sought to identify the building blocks (sets of relationships) that constituted Aboriginal society (or societies). For example, R.H. Mathews published a map in 1898 showing what he determined to be different cultural blocs, based on difference in types of initiation rituals as he had collected them from his correspondents (1898a). Mathews went on to publish several additional similar accounts (1898b, 1898c, 1898e, 1900). Mathews was not alone in this endeavour. Howitt (1904, 41) defined nations by reference to the terms used for 'man' by its constituent members, while Bates also mapped 'nations', inventing names for them and relying on kinship, social categorisations and totemism[25] to identify groups that she considered to share cultural commonalities (e.g. 1985, 39–61). Many of these 'nations' would be much larger in the extent of their country and constituent membership than most native title applications today.[26]

These early accounts are of importance in native title research since establishing a view as to the continuity of a social formation (a society) must rely, to a considerable extent, upon the accounts provided by early ethnographers. Those assisting or assessing an application for native title are likely to go to this early literature to see what was said about the society in question at or about the time of sovereignty.

Anthropologists writing post-1950 generally did not use the term 'community' and the word fell out of favour. Two exceptions are Meggitt (1962) and Hiatt (1996), which were discussed by Sutton (2003, 99–107). R.M. and C.H. Berndt (1993, 19) dismissed the term 'nation' on the ground that its use implied a degree of political unity that was never apparent. The word is not much found in the Australian anthropological literature today, although it has found its place in the vocabulary of some contemporary Indigenous political discourse.

Applications for recognition of native title have used a variety of different models of society as a means of establishing the parameters within which laws and customs were held in common (see Strelein 2009, 98–

---

25   I discuss the meaning of this word in Chapter 5, under the heading 'Religious beliefs'.
26   Peter Sutton has reviewed these and other attempts to map 'nations' and his account may be of interest to those seeking additional information on the subject. See Sutton 2003, 42.

105, 123–125). Peter Sutton (2003, 88) took the view that there were several kinds of Aboriginal groups that could be defined in relation to land. He observed that a choice in how a claimant community was to be defined reflected the reality of 'different landed entities' that would yield 'a number of overlapping "territories" for the same population' (ibid.).

Sutton also noted that there were different sorts of Aboriginal 'community': he identified two, one defined in relation to geography, another defined in terms of the relationships of its members (ibid., 89–92). Each was different and neither necessarily comprised members who were the same as members of a native title community – that is, a group who together shared rights in the same country. By this account, then, not all 'communities' will be relevant to a native title application. For the anthropologist there is choice in how the word will be applied. There is no absolute 'community'. The anthropologist needs to ensure that the sort of community chosen is relevant to the group understood to have customary rights to the application area.

The two-fold question in relation to any native title claim, then, is which sort of 'landed entity' is to be chosen and how broad a compass does its collective interest in land circumscribe?

It is not my intention here to review and categorise the types of society that have been presented in native title applications, even if this were practical. However, there are some sorts of societies that can be regarded as models and may provide useful starting points for the definition of the native title society in a particular claim. For the most part they relate to models that might be applicable to larger rather than smaller-scale social formations. All would appear to me to be anthropologically defensible in terms of meeting the requirements of a society for the purpose of a native title application.

Modelling society

Cultural bloc

The concept of a 'cultural bloc' as an aggregation of constituent tribes or other groups has been the subject of a number of early studies, including Radcliffe-Brown, who was interested in expansions of 'social solidarity' beyond the range of the local group (Radcliffe-Brown

1930–31, 445–455; Sutton 2003, 46). Similarly, Roth (1897, 41) characterised larger aggregates in Western Queensland as 'messmates', united by the use of mutually intelligible languages, 'bonds of comradeship', endogamy and cooperation in times of war.

Sutton reviewed other accounts that provided evidence of aggregations or 'nations' (2003, 92–98). In the context of a discussion of both Mathews and Howitt, Sutton (2003, 95) stated that the early accounts support the view that there were regional aggregations with substantial cultural commonalities:

> Certain extensive areas of south-eastern Australia, for example, were characterised by a widely reported classical complex in which were to be found matrilineal moieties, sections, matrilineal unlocalised social totems, single linguistic groups numbering several thousand (not just a few hundred people), a *bora* (sacred ceremony) type of initiation system, emphasis on site-bound increase rites, a prominent religious and social role for the medicine-men of high degree who were able to fly, a belief in an 'All-Father' figure located in the heavens, fragmentary evidence of primary recruitment to country through birth or, possibly, conception and, probably, a system of individualised life-time site or tract tenure resting on an underlying communal estate title system.

Sutton also noted that some later writers attempted to identify regional aggregations in relation to drainage divisions (ibid., 96; Peterson 1976, 50–71).

The 'cultural bloc' is sometimes associated with the Western Desert region. In 1959, R.M. Berndt published an account of local organisation for some Australian desert regions, suggesting that the term 'tribe' was 'not entirely applicable' (Berndt 1959, 104). Instead, he suggested that the use of a common language, with dialect variations, resulted in 'a common awareness of belonging to a cultural and linguistic unit, over and above the smaller units signified by these [dialect] names' (ibid., 92). Berndt identified such a group as a 'culture bloc' (ibid., 84). Berndt suggested that within the culture bloc was a 'wider unit' 'formed seasonally by members of a number of hordes coming together for the purpose of performing certain sacred rituals' (ibid., 104). These wider units would have changed composition over time and the degree of interaction would have been variable. There would not necessarily have been a consistency of horde membership of a 'wider group' (ibid., 105). He concludes:

> One might expect to find a number of these [wider groups] throughout the Western Desert, with some of their members interchangeable from time to time … Each one of these might be termed a society, with the main criteria being, (a) sustained interaction between its members; (b) the possession of broadly common aims; (c) effective and consistent communication between them. It is suggested, therefore, on the basis of material presented here, that it is more rewarding to speak of Western Desert societies, rather than ambiguously of tribes. (ibid., 105)

For Berndt, the Western Desert cultural bloc was made up of a number of societies – it was not a single 'society' in the sense that he used the term. The characteristics he ascribed to a society do not clearly equate to the characteristics of a society of native title law. The societies were both labile and ephemeral, so lacked corporate attributes and were social rather than land-holding groups. 'Broadly common aims' is the closest we get to any idea that the members of such a society might share laws and customs – although their social interaction might imply that they do.

In a later paper the same writer was to apply this concept to a non-arid region which he called the 'northeastern Arnhem Land bloc' (Berndt, R.M. 1976, 145–146). This identity was marked by a 'local recognition of a broadly common culture', an acceptance of dialect variation constituting a common language and acknowledgement of 'mythic' relationships – that is, relationships that existed between constituent groups or individuals that developed from spiritual ties between themselves, the land and each other (ibid.).

Berndt's comments on tribes and societies provide a useful introduction to what is, to my mind, a more problematic concept and one that Berndt found unhelpful, at least for Western Desert societies. I refer to the word 'tribe', which occurs with depressing frequency in native title discourse.

Tribe

The idea of the tribe lies deep within the popular psyche and has dogged much debate about local organisation and society, often without discrimination. Indigenous societies, it seems, must be made up of tribes, reflecting I think some arcane perception that employment of the term readily identifies Australian Indigenous systems, matching stereotypes of 'exotic' peoples in Africa or South America. If there was one word that should be banished from the native title discourse – published, unpublished, spoken or written – it should be the term 'tribe'.

Unfortunately, use of the term is not confined to lawyers, state bureaucrats and the occasional anthropologist. Claimants commonly press an identity by reference to a 'tribal name' and define their country by reference to a tribal territory. Such arrangements are not, as I will explain below, founded on customary systems of social or local organisation. Rather, they represent a telescoping of prior local interests into what is sometimes an undifferentiated whole, managed by reference to contemporary corporate structures that typify the administration of Aboriginal Australia at a regional or local level. Because of these canards 'tribes' are sometimes misrepresented as land-owning corporations, which (to the extent that the term might be used of customary systems in Aboriginal Australia) they were not. As a model for a native title society then, the concept of the tribe provides for more pitfalls than it does advantages, but it may have some facility if employed with definitional clarity and caution.

The term 'tribe' retains popular currency, in part as a result of Tindale's 1974 map and, to a lesser extent, because of subsequent reincarnations by Horton (1994) and others. There has been an assumption, common in lay thinking, that a set of language speakers may form a discrete community with an internal political structure that merited the appellation of 'tribe'.[27] Thus, the name of a spoken language becomes a 'tribal' name. A corollary of this is a view that the 'tribe' was the maximal territorial unit, whose members together held a defined area of land in common. There was also an assumption in much early Australian anthropological literature that this model was generally applicable.[28]

Anthropologists in Australia have not always been in agreement as to how best to characterise Indigenous societies in terms that can be shown to have empirical validity. This is a consequence of the fact that the social units that comprise Aboriginal groupings are not easily or simply identified. It is likely that within what was a hunting and gathering society there were several ways by which people identified, according to activity (economic, ritual or regional) as well as by reference to kin relationships. This multiplicity of referents presents a problem if a single unambiguous identity is sought. Moreover, some aggregations are likely to have been labile and so would have changed composition over time, providing an obstacle to the identification of enduring social formations.

---

27   For a comprehensive summary of this issue, see Rumsey 1993.
28   See, for example, Elkin 1945, 22ff.; Tindale 1974, 30–33.

The assumptions and preconceptions about Aboriginal political organisation are particularly common in the early Australian literature. They developed from conjecture that a 'native' society would take the form of a named 'tribe', with little or no understanding of the variety of social formations and the multitude of names applied by Aboriginal people themselves to social and regional groupings. For many early writers, a 'tribe' was explicitly or implicitly understood to comprise a community of people, with a classifying name, whose members spoke the same language and adhered to a system of government that included a chief or leader. In early (and, indeed, in some later) ethnographies, the use of a name to identify the 'tribe' was, then, a convenience born of a preconception that obfuscated a more complex reality. In any event, unless the term 'tribe' was being used in a narrowly defined sense, the field data did not support the existence of 'tribes' in the popularly understood sense of the term, as later writers were to show.

As far back as 1938, Davidson, who also provided an early example of a 'tribal map', stated that the largest political unit in Aboriginal local organisation was what he termed the 'horde'.[29] He understood:

> Larger groupings are recognised and named by the natives on the bases of dialect and cultural similarities and geographical contiguity. These larger units, which furnish a more practical basis for ethnological considerations, can be spoken of as tribes in spite of the fact that there is no semblance of centralized political authority nor any sense of political confederation. (Davidson 1938, 649)

For Davidson, then, the use of the term 'tribe' was a convenience, the term used to identify groups whose members recognised 'dialect and cultural similarities', furnishing a practical basis for 'ethnological considerations'.

For the native title anthropologist it is generally a short journey to Norman Tindale's classic map of Australian tribes, published in 1974. The Tindale map and its accompanying text has provided the basis for countless native title application boundaries and is often referred to by claimants and lawyers alike in justification for their claim. I will have more to say about Tindale's work in Chapter 7, when I examine the use of his 'tribal' materials in native title research and some of the difficulties

---

29 Generally later called the 'local descent group' (Berndt 1959, 102–103) and also called the 'country group' (Keen 2004, 277, Sutton 2003, 54–66).

that have developed as a result of his lack of clarity in relation to social groupings which have become prominent points of reference in the native title debate.

Tindale's characterisation of 'tribes' and 'boundaries' was examined in detail by Monaghan in a thesis presented in 2003. Monaghan sought to understand the extent to which Tindale's representations were in fact the result of his theoretical preoccupations and his ideas of linguistic and racial purity. While the focus of Monaghan's study was on areas identified as 'Pitjantjatjara', his arguments are relevant here.

> Tindale effectively reduced a diversity of indigenous practices to ordered categories more reflective of Western and colonial concepts than indigenous views. Tindale did not consider linguistic criteria in any depth, his informants were few, and the tribal boundaries appear to a large extent to be arbitrary. (Monaghan 2003, xi)

Monaghan counselled against accepting Tindale's research findings, 'at face value, as lawyers, anthropologists and linguists have done in the past' (ibid.).

Early ethnographers had found 'tribal' names to be sometimes 'vague' (e.g. Mathew 1910, 128) and boundaries to be drawn without 'exactness even on river frontages where land is most valuable' (Curr 1886, xviii). The indefinite nature of boundaries in Aboriginal local organisation has been remarked upon by a number of anthropologists, including Warner (1937, 18), Stanner (1965, 11), Hiatt (1965, 16), Peterson and Long (1986, 55) and Williams (1986, 83). Other writers have also pointed out the difficulties and errors of 'tribal' models. As mentioned above, R.M. Berndt had questioned the applicability of the term to Western Desert societies in 1959 (Berndt 1959, 91–95). Rumsey provided a helpful critique of the use of the term 'tribe' and exposed some of the assumptions related to its unquestioned use, particularly with respect to the relationship to both a single language and territory (1993, 191–195). Rumsey was of the view that the misconception regarding tribes is still current (ibid., 191), a conclusion which I think cannot be much in contention. 'Tribes' are well represented in NNTT research reports that reproduce maps produced by linguists (and others) – of which there would appear to be many, showing 'tribal' territories drawn onto maps by means of boundary lines. This would appear to confirm my view that 'tribes' are regarded by at least some of those involved in native title research as a valid unit in defining customary native title groups. This stems from the lingering popular misconceptions about 'tribes' in Aboriginal Australia.

Since the 'tribe' was not a political entity, it could not have a bounded territory. The territorial regime was, as Davidson pointed out, a matter for what he called the 'horde' or local group. Boundaries were a product of the assertion of rights by members of these groups. Where several groups recognised linguistic commonalities, it seems reasonable that boundaries might also be conceptualised in language-group terms, especially in a regional context. In some cases it is evident that language was imputed into country by reference to both place names and myth, further enhancing the association of language and country. However, it is not the case that this is only by reference to one language (ibid., 201–204). From my own experience, this process was not universal and was (and is) more strongly marked in some areas than others.

Some years later Ian Keen wrote:

> Many early ethnographers assumed that Aborigines were divided into relatively large and discrete 'tribes', each of which shared a common language, culture, and territory. This model survived through the first two-thirds of the twentieth century, adhered to, with variations, by Radcliffe-Brown, Elkin, Tindale and Birdsell … the tribal model had begun to unravel more than a decade before Tindale published his book and maps of Aboriginal tribes in 1974. (Keen 2004, 234)[30]

Keen noted that the early ethnographer Howitt wrote of 'mixed' language group areas and that some marriages took place between people of different language varieties, making their children, presumably, in his view, of mixed language identity (ibid., 149). More recently, researchers (in Queensland) have demonstrated that the relationship between language, social identity and community is complex (ibid., 134–135). People tend to be multilingual (or to speak several dialects of the same language), people sometimes marry those from other language or dialect groups and this language, while important, could not be seen alone as a diacritic of group membership. The formation of an identity also involved references to a locality or a relative appellation, like 'northerner' or 'coastal dweller' (ibid., 135).

---

30 See also Howard (1976, 17–19) for a similar view.

While accepting that much of the early literature casts Aboriginal social life and culture in terms of discrete 'tribes', Keen concluded that 'several critiques have cast doubt on the validity of a cellular model of Aboriginal society' (ibid., 6). With respect to the named 'tribal' groups that were the subject of his analyses, he warned, 'it should not be assumed that these names refer to societies or localised "social systems", especially given the degree of heterogeneity of both ecologies and cultural forms documented for some regions' (ibid.).

Defining what might constitute a 'society' or a 'community' in terms of the account of 'tribes' will need to accommodate these difficulties and avoid these obstacles. This is not to say that a 'tribal' model is not sometimes helpful. However, designation of a 'tribal group' cannot, of itself, assume commonalities of law, language and culture. Conversely, a society could comprise more than one 'tribe', since laws and customs transcend the territorial boundaries of country groups and commonly traverse a number of different language groups.[31]

Language groups

Given that 'tribes' are problematic for anthropologists, the characteristics of a group of people that have been labelled a 'tribe' might provide for a more profitable line of inquiry. Language spoken or used as a characteristic of group membership can be a useful tool in defining a society for the purposes of native title. In so far as a language group corresponds to the old fashioned notion of a 'tribe' there are likely to be ethnographic references resting on assumptions of 'tribal' unity to support the representation of the society as a relatively unified body of people.

Language variation, however, is an issue that has to be addressed in such cases. Pertinent questions include whether dialect variations are a means of asserting difference and what is the Aboriginal understanding of similarity and difference in this regard. Analyses effected by linguists can be misleading in cases where languages are shown to be technically similar, and so classed together, while social and political difference between speakers marks substantial difference. Conversely, there are instances where

---

31   There are examples of successful native title applications that have included members of more than one language-speaking group. See, for example, *Ward v Western Australia* (1998) 159 ALR 483, *Neowarra v State of Western Australia* [2003] FCA 1402, *Griffiths v Northern Territory of Australia* [2006] FCA 903 and *Watson on behalf of the Nyikina Mangala People v State of Western Australia* [2015] FCA 1132.

languages that are technically classed as being quite different are regarded by multilingual speakers as being much the same. Linguist Bill McGregor made relevant comment on the nature of linguistic classifications in this regard. Writing of the Kimberley, he distinguished between technical classification and how a speaker of a language understands the relationship between his or her own language and that spoken by another.

> It should be noted that speakers may classify languages quite differently from linguists, and may perceive similarities on the basis of cultural affiliations over and above formal resemblances of either typological or the genetic type, which are the basis of linguists' classifications. (McGregor 1988, 97)

Linguists and others have also made a distinction between language-speaking groups and language-owning groups (Walsh 2002, 233). The distinction between an ability to speak a language and being regarded as an owner of the language was first made over 35 years ago by Peter Sutton and Arthur Palmer (Sutton and Palmer 1980). In short, the former group are characterised by members who speak the language in question; the latter group by those who consider they are associated with a language name, but who do not themselves necessarily speak the language. It is, however, something that they consider they own and thus is a cornerstone of their common identity. This distinction is obviously of importance for many areas of Australia where a traditional language is no longer spoken. I find the use of the phrase 'language group' to be a convenient way of identifying those who claim commonality by reference to an ancestral language (often no longer spoken except as isolated words). Language groups, so understood, are a significant feature of the native title landscape and it is rare to be involved in a claim that does not have one or more language groups as core components of the concept of the society of its constituent members.

Cultural cohesion

A fourth model for a society is one characterised by close kinship, ritual and economic links, perhaps in relation to a unifying geographic feature, like a river or drainage system. Such an arrangement would not preclude the use of different languages, as multilingualism would be a necessary feature of the population's skill set where the society was comprised of speakers of more than one language. One such example was *Griffiths v Northern Territory of Australia* in the Timber Creek area. In his judgment

Weinberg J accepted that five discrete country groups, representing two different language groups, constituted the society whose members together held native title in the application area.[32]

Likewise, Sundberg J, in a determination of native title in the northwest Kimberley region of Western Australia, found that a number of groups together made up a community bound together through observance of a number of laws and customs. These were clearly enunciated in evidence.

> The body of evidence in pars [162]–[322] shows that the claimants regard themselves as part of a community inhabiting the Ngarinyin, Worrorra and Wunambal region. Throughout the evidence there is an emphasis on shared customs and traditions that transcend any particular dambun or language area. Central to this sharing is the belief in Wanjina; that Wanjina impressed themselves on the landscape, principally in painting sites. Wanalirri, though in Ngarinyin country, is regarded throughout the claim area as the source of the laws and customs laid down by Wanjina. This belief extends beyond the borders of the claim area into the claim region. The Wunggurr tradition also extends across the claim area and beyond, as do other practices and customs: moieties, the marriage rules, wurnan, wudu, rambarr, traditional burial, dambun and kinship rules. The evidence collected earlier is inconsistent with any description of the group or groups that hold the native title rights other than those who are members of the Wanjina-Wunggurr community.[33]

The Wanjina–Wunggurr community is substantially larger than the Timber Creek society, although the principle of recruitment would appear to have much in common. The commonalties that the groups were held to exhibit by the judges in question relate to the same sort of cultural beliefs, practices and norms as were outlined for regional aggregations by Sutton (see subsection 'Cultural bloc', above) and is perhaps a contraction of the regional aggregation model, which I also noted at the same reference above.

The application of models

Native title law requires recognition of a defensible society or community – one that is anthropologically viable in terms of both contemporary practice and past ethnographies. Thus, the proper society for an application

---

32   *Griffiths v Northern Territory of Australia* [2006] FCA 903 [6], [377].
33   *Neowarra v State of Western Australia* [2003] FCA 1402 [386].

must be founded upon a reasonably argued expert view that such a body of persons were united through observance of common laws and customs in the past.

The models I have discussed above may provide a basis for developing an idea of a community or society. It is possible that no single one will match the ethnography, and the final construct will be an amalgam of parts of more than one. A 'society' is a group (or body) of people who recognise themselves and are recognised by others to share commonalities developed and expressed through actual or potential social relationships. In this, they identify themselves as having more in common with their fellows than they do with others who may be differentiated as 'strangers'. Cultural commonality is underpinned by the observance of common laws and customs. Other factors may also play a part, but not invariably. For example, members of a society may use the same language (or dialects of the same language), or be multilingual, utilising a suite of languages with varying degrees of proficiency. Members may also feel themselves to be united by social bonds and recognise kinship links by reference to classificatory as well as consanguineal reckonings.

I have set out above some of the choices for a 'society' that have anthropological credibility. These have the potential, given the right supporting data and evidence, to have relevance to a consideration of native title. However, finding a fit between what might be a native title society or community, however understood, for the purposes of the *Native Title Act*, and a society or community defined by reference to the available ethnography, presents a challenge for anthropology. There are three reasons for this.

First, for anthropologists unqualified terms like 'community' or 'society' invoke a number of different and sometimes conflicting referents. This is true generally in relation to the discourse of the profession, which counsels strict definitional use of the words. It is also true in relation to Aboriginal studies in particular where many different terms have been used, without consistency, for different types of social formation – real or imagined. As Sutton has pointed out (2003, 88), this may afford some flexibility and choice over the type of social formation identified as apposite in the context of a native title application. On the other hand, the form of the society used to characterise the claimant community needs to be robust and defensible, clearly defined and substantiated by the field data. In short, anthropologists need to do a proper job in their application and definition.

Second, demonstration of continuity of a society necessarily relies upon ethnographic reconstruction. While the early ethnographic accounts for some areas of Australia are many, quality and reliability are both questionable.[34] This is a consequence of assumptions made by observers about 'tribal' organisation and other groupings, their often inconsistent use of terminology and the manner in which their data were collected – mostly at arm's length and second or third hand.

Given substantial difficulties in developing reasonable reconstructions of social formations, expert views about correlations between a contemporary community of native title holders and that likely to have been in evidence at the time of first sustained European settlement will be qualified. Moreover, they will, at least potentially, be subject to criticism on the ground that the contemporary society has little or no correspondence with that developed from the early ethnography. Again, the anthropologist needs to be aware of this potential difficulty and ensure that it is addressed in his or her account.

The third issue relates to scale. As a general rule, the smaller a society, the more likely will be the uniformity of observance of law and custom. Conversely, the larger the society, the greater the likelihood of internal variation. In the case of a clearly bounded society, discontinuity is identified as a boundary. Such is the case, for example, with the so-called 'circumcision line' that Tindale drew on his maps.[35] The line purports to show a discontinuity of a cultural practice (a law) within geographic space. On one side of the line people practised circumcision, on the other they did not.

Such a boundary is necessarily a cadastral and cartographic construct. It has the intention of demonstrating the incidence of cultural practice in geographic space, at least in general terms. At the boundary of two distinct societies there would be a defined representation of difference. However,

---

34 Sansom has disagreed, arguing in relation to the Yulara ethnography that 'earliest sources are best' (2007, 79). It was a view challenged by some other anthropologists (Burke 2007, 164; Glaskin 2007, 167; Morton 2007, 172).
35 See, for example, N.B. Tindale 1940a and 1974.

social space is not always so clearly bounded.[36] In an arrangement where aggregations of groups recognise commonalities between themselves and their near neighbours, bounded cultural space as a recognition of cultural correlation is going to be a function of relative proximity. In such a case, distinctive commonalities would diminish gradually across space. At opposite ends of a spectrum would be those who understood one another to be observers of different laws and customs while those at various intervals in between might appreciate more or less difference, a greater or lesser degree of correlation.

The question then is this: at what point, for the purposes of a native title application, is cultural dissonance tantamount to disunity and the admission of two or more different societies? Were this the case there would be two (or more) sets of laws and customs relating to rights in country, resulting in different groups of rights holders for the same country. Again, these issues must be addressed in any expert anthropological view, although, as I explore below, issues of cultural process sit with some difficulty with many aspects of the native title legal process.

Anthropology and law: disjunction or snug fit?

An essential task for the court – or for the state if it is considering the acceptability of an application for a potential consent determination – relates to a necessity that certain criteria have been met. This is, like any matter of proof, a question of examining whether requirements set down in statute and encased by judgment can be understood to have been attained. In this activity, evidence is judged (by the court or by another set of persons) either to have satisfied those conditions or not. While native title law can accommodate the notion that things have not stood still in relation to the form and structure of a society over time, the essentially synchronic process of adjudication remains fundamental to the enterprise.

---

36   Indeed, Bates tells us that, along the line that marked the circumcising people of the southwest of Western Australia from the neighbours to the north and east, 'On the borders of this line, right through to its north-western point, the local groups appear to become mixed' (1985, 45). See also Palmer 2016, 76.

I noted above, in my discussion about the extent of a society, that forming a view of commonalities can provide a challenge for anthropologists. This is because an anthropological account often understands societies to be moving, vibrant entities, which do not remain the same from one moment to the next. Moreover, seeing societies as discrete entities is neither a part of our contemporary discourse nor a reflection of the manner whereby our science makes sense of and comprehends them.

There is, then, a difficulty between a mode of thinking that sees a society as a thing and a snapshot in time, and a society seen as sets of relationships that are likely to be in a constant state of flux and to change in some ways most of the time. It is not that native title law admits no change: it can accommodate significant change and adaptation provided there is a clear connection with pre-sovereignty formations. Thus, in native title law the structure is the focus of attention and interrogation. Typically in anthropology it is relationships and meanings and their social construction, perpetuation and transformation that are our concern. The study of structure does not, of itself, comprehend the complexity of the social universe we seek to explore and explain.

The ideas I have explored in this chapter about community and society have one thing in common: they are all descriptive of structures. That is, they represent a view of a social formation during a single slice in time. While what I have called 'cultural cohesion' exhibits some propensity toward a diachronic analysis, it is still essentially a description of a society at a point in time. This fact is what makes these descriptive structures helpful in the context of the consideration of applications for the legal recognition of native title.

The sorts of social formations that I have set out above that could correspond to a 'society' for the purpose of an application for the recognition of native title are what could be termed models. A model is (amongst other things) a small scale replica founded after reality. It is also, by virtue of its replicated but small scale construction, both an ideal and a representation of that reality presented at a particular moment in time. For an anthropologist, models are useful heuristic devices. But in the sense that I use the term here, models cannot easily accommodate social process: the ebb and flow of relationships, the fluctuations in identity in response to political motion, the rise of one man and the demise of another, and the essential uncertainties these vacillations generate. These are the sorts of things that provide the basis for an understanding of social process over time. The use of models, a legitimate instrument for the preparation of an expert view for an anthropologist, provides then for a means of mediation between a requirement of the legal process and the tools available to the anthropologist. It permits the anthropologist to provide expert views in a manner that will be comprehensible to the requirements of a legal process. Because models are founded after the ethnographic reality (and will be tested in court to see if indeed they are so), they are the product of the anthropological endeavour. In this way there is a clear differentiation, but no necessary disjunction, between doing anthropology (understanding social process and meaning) and being an expert witness (furnishing a synchronic model based on that research).

What the court requires is an understanding and a view that relates to the particular constructs and technical requirements of the law – in this case, the *Native Title Act*. The focus of an expert view needs to be a clear understanding of that requirement. The anthropologists' view, then, relates to the field of endeavour that is set and defined by the legislation and the legal process. The apparent difficulties that develop in this regard relate to anthropological and legal fundamentals. Social process is never discrete, final or absolute. In contrast, forensic determination is the absolute product of relating completed evidence to a defined claim. In this chapter I have argued that it is beneficial for anthropologists to pay heed to these facts and differences and so to recognise the process with which they are engaged. In the adoption of models it is possible to follow the anthropological discipline while developing methodological discriminations that mediate between the fundamentals of social inquiry and the legal requirements for expert opinion and evidence.

3

Customary rights to country

Owning rights

At the heart of any native title inquiry is a thorough examination and understanding of the ways the claimants gain rights to the country they call their own. For reasons that should by now be evident, the system of gaining and perpetuating rights to country must be based on customary practices, if they are to be capable of recognition by the court. So fundamental is the notion of elucidating the system of Indigenous rights to land in native title matters that one lawyer has argued for a primacy of its consideration, implying perhaps that other ethnography is of secondary or only minor importance (Hiley 2008). This may have some justification from a legal point of view, but anthropologists who have studied Australian Aboriginal systems of law and land would find it difficult to separate out the strands of spiritual belief and practice, kinship relationships and hunter gatherer economics as isolated and discrete subjects of study. Rather, land and a person's relationship to land is enunciated and codified by reference to spiritual relationships, totemic referents and interpersonal relationships, making separation impractical. Moreover, as I have discussed in earlier chapters of this book, native title law demands that the laws and customs of a society be shown to have continuity as practised by members of the relevant society. Arguably, demonstration of the practice and observance of laws and customs adds to the evidence that the society remains extant, vigorous and viable.

Anthropologists, perhaps like many of their non-legal colleagues, are not always clear as to what exactly is meant by the use of terms of ownership and possession. Thus it is commonplace enough to state that you 'own' something or to refer to another as the 'owner' of a piece of property. We also use the word 'own' to identify a relationship of possession with a thing by saying, 'That's my own …' article or whatever, as opposed to acknowledging that it belongs to someone else. These generalised statements allow us to communicate on a daily basis, usually without much misunderstanding. However, the terms 'own' and 'owner' are inadequate for the purposes of developing a comprehensive understanding of an Indigenous system of tenure or possession. This is because the words do not reflect the complexities of the process whereby human beings have appropriated to themselves certain objects or lands according to a normative system of rules and regulations that are accepted by others to hold good for themselves and others with respect to property. In short, 'owning' something is not as straightforward as the use of the word might imply. The desire to gain clarity in this regard has been seen as important by Sutton (2003, 15–17) who examines some of the same materials as I consider here.

Anthropologists have visited this issue and can contribute to the present discourse. Max Gluckman, an anthropologist who was particularly interested in customary law, noted the evident but implicit imprecision of the term 'ownership'. In this regard, he cited a classic work of jurisprudence:

> Ownership, in its most complete signification, denotes the relation between a person and any right that is vested in him. That which a man owns is in all cases a right. When as is often the case, he speaks of ownership of a material object, this is merely a convenient figure of speech. To own a piece of land means to own a particular kind of right in the land, namely the fee simple of it. (Salmond 1920, 220, quoted by Gluckman 1943, 8)

Discussing land tenure of the Lozi of southeast Africa, Gluckman commented, 'The so called owner of a thing has one particular set of rights in it; some of these may be abrogated, limited, or opposed, by other rights held by other people, and the State always has certain ultimate rights' (Gluckman 1943, 8). Later, but in similar vein, Gluckman expanded this account:

> We say that a person or a group 'owns' a piece of land or some item of property. We are speaking loosely when we use this sort of phrasing: what is owned in fact is a claim to have power to do certain things with the land

or property, to possess immunities against the encroachments of others on one's rights in them, and to exercise certain privileges in respect of them. But in addition other persons may have certain rights, claims, powers, privileges and immunities in respect of the same land or property … land … may be subject to a cluster of rights held by different persons in terms of their relationship within the network of kinship ties. (Gluckman 1977, 36)

Gluckman noted that that 'ownership' is seldom absolute (ibid., 45). What is generally termed 'ownership' is a right to claims, powers, privileges and immunities. The exercise of these rights also involves a duty (ibid., 36). Where rights are not absolute they are exercised in accordance with the rights of others and are burdened by them (ibid., 49–50). It follows from this that the exercise of rights may also be subject to obligations to others while more generally there are rules that govern how rights may be exercised and so also burden those rights.

Radcliffe-Brown understood ownership in terms of what he termed the 'social usage' of the exercise of control (1952, 32). He wrote, 'A right may be that of an individual or a collection of individuals. It may be defined as a measure of control that a person, or a collection of persons, has over the acts of some person or persons, said to be thereby made liable to the performance of a duty' (ibid.).

The implications of these definitions are substantial and pertinent to any inquiry into a customary system of rights to country. So-called 'ownership' is, in fact, an expression of a right that is not likely to be exclusive, meaning that it exists alongside rights that are exercised by others, in which case it is 'burdened' by the rights of others. 'Rights' are manifest as complex social arrangements that characterise a system whereby the use and access to property is organised. Anthropologists attempt to understand the system relevant to the native title claim that is the focus of their inquiry. An ability to distinguish clearly the nature, origin and potential of rights within the cultural context is essential.

Distinguishing rights in cultural context

Rights determinative and contingent

It is helpful to distinguish two sorts of rights discussed in this chapter. The distinction has implications for the perdurance of rights through the generations and so is important to native title inquiries. Understanding how rights are endorsed by and sustained by social exchanges and adherence to a normative system are essential to any native title inquiry that seeks to show that there is a system of rights to country rather than a haphazard, ever-changing disarray in the social organisation of relations to country. In any social system the continuity of rights depends upon acceptance of the process that characterises the transmission of rights over time and generations by participants. Thus, the mode of derivation of a right may have important implications for the nature of that right, its transmissibility and perhaps its relationship to rights gained by other means.

A very common way whereby rights to country are gained is through descent. Claimants will often say that they own an area of country because it belonged to their father (or sometimes their mother) and grandparents before them. An expression I hear quite often in my fieldwork is that rights to country are 'in the blood'. Just as a person is understood to have the same 'blood' as their mother or father, so too they share a common bond with the country of their parents. Rights gained by descent are determinative rights. By this I mean that they are determined by the fact of one's birth and cannot be altered or changed. If the rule of descent is applicable a child gains rights to the country of his or her father and is a member of the father's country group. He can leave the group only on his death. There is no other way out. Generally it seems that rights gained through descent are always transmissible – that is, they are automatically passed on to the next generation, the rule of descent (unilineal or cognatic) determining the extent of their exercise in descendent generations.

In contrast, rights that depend upon the attainment of some qualification, such as a command of ritual knowledge or objects, are contingent rights in that they depend upon the satisfaction of a contingency. The child of a man who enjoys a contingent right does not gain that right automatically but would in turn have to gain that qualification on his or her own account. Contingent rights are, then, generally not transmissible in customary arrangements. Place of birth or conception probably also falls into this category since the rights develop from the belief that the individual gained a spiritual (totemic) attachment to country through their place of birth. It might be argued that this spiritual connection was passed on 'through the blood' by descent, but I think this is a matter that would require further testing against the ethnographic materials available both from contemporary field data and from the earlier literature. When undertaking research in relation to such asserted rights, care must be exercised to ensure that the command of ritual knowledge or place of birth or spiritual conception translates to a real exercise of right and not merely a personal connection or responsibility. Rights that do inure by reference to such contingent acts or incidents may relate to specific areas or places, rather than to a whole estate of the country group.

Other ways to classify rights and the importance of duty

In Western legal systems some rights are generally not available to minors (drinking alcohol, owning real property) but are potential rights that become exercisable upon an individual reaching adulthood, at whatever age that is recognised. Others again depend on gaining a particular qualification prior to their exercise (driving a car is the most obvious) and in this sense have to be realised by gaining the required qualification. Generally, it seems that some rights are given greater centrality in social arrangements and these might be termed 'core' or 'presumptive' rights – that is, those that are probably not dependent on gaining qualification or contingent circumstances but are generally regarded as automatic – although according to this analysis it can be appreciated that no right within a social system is automatic. A right that is understood to afford less direction or control over something than another sort of right might be understood as a 'secondary right', in contradistinction to a 'primary right' to which it is inferior. This is a distinction to which I will return later as its use raises some difficulties in native title inquiries. A person who owns a right may also be able to license that right to another person, perhaps on certain terms and conditions, including the ability to revoke the licence should they choose to do so.

In a social system that provides the structure whereby a proprietary interest in something is articulated, the exercise of the right generally implies a duty so that the duty is a concomitant of the right. In Aboriginal discourse a duty of this sort relating to land is often expressed in terms of 'looking after' the country, that is, keeping it regularly burnt or free of rubbish and preventing it from being damaged or entered by those who have no permission to do so. The exercise of a duty may then be an indication of the presence of a right and can provide evidence of the latter's vitality.[1] Another example of a duty commonly found in Aboriginal discourse is the requirement that a right holder takes care of visitors, who are understood to be his or her responsibility. This may include advising them of places within the country that are believed to be spiritually potent and consequentially potentially dangerous and performing a ritual that introduces the visitor to the country so that the spirits will be more accepting of his or her presence there.

These types of rights and associated duties take us a long way from the simple and potentially misleading idea that a person 'owns' something, implying in much common thinking the ability to do with it more or less as the 'owner' pleases. Rights of possession are complex expressions of relationships developed and codified within a culture. In native title dealings these codifications are often referred to as the 'laws' of the society in question and represent an accepted and agreed way of ordering social relationships that relate to property, including land. For those who gain their livelihood directly and solely from the land (as is the case with hunting and gathering societies), having a right to country which is acknowledged and accepted by others legitimated by reference to an accepted set of rules is immensely important since it helps to give certainty in an aleatory environment. The system that encapsulates this regulation, comprising the laws, customs, mores, and emotional and spiritual values of the society, can be referred to as a 'normative system'.[2]

When is a 'right' a 'rule'?

In an oral tradition, the rules that determine and define rights are expressed through practice and the enunciation of dogma. In this, we must examine the ethnography carefully to gain an understanding of the particulars of the normative system in question. The complexities inherent in the sorts

---

1   Presumably, it is possible in a normative system for there to be a duty without a right. Those holding rights recognise the rule that they respect the duty and accommodate its exercise. I thank Robert Blowes for this observation.

2   This term is not found in the *Native Title Act* but is a product of the ensuing jurisprudence (*Members of the Yorta Yorta Aboriginal Community v Victoria* [2002] HCA 58, [37] and following).

of systems that may be revealed in native title research relating to rights to land and sea country present some challenges when they are translated into an alien legal framework that is native title law. For example, a contingent right has to be understood as having legitimate potency in and of itself and not dependent upon or a benefit of the exercise of a superior right. The contingent right has to be capable of exercise without the need for permission or licence from a person who holds a determinative right to the same area – although it may be exercised with due regard to their needs, desires and obligations as it is burdened by that other right.

While this distinction may be helpful, in practice the field data may provide for some ambiguity. For example, a person with rights to country by descent may say of another, 'Well, he's got something to say for my country because his spirit comes from there, but he's got to stand behind the real owners'. The question for the anthropologist is, then, whether the 'real owner' is the one with the right, while the person who has 'something to say' is awarded a certain privilege but that this does not amount to a right. The matter becomes more complex in situations that I have encountered where a claimant says of another that they lack a 'right' to the country in question. The assertion is then qualified (usually on further questioning) by the admission that the leverage exercised by the person in question upon the country (say, through place of spiritual conception) is such that their accommodation must be afforded because to deny it would be contrary to customary practice (usually expressed as 'the Law').

The anthropologist will need to consider questions about the relationship between rights and duties prescribed as rules. If access to country is gained by virtue of the existence of a rule that they be permitted to do so, that does not mean that the person who so accesses the country has a right to do so. This is an important distinction and one that has to be explored in the field data collected during the research for a claim. In separating out 'rights' from 'rules' it may be helpful to bear in mind a fundamental characterisation of the derivation of rights in Aboriginal systems of land and sea tenure. The right has to be derived from a relationship between person and country: descent, which is believed to carry such a link through the blood, totemic spiritual connectedness, ritual qualification or some other social or metaphysical construct that legitimates an essential and noumenal connectedness that lies at the heart of the relationship between Aboriginal people and the country wherein they exercise customary rights. The classic pathways identified in the anthropological literature whereby rights to country are gained (whether descent-based or founded on other spiritual relationships) all articulate the metaphysical correlation between a person and country. It is upon that principle that a right is understood to exist. In a later section of this chapter I review how anthropologists have identified these different ways of gaining rights to country and the implications that this developing literature has had on our understanding of the complexities of the system whereby rights to country were both gained and exercised.

A rule, on the other hand, is not expressive of this fundamental correlation between a person and country. The application of a rule which, for example, requires that access to country be afforded to certain persons, while mandated and likely to be reflective of social relationships, is a concomitant of the right. It is a feature of the exercise of the right but does not, of itself, represent or reflect the spiritual relationship between a person and their country. It is also a matter of social dealing and even though it may be normatively a part of the exercise of rights is ultimately negotiable.

In my experience, these complexities and their associated complications and obstacles to the successful resolution of the claim arise when there is competition or dispute about the integrity of an asserted right. These are matters that will ultimately be a matter for the court. While the legal process must pay due regard to the Indigenous system of law, this is not necessarily easily or accurately translated into the provisions of the *Native Title Act*.

Succession to deceased estates

Country groups were subject to the vicissitudes of life and, just as families do today, waxed and waned, grew in numbers or declined. Factors that affected the viability of a country group would have included disease, warfare, infertility and probably natural disasters. Inevitably, then, some country groups would have been wiped out or diminished until eventually the last member died, leaving the group with no living representative. The country of that group became then a deceased estate. While the advance of the frontier, with introduced diseases and sometimes significant violence, undoubtedly increased the numbers of deceased estates, early commentators did not generally describe country without an owner as the sole product of European settlement. In a short but classic paper that addressed the issue of 'succession to land' (Peterson, Keen and

Sansom 1977) the authors wrote of the 'extinction of clans' as a 'recurrent problem'. They suggested that the relatively small size of a clan rendered it vulnerable to extinction. It was their view that 'the Aborigines have evolved mechanisms to deal with' this eventuality (ibid., 2). Peterson, Keen and Sansom cite Spencer and Gillen, writing in 1899, who reported of a clan country:

> if it happens that all the individuals associated with it die, then a neighbouring group will go in and possess the land. It is not, however, any neighbouring group which may do this, but it must be one the members of which are what is called *Nakrakia* to the extinct group – that is, they belong to the same moiety of the tribe as the latter. (Spencer and Gillen 1899, 153, cited in Peterson, Keen and Sansom 1977, 1004)

The early ethnographic observer Daisy Bates was also aware that country could become 'vacant'. That is, a last surviving owner had died, leaving the area without a hereditary successor. She noted the term for this in the Bibbulmun language of the southwest of Western Australia as *bindardee*. She wrote, 'it is the "Bindardee" country when the nyungar[3] dies who owned it. Nilgee's house is called Bindardee because it has "no father"'.[4] In South Australia, probably amongst the Wirangu with whom she camped at Ooldea, Bates recorded the term *narruri* to mean 'orphaned country'.[5] Bates's account lacks the insightful detail provided by Spencer and Gillen and the rich ethnography relating to sacred objects that could eventually be given over to a person believed to have their spiritual quickening from the country in question, so restoring what was believed to be an autochthonous clan (Spencer and Gillen 1899, 154, 302). However, Bates confirms that the idea of country without owners due to the demise of the local group found expression in their language. Taken together these accounts strongly support the view that extinction and subsequent succession were a part of customary dealings prior to the arrival of Europeans.

Peterson, Keen and Sansom (1977) defined succession as a process contingent on the possession of some sort of right in the country in question. They differentiate in this regard 'primary rights' gained for the country by patrilineal descent from 'secondary rights' gained by other means including place of conception, birth, death/burial, kinship

---

3   Footnote added: Aboriginal person.
4   Bates n.d., typescript from notebook 15, 54.
5   Bates n.d., typescript from notebook 5c, 63 (Bates folio 68, 23).

and ritual ties and matrifiliation (ibid., 4–5). They go on to document a process of succession that was brought to light during the Yirrkala land rights case where a clan comprising two old women was 'looked after' by members of a clan of the same moiety (ibid., 6). Senior members of that clan went on to assert ownership of the country in question – and of its substantial resources – an arrangement that resulted in a longstanding dispute (Altman 1983, 22, 116–117).[6]

Sutton provided additional commentary on the distinction between 'primary' and 'secondary' rights in relation to succession. In Sutton's view:

> 'secondary' forms of connection to an estate may become activated as acceptable bases for claims of succession to estates whose owners have died out. Those who succeed in this way, a process which often takes many years or even decades, convert their interest in the relevant estate from a secondary one to a primary one, or at least ensure that the interests of certain of their descendants in that estate are recognised as primary ones in due course. (Sutton 2003, 4–5)

Sutton understood the process of succession to reach its endpoint when 'a "normal" situation has been restored whereby at least some people again enjoy unmediated rights in the country, and their precise origin is forgotten' (ibid., 5, 121–122).[7]

Sutton has also provided a helpful distinction between an individual or 'a close-knit set of siblings' who forge their succession to an estate and that effected by a group (ibid., 5). The latter case applies when a whole subset of a language group becomes extinct as a result of catastrophic population collapse due to colonisation, killings, poisonings or disease, leading to sudden or eventual extinction. Given this territorial vacuum, the country is 'subsumed by one or more extant groups' (ibid., 5). Sutton provided examples that included the Ganggalida, who subsumed country of the defunct Min.ginda (Burketown area); the Waanyi, who subsumed country of the Injilarija (Lawn Hill region); and the Pangkala, who subsumed part of the territory of the much depleted Nauo (Eyre Peninsula) (ibid., 5). Sutton distinguished this 'group succession' from 'small genealogical subgroup succession' by reference to the scale of the event. However, both

---

6   See, for example, www.theguardian.com/australia-news/2017/mar/23/indigenous-land-rights-arnhem-land-bauxite-royalties, accessed 22 August 2017.
7   Sansom has called this process of forgetting 'strategic amnesia' (Sansom 2001).

rely on some form of existing relationship including common language, geographic unity, moiety affiliations and ritual commonalities (ibid., 6–7). He further remarked:

> These cases do not involve the extinguishment of pre-colonial rights of surviving groups so much as their transformation – usually involving considerable simplification – and their generalisation to wider 'tribal' areas. One cannot exclude the possibility that similar catastrophic population losses may have occurred before the colonial era, where epidemics could have wiped people out in big numbers from time to time. (ibid., 6)

Other writers have also added to our understanding of the processes of succession and, to some extent, how they have interacted with the legal processes that have contextualised their ventilation (Glaskin 2017, 175, 178, 193). In 2015, David Trigger wrote a paper that features instances of succession in native title cases, while providing a summary of some of the anthropological accounts relevant to their consideration (2015b, 53–55). I return to Trigger's case studies below.

In the context of a native title inquiry, the fact of a succession to country raises important issues regarding continuity. The processes of succession I have reviewed above all involve a change of owners – rights to country that were vested in one group become vested in another. That such a change happened post-sovereignty means that there is no continuity of ownership according to the principle of descent – given that that is the relevant means whereby rights to country are perpetuated. However, it is the operation and perdurance of the 'laws and customs' of the society in question that is a key to the question of continuity in a native title case. Consequently, a change of owners, *per se*, is not inimical to the recognition of native title by the court. However, a succession event is seen by some legal experts as potentially problematic. During a panel discussion, Senior Counsel Vance Hughston commented that, under native title law, 'The requirement to demonstrate that members of the claimant group are part of a society and that that society has continued to exist since sovereignty united by its acknowledgement and observance of the laws and customs under which the rights and interests claimed is possessed is central' (Blackshield, Sackett and Hughston 2011, 109). Laws and customs are, in native title thinking, a creature of a particular society. Consequently, an act of succession whereby members of one society take over the country of the members of another society would upon the succession render the laws and customs applicable to the country so taken over different to those evident at the time of sovereignty. Based on this reasoning, Hughston stated:

On the current state of the law, the likelihood is that succession will only be recognised by the courts if it is intra-societal, that is, if it is within the one society. The courts have shown a distinct reluctance to accept that the members of one society can succeed to the country of another society (*Dale v Moses* 2007 at [120]). So, in *Sebastian*, the claimants had to demonstrate that the Djugan were part of the same society as the Yawuru, despite different languages, distinct territories, separate self referents and somewhat different legal traditions. (Blackshield, Sackett and Hughston 2011, 110)

Following Sutton's lead, Trigger provides an analysis of the Ganggalida group succession to the country of the Mingginda[8] people in the vicinity of Burketown – based on his own long-term field research in the area (2015b, 55–59). Trigger was able to document the demise and eventual extinction of the Mingginda people through disease and frontier violence (ibid., 56). While older informants recalled the group, younger members did not (ibid., 57). Members of the Ganggalida group had moved into the area (around Burketown), claiming rights to it through birth conception and subsequently through Dreaming associations represented as mythology integrated into Ganggalida traditions (ibid., 57–58). Trigger called this 'a case of completed succession' (ibid., 57). It was based on customary principles and won favour with the court. His Honour, Justice Cooper, stated:

130 The second respondent submitted that the interest claimed by the Gangalidda[9] peoples in the former land and waters of the Mingginda peoples was not a right or interest held at sovereignty under the traditional laws and customs of the Gangalidda people. That is, it was an interest acquired post-sovereignty which was not recognised by s 223(1) of the Act.

131 In my view, the submission of the second respondent is incorrect. The new legal order at the time of sovereignty recognised both existing rights and interests in relation to lands and also '*the efficiency of rules of transmission of rights and interests under traditional laws and traditional customs which existed at sovereignty.*': *Yorta Yorta* at [44]. If the rights and interests in respect of the Mingginda peoples' countries was acquired under traditional laws and customs which provided for such a succession

---

8   Sutton's 'Min.ginda'.
9   His Honour chose the spelling 'Gangalidda', which reflects the name of the application in contrast to Trigger's published spelling, 'Ganggalida'.

and those laws and customs existed at sovereignty, then the interests of the Gangalidda peoples in respect of those lands and waters will be recognised and protected under the Act.[10]

In reaching this opinion, his Honour relied on the evidence of the anthropologist (Dr Trigger) that the succession had occurred 'under traditional rules and customs which were acknowledged and observed at the time of sovereignty by both peoples' and so were 'capable of recognition and protection under s 223(1) of the Act' (Lardil Peoples [132]).

Trigger added what I think to be an interesting and relevant observation. He wrote, 'few if any living Aboriginal people disputed the fact that for many years the Burketown, Albert River, lower Nicholson River area had been Ganggalida country. This conviction was evident even among the few who nevertheless knew they had a likely Mingginda forebear in their own ancestry' (Trigger 2015b, 59). A footnote qualifies the observation: 'However, this is not to conclude there was complete agreement of this kind in relation to other inland parts of Mingginda country' (ibid., fn. 4). This raises an important question: would the matter have been so positively settled (for the applicant) had the matter been in dispute?

Trigger's second case study also echoes Sutton's earlier observation regarding the Waanyi. Trigger reports that the Waanyi people moved historically 'eastwards into Nguburindi territory and southwards into parts of Injilarija country' (ibid., 59). He observes that both areas were 'believed by claimants to be culturally familiar, and since European arrival taken over according to Waanyi traditional law and custom with the demise of these two groups' (ibid.). Trigger documents the cultural commonalities of the groups, even though their languages were distinct (ibid., 59–63) and considered that there was some evidence that these demographic changes occurred in part prior to the date of effective sovereignty (ibid., 60). Land-based mythological traditions were incorporated within the landscape as part of the Waanyi's succession eastward and their 'associated cultural assimilation of the landscape' (ibid., 63). Trigger concludes that, 'the Waanyi research, in the context of the native title claim, indicated a completed case of adaptation and succession according to tradition-based law and custom in relation to land and waters' (ibid., 65).

---

10 *The Lardil Peoples v State of Queensland* [2004] FCA 298 [130–131].

The application was settled by consent.[11] Trigger does not tell us what the judge found in relation to this succession for the matter is not addressed in any of the judgments I have viewed, except in passing in relation to a contentious issue of claim group membership.[12]

Trigger is sanguine about the potential for accommodation of changing rights to country within the Australian native title legal system. He wrote, 'substantial change has occurred, yet forms of contemporary connection with country are also continuous with adaptations in the previously operating system' (ibid., 66–67). In order to achieve recognition of these new-order rights in native title law, he takes the commonsense view that what is required is good research and thoroughly documented accounts of the process or processes involved. This would seem to be sage counsel applicable to all our anthropological research.

Part of the reason why anthropologists should pay particular attention to instances of succession is that they present an evident vulnerability in the proof of native title. In the Waanyi case discussed above, the Queensland Government and mining giant CRA argued that there was no evidence of transfer of native title from the Injilarija to the Waanyi (ibid., 67). In the Gangalidda case, as I noted above, the second respondents argued that the rights now asserted were not rights held at sovereignty but rather an interest held post-sovereignty. Research into instances of succession in relation to a native title claim must, then, tackle the fundamental question of how the transference of rights from one group to another has taken place consistent with the claimants' laws and customs, as well as those which may reasonably have been supposed to have been those of the extinct group. It would appear that the laws and customs must be a product of the same native title society, otherwise they would necessarily be different and the issue of their continuity brought into doubt.

The task of researching and providing a positive opinion in relation to these matters is made much easier if the matter is not subject to rigorous challenge by respondent parties. Conversely, it is made much more difficult if it is subject to disputes between Indigenous parties. Trigger remarked in this regard:

---

11 *Aplin on behalf of the Waanyi Peoples v State of Queensland* (No. 3) [2010] FCA 1515.
12 *Aplin on behalf of the Waanyi Peoples v State of Queensland* [2010] FCA 625 [87], [100], [119].

Where disagreement emerges between contesting Aboriginal parties about whether or not succession has been licit in terms of law and custom, or whether it is a completed process, it can be difficult to determine a resolution. This can involve quite bitter disputes that continue over decades, as in the Finniss River area of the Northern Territory. (ibid., 67)

The process of succession to a deceased estate marks a hiatus in the seamless succession of rights through descent. When the process of succession is in train and knowledge remains of the original owners, those pressing claims through lesser rights or merely consocation are vulnerable to challenge. In the native title era, where claimants have increasing access to archival records, genealogical data and earlier ethnographies, the period of selective amnesia is simply illuminated. While the studies I have discussed above show that, under the right circumstances and with good research, succession to country can find recognition within the native title process, it represents a vulnerability and is ripe for the articulation of disagreements. It is not, then, an area of research for the inexperienced or the unwary.

Linking local organisation and title

In terms of property, 'title' refers to the legal basis of the ownership of that property. 'Native' title in the Australian context requires that there is a customary identifiable system of law and normative regulation that provides a basis for the allocation of rights to country that has legal-like qualities. These rules and regulations must be shown to relate to rights or obligations and be accepted by members of the society as ordering the allocation of rights to country. The recognition of native title today requires that the rights of the original Indigenous owners of the land and the system that sustained them have endured, substantially unaltered, since the time of sovereignty. As with other issues of continuity the anthropologist as expert must apply the 'then and now' test. By this, I mean that there must be a reliable account of the system of local organisation as it is likely to have been at or close to sovereignty, compared with the system that is avowed now by the claimants, as documented in the fieldwork data upon which the anthropologist founds his or her views. This is typically no easy task. Descriptions of local organisation found in the early settler literature are not only elusive but also were sometimes based on naive and inaccurate accounts of a system of land tenure that was poorly understood and incompletely recorded. Early accounts were also sometimes prejudiced by preconceptions relating to 'tribes' (a matter discussed in the previous chapter) and hostility to the notion that the Indigenous inhabitants of Australia actually recognised property rights at all. As the frontier advanced, the subject was the focus of attention by anthropologists but there were misunderstandings and preconceptions here too. Radcliffe-Brown was a pioneer in this regard and some of his data go back as far as the beginning of the second decade of the last century and I consider some of his writing in this regard below. Anthropologists have not been in agreement as to the details of Aboriginal local organisation, although research in recent decades has probably developed what might be termed an 'anthropological orthodoxy' that has gained general (although not universal) acceptance amongst practitioners.

I do not trace all aspects of the anthropological debate here as this has been done by a number of other writers whose work can be consulted (Peterson 2006; Peterson and Long 1986; Sutton 2003, 38–53). A number of anthropologists who undertook fieldwork in Australia prior to the 1930s developed understandings of how the customary system of rights to country worked, according to their observations and field data. Of these, A.R. Radcliffe-Brown was one of the first anthropologists to set out an understanding of local organisation in Australia (1913; 1930–31, 34–37; 1952, 32–36). Based on a single and probably quite short period of fieldwork in 1911 amongst the Kariyarra of northwest Western Australia (not far from the present site of Port Hedland), Radcliffe-Brown attempted to reconstruct systems of land tenure for the Kariyarra. The paper he published in 1913, following his return from the field, has become a citation classic amongst anthropologists because of its succinct statements relating to local and social organisation as well as its comparatively early date in the history of Australian Aboriginal studies. Consideration of his findings are helpful because they were central to a debate that ensued about the defensibility of his conclusions and so too to the development of a better understanding of customary systems of rights to country that are broadly applicable to other areas as well.

Radcliffe-Brown

The people who Radcliffe-Brown identified as Kariyarra[13] had been living on station properties for about 50 years by the time he undertook his research. Consequently, it is likely that most of his informants had not known a complete hunting and gathering lifestyle, although some older individuals may have recalled a time before European settlement. Radcliffe-Brown understood that the tenurial system was based on 'Local groups, each with its own defined territory' (1913, 145). Membership of a local group was determined by descent in the male line. The country of a local group was identified by reference to an important place or places within the country of that group (ibid.). He drew a map showing the location of some of these local groups (he admitted that his data were not complete) within Kariyarra territory that he represented on the map by means of an idealised boundary (ibid.,145).

According to Radcliffe-Brown, the 'normal'[14] Australian type of local organisation comprised a local group with rights to a defined area of country. Members of other hordes were required to seek permission to use another horde's country, or be invited into it, so rights of ownership within the local group area were exclusive to members of the local group. He wrote:

> The country of a local group, with all its products, animal, vegetable, and mineral, belongs to the members of the group in common. Any member has the right to hunt over the country of his group at all times. He may not, however, hunt over the country of any other local group without the permission of the owners. (ibid., 146)

Pursuit of game seems to have constituted a permissible exception to this rule, but otherwise trespass was punishable by death. Despite these strictures, Radcliffe-Brown noted that visiting and sharing of food was common (ibid., 146–147) such that there was 'a perpetual shifting to and fro both within the country of the group and from one group to another' (ibid., 147). Connubial relations also expanded the potential for

---

13   Radcliffe-Brown spelt this language name 'Kariera'. I here adopt the spelling employed by members of this group today (Kariyarra) but retain Radcliffe-Brown's spelling where I have quoted from his writings.
14   Radcliffe-Brown 1930–31, 29.

the enjoyment of country. Radcliffe-Brown found that local groups were exogamous, so a man had to gain a wife from a local group different to his own.

> A woman seems to have retained a sort of right over the country of her birth, so that a man and his wife were generally welcome to visit the wife's local group whenever they wished. A man seems also to have a sort of secondary right over the country of his mother, that is the country to which she belonged by birth. In a large number of cases this was the same as the country of his wife. In both cases, however, it seems to have meant no more than that a man was sure of a welcome in the country of his wife or his mother. (ibid., 147)

For Radcliffe-Brown, then, rights to country were a matter of descent, exclusive to the local group and vigorously enforceable. While his opening position was that local group membership had to be descent traced through patrifiliation (to the father and father's father), he also recognised that a man had rights in his mother's country and perhaps in his wife's country too. Whether a man could be denied access to his mother's country is not clear. Presumably in company with his wife he could freely visit her country. In any event, he reports constant free movement between estates, indicating that, while there were evident rules relating to how rights to country were obtained, there was flexibility in their exercise since the country was not as compartmentalised as he had first stated. Such flexibility would have been an important factor in sustaining the economy of a hunting and gathering society, as Radcliffe-Brown shows each estate to have been quite small. I return to the question of size below.

One difficulty with Radcliffe-Brown's early analysis is that he conflated two social formations: the descent group and the residence group. This distinction was later shown to be critical to a proper understanding of Aboriginal local organisation (Berndt 1959, 95–96) and remains so today when writing native title reports. The descent group, as the name implies, was recruited according to principles of descent; the latter by choice, kinship ties, commensality and perhaps circumstances. The residence group, whose members moved round the countryside hunting and gathering (and were therefore visible within the countryside), would likely have been made up of a man and his wife (members of two descent groups), the man's affinal relations and perhaps those who were not directly related through blood ties at all. There are records of the composition of these groups available in the ethnographic literature (e.g. Peterson and Long 1986; Palmer 2010a, 74–80). The descent group, on the other hand, was not in evidence as a reality on the ground except in so far as a residence group might in part comprise a father, his sons and daughters and perhaps grandchildren.

In response to this difficulty Radcliffe-Brown was to revise but not substantially change his views based on his 1911 fieldwork with the Kariyarra and others of the Pilbara region. In 1931, he published a monograph that sought to define the social organisation of Australian tribes and examined many groups in addition to the Kariyarra (Radcliffe-Brown 1930–31[15]). In this he generalised from the particular, attempting to set down a definitive account of Australian systems of social and local organisation. He introduced a new term, 'horde', to his account, which he hoped would clarify what he meant by use of the word 'clan':

> The horde is a small group of persons owning a certain area of territory, the boundaries of which are known, and possessing in common proprietary rights over the land and its products – mineral, vegetable and animal. It is the primary land-owning or land-holding group. Membership of a horde is determined in the first place by descent, children belonging to the horde of their father. (ibid., 35)

He sought to clarify membership in reality ('an existing group at any moment') by accommodating wives of local group members:

> The horde, therefore, as an existing group at any moment, consists of (1) male members of all ages whose fathers and fathers' fathers belonged to the horde, (2) unmarried girls who are the sisters or daughters or son's daughters of the male members, (3) married women, all of whom, in some regions, and most of whom, in others, belonged originally to other hordes, and have become attached to the horde by marriage. (ibid., 35–36)

Later, and in the same article (ibid., 59), he attempted to distinguish the horde from the clan. His initial proposition was that, for the Kariyarra, 'all the men of any given horde belong to a single line of descent' (ibid., 59). Since the horde is based on descent, ego's[16] father's horde is different to ego's mother's horde. Recognising perhaps that the two hordes would

---

15 Published as a monograph in 1931; parts were published in the journal *Oceania* the year before.
16 'Ego' is the 'I' of a genealogical account. This is often the person from whom the genealogy has been collected or the person who defines the relationships set out in the genealogy or discussed in the accompanying account. See Sutton 2003, 186.

then constitute a single social unit (the family or group that lived together on a daily basis), he suggests using the term 'clan' for the residential group. His conclusion in this regard is, however, not evident:

> We can therefore say that in the Kariera tribe, connected with each horde there is a clan. I have defined a horde as consisting of all men born into the horde together with their wives and unmarried daughters. The clan connected with the horde consists of all persons born in the horde. The male members of the clan all remain in the horde from birth to death. The female members of the clan remain with the horde till they are married and then are transferred to other hordes. (ibid., 59)

Radcliffe-Brown adds a footnote to the end of this paragraph in which he seeks to clarify further his choice of the terms 'horde' and 'clan':

> This distinction between the horde and the associated local clan is, I think, a very important one to make and to keep in mind. A horde changes its composition by the passing of women out of it and into it by marriage. At any given moment it consists of a body of people living together as a group of families. The clan has all its male members in one horde, but all its older female members are in other hordes. It changes its composition only by the birth and death of its members. (ibid., 59, footnote 8)

Radcliffe-Brown's shifting terms do not make for clarity. He understood that there was a difference between the filiative relationships of the descent group whereby rights to country were transmitted and the 'body of people living together as a group of families'. His lack of precision was to give rise to a substantial debate that has been discussed by others (Hiatt 1962, 1966; Stanner 1965). However, so it seems to me, despite the shortcomings of the account, Radcliffe-Brown was probably heading in the right direction. It was left to others to clarify the system, introduce better defined terminology and recognise that as hunters and gatherers residential groups were reliant on a sustainable economic base that was unlikely, except in the better watered areas of Australia, to have been afforded by a single hermetic estate. Of direct relevance to native title and an understanding of the allocation of rights to country were his tantalising observations about what appear to be the ability of a man to exercise rights in his wife's country and in the country of his own mother. While Radcliffe-Brown appears to suggest that these were either lesser rights, indulgencies or some sort of standing permission on the part of the relevant local descent group, this is not pursued. In his 1952 account Radcliffe-Brown elevated rights gained through matrifiliation, previously described in 1913 as 'a sort of secondary right over the country of his mother', by stating, 'in the Kariera tribe a man had certain quite important rights over his mother's horde, over its individual members, and over its territory' (1952, 36). From a practical point of view, right of access to several estates made sense. Radcliffe-Brown had produced a map of the 19 estates of Kariyarra country (1913, 144), some of which lay in quite dry country and well away from the coast, which has a more temperate climate than the interior. In all, Radcliffe-Brown had estimated Kariyarra country to comprise between 3,500 and 4,000 square miles (ibid., 145). This computes to an average area for each estate of between 184 and 210 square miles (477 to 544 square kilometres[17]). At its largest, then, an estate would be only some 23 km× 23 km. It seems unlikely that, in practice, exploitation limited to the country of a single descent group would be economically viable.

Phyllis Kaberry

Phyllis Kaberry undertook fieldwork in the Kimberley region of Western Australia in the mid 1930s, so she came to her ethnography over two decades after Radcliffe-Brown. As a student based at the University of Sydney she was undoubtedly influenced by Radcliffe-Brown's work, although her supervisor appears to have been A.P. Elkin.[18] Kaberry's principal interest was in the role of women in Aboriginal societies, so systems of land tenure were not her primary concern. However, she would have been aware that Radcliffe-Brown had adopted a somewhat male approach to his analyses of Aboriginal society, such that Sutton stated that his sexism was 'a problem for his analysis' (2003, 52). Kaberry was, then, ideally suited by virtue of her sex and research focus to provide a corrective. As a graduate anthropology student Kaberry was aware that Radcliffe-Brown had set down that the 'normal' method of recruitment to the horde (land-owning group) was patrifiliation (e.g. 1930–31, 44, 55, 73; Kaberry 1939, 136–140). Kaberry questioned Radcliffe-Brown's justification for accepting patrifiliation as a given, based on economic determinants (1939, 136–137). She cited other researchers (Stanner and Warner) to support her view that a man might live in his mother's country, presumably as of right, as well as his father's (ibid., 137). The real tie to patri-country, she argued, was a result of ritual and spiritual ties that develop as a result of a man's relationship with his father (ibid., 138).

---

17   Where 1 square mile = 2.58999 square kilometres.
18   Elkin 1939, xli.

However, Kaberry also distinguished rights in at least two other countries: country (or area) of birth and mother's country (ibid., 31, 137, 194–195). Accordingly, Kaberry wrote that the children of a marriage 'inherit their father's country and the right to participate in certain horde ceremonies, but the relationships with the mother's group are retained and emphasised, as opposed to the view that the society is purely patrilineal' (1939, 133). Kaberry, who undertook fieldwork across the Kimberley region, made a similar distinction between father's and mother's country for areas of the east Kimberley, recording different terms used for father's and mother's country, 'a usage that points to different horde countries for the parents' (1939, 125).

Like other writers at this time, Kaberry did not distinguish between the country group and the residence group, using the single term 'horde' to obfuscate any distinction. Kaberry defined the horde at one point as 'the patrilineal group of men and women who own a stretch of territory' (ibid., 136). She added that 'some of them [members of the patrilineal group] may be living elsewhere' (ibid.) and thereby implied the distinction that she did not make: the horde or land-owning group was not always the same as the residence group.

Despite these points of variance with Radcliffe-Brown, Kaberry recorded that 'over a strip of territory a patrilineal group exercises well-defined rights which are guarded and enforced by the headman. The body of totemic myth not only strengthens these, but provides a legal and religious charter for land tenure in these tribes' (ibid., 140). For Kaberry, then, rights to country were about far more than a descent of rights, but relied upon totemic links, ritual and religious beliefs that together formed a system (she called it a charter) for land tenure.

While undertaking her fieldwork, Kaberry had written to Elkin from the small town of Fitzroy Crossing in an early attempt to relate social categories to country, but this led her to consider how rights to country were gained.

> All the subsections may belong to one horde country, and this is borne out by the fact that a person's country is determined by his birth. Normally that would be his father's country, but not necessarily so. The term for country is <u>noa:ra:</u>. If a man is born in another country than that of his father, then he still has a right to live in his father's, but the latter is called

'half-country' or <u>kamera</u>. A man also calls his mother's or his mother's mother's, or his father's mother's, or his father's father's country his <u>Kamera</u> [sic]. (Letter to Elkin, 22 March 1935, 1–2)

Writing from Moola Bulla, some 160 km east of Fitzroy Crossing, she noted later in the same year that, 'sometimes a man gave as his country as the place where he was born, and laid claim to this, even if different from that of mother and father' (letter to Elkin, 8 December 1935, 3).

Kaberry published a paper (1938) documenting the importance of a person's relationship to country through a belief in spiritual conception and place of birth. Writing of data she had collected from the east and south Kimberley she reported the belief that spirits enter the prospective mother as a result of propinquity, while an animal association is established through some incident whereby the animal in question (usually as meat) causes illness to the mother (ibid., 278). The belief serves to link a person with a place and a natural species, founded upon a conviction in the pervasive spirituality of the great creative period of the Dreaming, when the spirits were ordained within the pools (ibid., 279; 1939, 30, 195). Daisy Bates had recorded a similar belief for areas of the west Kimberley two decades before.[19] Consistent with these accounts, Kaberry understood a person's territory to comprise different sorts of 'country' – a term she glossed as *da:m* that was used in the eastern Kimberly and was the equivalent of the term *ngura* that was used in the central parts of the region. These terms (*da:m* and *ngura*) could also be used to mean 'camp'.

> The comparison of the word for camp – da:m, with those for horde-country – noera:m da:m, big camp, and spirit centre – wanyagoara da:m (little camp), can be taken up at this point. The repetition of da:m would seem to indicate a similar attitude adopted toward all three localities. They are places where a native makes his fire, sleeps and searches for food. This is borne out by the difficulty, frequently encountered, of discovering a man's or a woman's noera:m da:m. (Kaberry 1939, 30–31)

My reading of Kaberry is that when she asked people where their country was, the answer was not always a simple one that made reference to their ancestral (and presumably patrilineal) country. Rather, those with whom she worked might refer to one or more of the following: the country they occupied – presumably, as of right; ancestral country; or totemic

---

19   Bates (1913, 389–391) wrote of spirit children for areas to the west of Nyikina country.

country. In short, country (*ngura, da:m*) could comprise a suite of country gained through different customary means. She wrote that although the horde country had 'well defined boundaries and is named' (ibid., 31), her informants sometimes gave her the names of:

> half a dozen pools, i.e. places where he had camped and which offer a plentiful supply of game and food. They are vital points in his territory; in part they constitute its significance and value for him. Of these, one generally is more important than the others – his *wanyegoara daam*, the pool where his father found him as a spirit child. This he regards as peculiarly his own though others may camp by it. He visits it frequently, mentions it with pride and will be buried with his head pointing towards it. The tie is a spiritual rather than a purely economic one. Occasionally the spirit centre may lie outside his horde territory, in which case he is allowed to hunt there. (ibid., 31)

In summary, Kaberry presents a system of local organisation whereby rights are to areas of country, principally defined in relation to camping sites (or other significant places) within it, rather than to lineal boundaries. Some rights to country derive from the father. Father's country is identified both by a generic term (*ngura* for the central Kimberley region) and an area name. A person also has rights in areas of land associated with that person's spiritual conception, these being areas generally of smaller extent than the totality of what is conceived of as being a country area. Thirdly, a person has rights in their mother's country, which she termed *kamara*. It is evident from her account of rights to country in the Kimberley that rights did not develop from a unilineal system to just one area, but were multiple and composite.

Kaberry provided detail as to the range of rights that people legitimately exercised in country. This included the right of access, hunting and camping (ibid., 30) and the right of exclusion or invitation (ibid., 31, 139). She wrote that those with rights in country knew their country intimately (ibid., 136–137) and this included knowledge of the spiritual dangers of country and how to avoid them (ibid., 138–139, 203–204). Without such knowledge the exploitation of country was fraught with spiritual danger. Kaberry also reported that senior members of country groups (and their wives, should they have sufficient seniority) had the right and duty to conduct increase rituals[20] at renewal sites in their

---

20   Rituals performed to sustain and increase the fecundity of a particular plant, animal or natural phenomenon.

country (ibid., 138, 203–206). Kaberry stated that ritual duties and responsibilities with respect to the country of a local group could only be exercised by members of the patrilineal group (ibid., 138–139). Later, when discussing 'increase rituals' she stated that totemic sites are 'worked up' by a 'headman' or his wife, if she was old enough – although she would presumably belong to another descent group (ibid., 205). Kaberry concludes that local group members had a duty to undertake the rite on behalf of all others and that this indicates the strength of the cultural interdependence of the hordes (ibid.). In this Kaberry was recognising that the system she recorded involved not only rights and duties but also rules about the exercise of rights and duties as well.

A developing orthodoxy

There were other researchers from the Sydney University anthropology department who also reported a more complex situation. For example, M. and R. Piddington, who worked amongst the Karajari south of Broome in the 1930s, wrote of the coastal Nadja Karajari that Radcliffe-Brown's rule of exclusive ownership of the horde did not apply to their field data. They wrote:

> this rule does not exist. Certain small exogamous groups exist, but they lack the solidarity which characterises the normal Australian horde; small parties composed of less than a dozen individuals from any horde may go on hunting expeditions lasting several months, over the territory of any other horde, without asking permission of the owners, who would not object. (Piddington and Piddington 1932, 351)[21]

Elkin disagreed with M. and R. Piddington, suggesting that since the Karajari had been 'under white influence for some sixty years' this made reconstruction 'difficult' (Elkin 1933, 279) and that failure to ask permission was due to the 'decadent condition of this part of the tribe' (ibid., 280). But Elkin's own field data demonstrated, in fact, that while patrifiliation was an operative principle in the descent of rights to country, it was not the only pathway to gaining rights to country in Aboriginal Australia. Elkin recognised the importance of a totemic connection in this regard and the fact that there was no necessary or neat fit between an individual's totemic affiliations and his or her father or father's estate. This is a matter I have discussed in detail elsewhere (Palmer 2010a, 88).

21   See also R. Piddington 1950, 80.

W.E.H. Stanner's 1965 paper contributed to the debate about the correctness of Radcliffe-Brown's anthropology. His paper is better remembered (and now widely quoted) because Stanner presented his views as to how groups of Aboriginal people used the land over which they claimed rights and how this determined the economic resources they exploited, which in turn was a product of the natural environment. Stanner, like Berndt before him, identified the local group or clan as the group with rights to the estates. Bands were the land-occupying group whose range included the estates of several local groups (1965, 2). He thus succinctly overcame the difficulty of the exclusive patrilineal band and its relationship to country by recognising the practical aspects of the use of country by a band and its constituent members. Stanner wrote:

> Each territorial group was associated with both an estate and a range. The distinction is crucial. The estate was the traditionally recognised locus ('country', 'home', 'ground', 'dreaming place') of some kind of patrilineal descent group forming the core or nucleus of the territorial group. It seems usually to have been a more or less continuous stretch. The range was the tract or orbit over which the group, including its nucleus adherents, ordinarily hunted and foraged to maintain life. The range normally included the estate: people did not usually belong here and live there, but, in some circumstances, the two could be practically dissociated. Estate and range together may be said to constitute a domain, which is an ecological life-space. (ibid., 2)

Stanner was of the view that a number of local groups, represented in the countryside as bands, together made up language speaking groups. In a way of speaking, 'tribes' were congeries of bands (ibid., 21). Stanner's focus on bands comprising several local groups and the estate and range distinction meant that '"tribal" or language-divisions' (ibid., 13) were not central to developing an understanding of how rights to country were articulated.

There have been some modifications suggested to these ideas, as subsequent studies continue to confirm that patrilineal descent may not have been the only means of gaining rights to country. Evidence produced as a result of land claim research has shown that unilineal descent may not have been the case everywhere, particularly for the less well-watered areas.[22] Field research supported the conclusion that rights to country could be

---

22 For views developed from land claim literature, see Hamilton 1982; Layton 1983; Maddock 1981; Myers 1986. See also Peterson and Long 1986, 59–61 and Sutton 2003, 196–199.

gained through a number of ways, patrifiliation being just one (Peterson 1983, 137–138; Stanner 2001, 112–114). Myers, writing of the Pintupi of Central Australia, showed that rights in estates were multiple and perhaps differentiated as to degree rather than singular in relation to one patri-estate only (1986, 138–140). Cane (2002, 115–140) documented five ways by which rights to country could be gained, again for desert regions of southern Australia (ibid., 137). Sutton has shown there to be multiple 'pathways' whereby rights to country can be pressed, again for desert regions of Central Australia (2007, 178–187; 2015, 38ff.). In this regard, Hiatt wrote well before the advent of the native title era:

> [S]tatements by anthropologists and Aborigines during land claim hearings, together with academic field research carried out during the last decade [i.e. prior to 1984] consolidate the case against Radcliffe-Brown's conception of the patrilineal patrilocal horde as the basic unit of Aboriginal local organization. But it is not only that patrilineality can no longer be regarded as a principle uniformly governing residential associations and access to resources; we must now ask, in the light of new evidence, whether patrifiliation was everywhere the basic principle of ownership. My own view is that throughout Australia it was an important credential, and probably in many areas the most important. But, in competing for scarce goods and social status, individuals (in traditional times as well as in contemporary land claims) appealed to various other recognized credentials, such as matrifiliation, birth-place, conception-place, father's burial-place, mythological links, long-term residence, and so on. (Hiatt 1984, 9)

The evidence supports the view that these researchers had found field data to support the conclusion that proprietary interests in country were multiple and complex, depending on a number of relationships. Permission and the exercise of rights were best understood in the context of the relationships that legitimated their expression. The operation of such a system may account for the fact that at least some of the earlier ethnography demonstrated that people exercised rights to access country well outside their patrilineal estate, perhaps legitimated by other attachments to country that were pressed into service to justify the use of a range of country for economic and social reasons. The ideal of the patrilineal descent group whose members exercised exclusive rights within a single estate was not a satisfactory or adequate representation of the ethnographic reality.

Based on these accounts, it is evident that in arid regions, where maximum flexibility was required to ensure continuity of inheritance in an uncertain environment, more open systems were to be found, favouring multiple pathways of descent and the acquisition of rights to country through means other than descent (Keen 1997, 66). However, there appears to be much variation in the ethnography (cf. ibid., 73) and perhaps the best conclusion is that no model fits all. For the native title anthropologist, then, it is not a simple question of stating that the system was universally uniform. Rather, what is required is the provision of a view as to what was likely to have obtained at sovereignty and whether present laws and customs reflect a continuity of the same system. Above all, however, is the fact that in customary systems it is unlikely that rights were to be gained through descent alone. Other ways of gaining rights to country were also likely to have been important and a part of that customary system.

Consideration of the ethnography provided by Radcliffe-Brown and Kaberry shows that there has been some progress made over the decades with respect to our understanding of customary systems of rights to land in Aboriginal Australia. Radcliffe-Brown's initial view was elementary and disarmingly simple: a man gained rights to the bounded estate of his father and so on from one generation to another. The estate was (like an English country estate) bounded and members of other groups had to seek permission before entering it. Kaberry and the Piddingtons were less sure of this 'normal' type of local organisation. Later writers and researchers have shown that generally in Aboriginal Australia rights may be gained by reference to several principles, while in many desert systems there are multiple pathways whereby rights can be asserted according to customary principles and beliefs. In addition to descent, then, place of spiritual conception or some other totemic link commonly yields rights to country. So, too, may ritual links to a Dreaming that traversed the country, particularly with respect to specific places or sites or command of ritual objects believed to embody the country in question. In my experience these are all quite common principles that provide legitimation for the assertion of customary rights to a range of country. Examples of the free use of a much wider range of country than a man's single estate reflected the reality that, from a practical point of view, hunters and gatherers need a wider range of country than would have been afforded by a single estate, except perhaps in the richest tropical environments. Even if an estate provided an economically viable living space, social imperatives and bonds of kinship would have mandated a system that facilitated social intercourse, free visiting and access rather than impeding it. This instructs that systems of rights to country are neither singular nor simple. They undoubtedly exhibit regional variation but common principles are found throughout. They are the product of social relationships just as much as of jurally endorsed title and are consequently flexible to changes in those relationships as families and groups wax and wane over time.

Native title rights (and interests)

The native title anthropologist has as his or her primary task the job of seeking to explain the system whereby claimants assert rights to country and the extent to which this might demonstrate continuity with past systems. While a 'right' is fundamentally a legal concept, it has been variously understood by anthropologists, and unpacking the term, as I have done above, will assist in gaining a better understanding of what is meant by the use of the word. This, in turn, may assist in deciding whether something is a right or interest at all, as well as whether it is 'possessed' under traditional laws and customs. Attempts to classify types of rights (determinative, contingent) are helpful to the extent that they will assist in coming to an understanding of the social interplay that defines and distinguishes rights. This is particularly important where there is competition or disagreement between claimants (or would-be claimants) as to the status of one sort of right over another. In bringing some social analysis to bear on these disagreements, anthropologists can perhaps proffer a view as to the customary bases of such assertions – should they have the need or be impelled to do so.

While Australian anthropology has produced what I have termed above 'a developing orthodoxy', the matter is not without contention, particularly with respect to the mode of descent that might most usually have been in evidence in Aboriginal Australia. However, I have discussed above how some more recent Australian anthropologists have taken a much broader view of the allocation of rights to country than some of the earlier writers and shown the richness and complexities of the system. These are all issues that must be treated in any native title inquiry. Assessment should be made of the system today (based on the empirical field data) and the likely system in operation at sovereignty where this can be deduced from the early literature or developed through inference from work undertaken elsewhere. Perhaps above all else, this chapter serves to demonstrate how complex is the system of possessing, exercising and managing rights to country in customary arrangements. In my view, a proper explication of the complexity is a necessary part of advancing an expert view in relation to a customary system of rights to country.

4

Exercise of native title rights

Modern anthropology is founded on observation – anthropologists should seek to study what goes on around them. In a native title inquiry the focus of that observation should be the claimants' relationships with their country and their activities and behaviour in relation to it. With respect to proprietary interests in land, rights are manifest through their exercise. Some customary actions then, performed in relation to country, are significant signals of the exercise of rights or duties and potentially, then, also to the continuity of that exercise and the system that underpins it over continuing generations. Consequently, doing the anthropology for a native title claim should ideally involve observation of the exercise of rights to country by the claimants. However, in practice it may only be possible to record how claimants assert that they exercise certain of their rights to country. Both sources of data provide a means whereby the anthropologist can create a representation of the social interactions and normative values and principles that determine how rights and their exercise are managed. It is from these data that the system of land tenure is explicated.

Before I turn to an examination of these practical manifestations of the exercise of customary rights to country, there are a couple of preliminary matters that require attention. The first is definitional; the second a creature of native title law.

Understanding the anthropology in a native title context

Groups local and residential

As studies of local organisation in Australia developed it became evident that there was a necessary differentiation to be made between the form and structure of two quite different groups. One was the exogamous descent group (or 'local descent group', 'local group', and sometimes a 'clan' or 'country group'). The other was an extended family group or those who recognise bonds of kinship (sometimes the 'band' or 'horde'[1] or 'residence group'). I noted above that Radcliffe-Brown's account of local organisation resulted in some ambiguities and lack of lucidity. These developed from his failure to distinguish these two key components of customary Australian Indigenous local organisation.

The distinction between the local group and the band was regarded as fundamental by R.M. Berndt (1959, 96) and L. Hiatt (1962, 284). Berndt concluded that it was the local group that was the land-owning group while the band was the land-occupying group (1959, 98, 103). Keen (acknowledging Sutton) called the descent group a 'country group' (2004, 277) in recognition of the fact that not all land-owning groups were strictly speaking descent groups – that is, recruited according to filiative links to forebears but members could be enlisted by means other than descent, as I have discussed in the previous chapter. Keen termed the band (ibid., 427) a 'residence group' in recognition of the fact that its membership was potentially impermanent and could change over time. The members of the residence group went about together hunting and gathering and are sometimes termed the 'band' or 'horde'. The band was likely made up of two or more descent groups since the rule of descent group exogamy requires that spouses come from different descent groups.

Based on this analysis it is evident that the country group and the residence group are different types of social formation. While both are identified with respect to relationships of constituent members, country groups comprise those who recognise filiative, kinship or spiritual relationships with one another and with an area of land held in

---

1   The term 'horde' was used by Radcliffe-Brown and other earlier writers, rather confusingly, for what later writers termed the local descent group.

common by country group members. Residence groups comprise those with lived social relationships engendered from daily economic activity and lived experience. The former is a description of how relationships are calculated and thought out. The latter is a description of how relationships are actuated.[2] Early observers of Aboriginal Australia witnessed residence groups moving across the countryside as hunters and gatherers. While the residence groups comprised two or more country groups, it was the latter not the former that represented land-owning corporations by virtue of their members' spiritual or filiative relationships to country. Thus, members of a residence group together as congeries of members of several country groups were likely to have claim to rights in more than one estate. To the extent that a member gained rights to different country through more than one pathway, members of the hunting and gathering residence group together were likely to claim rights to multiple estates. This arrangement would explain why the Piddingtons found that the exercise of rights to country was not effected with respect to singular hermetic estates.[3]

Claim groups and local groups

In native title law, application for recognition of prior rights is generally made by a claim group whose laws and customs are the subject of examination by the court. In this it is the claim group that makes the application and, in the event that there is a subsequent determination in their favour, it is the group as a legal entity that will enjoy the native title rights that have been recognised. The relationship between the country groups and the claim group is oblique: the former is a product of the anthropology and our understandings of how customary systems worked. The latter is a product of the native title law. This means that while the anthropology may instruct that, according to customary systems, rights were (and are) not spread homogeneously across those who comprise the claim group, this is not a matter that the court needs to consider. The rights are allocated in native title law equally between those who made

2   Sutton considered that country groups were 'typological units' defined in relation to types of relationship. Residence groups were 'land-utilising aggregates' (2003, 96).
3   Some years later Norman Tindale reported that, for the Yindjibarndi in the Pilbara region of Western Australia, 'there are no separate family territories, all people may hunt over the whole of Indjibandi country. Adults may hunt unquestioned. Young men may hunt but there are restrictions on some foods they may eat' (1953a, 333).

application for recognition of native title. Thus, the court generally takes the view that the intra-mural allocation of rights within an application area is not a matter for its consideration.[4]

This issue was raised in the Daniel claim where Nicholson J made comment on Professor K. Maddock's, one of the experts, view:

> [Maddock] was sceptical a language group had been regarded as having owned land although there would be some correlation with the area within which a language is spoken or mythologically identified. However, Professor Maddock was not prepared to start from a *priori* position of estate groups.[5]

His Honour continued:

> I do not consider it is necessary to explore further these aspects of the anthropological evidence. Following the decisions in Ward HC and in Yorta Yorta it became apparent that the concentration on notions of composite community and estate groups, which had featured so heavily in the anthropological evidence given earlier in the trial, were not to be the central focus of the inquiry.[6]

The appeal judges did not find that the trial judge had erred in relation to the groups that held native title rights and that these were not held 'at the estate group level' (*Moses v State of Western Australia* [2007] FCAFC 78 [344]).

> Sections 223 and 225 do not require the Court to search for an anthropologically identified form of community or group. The NTA [*Native Title Act*] makes clear the Court is to examine the evidence to see who holds native title, if anyone, and so whether there are communal, group or individual rights and interests. Anthropological theory and research may inform that examination but cannot determine it.[7]

This manner of treating customary systems does not mean that the proper characterisation of local organisation is unimportant. Understanding how Aboriginal systems of land tenure worked and how rights were transmitted through time is an essential driver to the process whereby native title can

---

4   However, determinations also record that the rights are 'exercisable subject to and in accordance with traditional laws and customs' and courts may acknowledge that the rights are not shared equally. I thank Robert Blowes for this information.
5   *Daniel v State of Western Australia* [2003] FCA 666 [241].
6   ibid., [244].
7   ibid., [334].

be proved. Establishing that the system remains substantially intact is a key component in any evidence of the continuity of laws and customs – as they relate to land and rights in country. Moreover, the intra-mural allocation of rights within the different constituent estates of the claim area will be significant in the post-native title administration of the country of a determined application – notwithstanding the court's lack of interest in such matters when considering the application in the first place.

There is a related issue where the framing of a native title claim can perhaps too readily accommodate substantial changes in the system of gaining and asserting rights to country and so neglect the customary arrangements. In places where the estate system has more or less vanished, rights are often conceptualised by claimants and their advocates as being universally and evenly spread across all members of a claim group. Members of the claim group say that they recognise commonalities and so are a 'society' in native title terms. They comprise, then, an undifferentiated modern day 'tribe'[8] and may also be a language group. According to this view, all members of the claim group can freely exercise rights to the country of the former estates of the language group members in aggregation. There is reason to conclude that this is based on a customary system by reference to the multiple pathways I have discussed above. However, to be shown as a customary system, based on rules and principles, there can be no automatic right to the country of others simply because they share commonalities and are, for the purposes of a native title claim, a single society. In the system as I have described it in the previous chapter, the extent of a person's range would be defined by reference to legitimating references as well as the rights of fellow residence group members who could bring their kinsfolk into country wherein they were, in fact, visitors not owners. Proof of native title requires continuity with the past. This means that the present-day arrangements must be shown to have some connection with the customary system such that it can reasonably be argued that the contemporary structure is based upon and rooted in past

---

8   Sutton (2003, 133) wrote in this regard, 'In regions heavily impacted by colonial and postcolonial developments, it is sometimes the case that some people maintain proximate entitlements to small areas such as classical estates as well as an identification with more widely-cast landed entities such as language groups, but at the same time others from the same region may maintain only the wider form of identification with land'. Sutton goes on to note that the neglect of a distinction between estate groups and a wider society or group may sometimes lead to disputes.

practice. A substantial or total move away from country group ownership to claim group ownership, should the ethnography reveal such, would weaken the case for recognition of native title.

Exercising and asserting rights in a customary system

Given the potential to benefit from a right to several different estates, by reference to a number of different governing principles, it is likely that there were in customary systems arrangements in place to order the acquisition of rights and their command. These worked to ensure governance and management of real assets in an orderly fashion. In short, it seems reasonable to assume that people knew where their country was and who commanded authority with respect to it as well as to all other areas known to them. Native title research needs to establish which principles are evident in the ethnography and how rights develop and are differentiated with respect to their originating belief and associated rules. Given this complexity, it is also essential to understand how the allocation and exercise of rights to country are a part of social process and the product of social relationships. It is important, then, to take a closer look at how rights to country were ordered in customary systems and gain an appreciation of the implications of this system for contemporary bids to gain recognition of customary title to land.

Descent, cognatic descent and the exercise of choice

What emerges from the Australian ethnography is that descent played a central role in how rights to country were transmitted. As Hiatt pointed out, this may not have been the only way to gain rights to country, but it was probably, in most cases, 'an important credential, and probably in many areas the most important' (1984, 9). Systems of descent that recognise filiative links through both the mother and the father (patrifiliation and matrifiliation) are sometimes called 'cognatic'. The implications of a cognatic system are that rights to country can be gained through both matri- as well as patri-filiative links, effectively giving ego the right to two countries gained from their parents – as Kaberry reported for the Kimberley. Potentially in a cognatic system ego gains rights in the country of four grandparents and eight great grandparents, assuming each had a different country. With each ascending generation the number of possible estates increases exponentially. This means that ego could potentially claim rights to up to eight different countries over three ascending generations from ego. I have drawn a diagram to illustrate the theoretical descent of rights in a cognatic system over three generations (Figure 4.1).

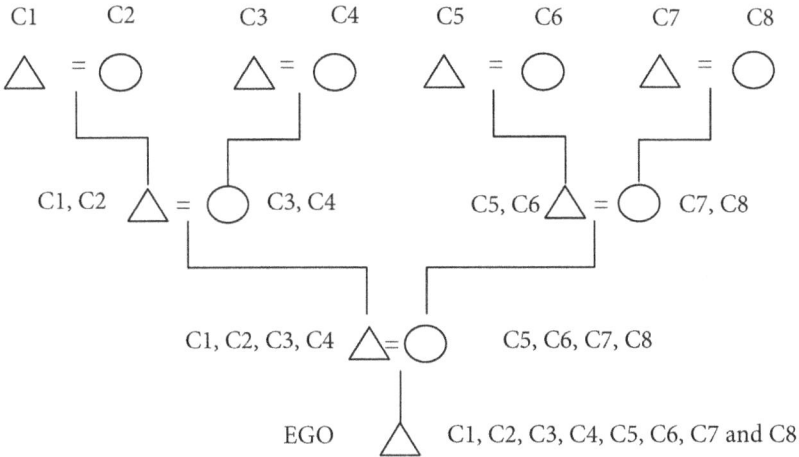

Figure 4.1: Cognatic descent over four generations

Note: 'C' denotes the country or estate wherein an individual gains rights through descent

Source: Diagram designed by author.

According to this account, then, a person potentially might claim rights in many countries through descent. Add to this a system that recognised that rights to country could be gained via other pathways and there develops, on the face of it, potential for a situation where there is no clear rule as to who was the principal owner of the country. Were such an open-ended system to be the ethnographic reality, claims to rights to country would have been open to a seemingly never-ending spectrum of individuals. This would have made the management of rights to country according to an ordered system next to impossible. Rather than a principled system there would be a seemingly random set of options and choices that might be selected without discrimination on the whim of the individual. Subject to no normative principles the arrangement would be no system at all. As such, it would run the danger of failing to qualify as a system of laws and customs, subject to normative values, and so would be incapable of being recognised in Australian native title law as a continuing system of native title.

Radcliffe-Brown identified this as a difficulty for a cognatic system which he considered had the potential to become dysfunctional. He wrote:

> If any society established a system of corporations on the basis of kinship – clans, joint families, incorporated lineages – it must necessarily adopt a system of unilineal reckoning of succession …

> Thus the existence of unilineal (patrilineal or matrilineal) succession in the great majority of human societies can be traced to its sociological 'cause' or 'origin' in certain fundamental social necessities. Chief amongst them, I have suggested, is the need of defining, with sufficient precisions to avoid unresolvable conflicts, the rights *in rem*[9] over persons. The need of precise definition of rights *in personam*[10] and of rights over things would seem to be secondary but still important factors. (Radcliffe-Brown 1952, 46)

Radcliffe-Brown postulated that there had to be a normative system of laws that regulated the rights of a horde (country group) to its country and in relation to each other (ibid.). He considered such an arrangement to rely upon a principled system of succession that would avoid 'unresolveable conflict'. He thus sought to establish that unilineal systems had a functional origin that if absent would have dysfunctional consequences.

In summary then, recognition of the fact that multiple pathways to country is a part of the Australian ethnography must be understood in the context of its operation and the social process whereby rights to country are gained and perpetuated. Accepting cognation and multiple pathways requires that the system in evidence exhibits some mechanism that would counter the potential for this 'unresolveable conflict'. Generally in the Australian ethnography these mechanisms are evident as qualifiers to the exercise of rights, whether by reference to descent or other means. Meeting these qualifications is a necessary requirement before the rights can be exercised in practice. These operational requirements have the quality of a normative system of rules in that they are accepted within

---

9   Radcliffe-Brown defines what he means by 'rights *in rem* over a person' earlier in his paper. He states, 'rights over a person "as against the world", i.e. imposing duties on all other persons in respect of that particular person. This is the *jus in rem* of Roman law in relation to persons' (1952, 33). However, the definition provided by the Merriam-Webster online legal dictionary for *jus in rem* reads, 'a right enforceable against anyone in the world interfering with that right founded on some specific relationship, status, or particular property accorded legal protection from interference by anyone (as the right to be free from slander or to enjoy one's property)'. www.merriam-webster.com/dictionary/jus%20in%20rem, accessed 16 July 2014.

10   'Rights over a person imposing some duty or duties upon that person' (ibid., 32).

a population as being mandated by past practice and typically are believed to have been sanctioned by metaphysical forces in the distant past. They are, in the claimants' parlance, matters of 'the Law'. These are as much a part of the system of the acquisition of rights and their exercise as are the means whereby the rights are gained in the first place.

One fundamental example of a requirement to be in evidence before a right to country can be realised and so exercised according to customary belief is an acknowledgement of a spiritual relationship between a person and their country. This may be understood in terms of a totemic bond or the product of descent itself where a person is believed to be linked 'through the blood' to the ancestor and the country from time immemorial. In any event, rights to country are not exercised in a spiritual vacuum. Rights are seldom unqualified in their exercise and may require that other conditions be met before they can be put into effect. Additionally, and in the ethnographies with which I am familiar, not all rights are regarded as yielding the same degree of entitlement and their manner of acquisition is generally important in this regard. Not all who command a right are equal and the pressing of rights is a part of social process that is characterised by relationships between people. The manner whereby these relationships are socially constructed is an important factor in the way rights were (and are) asserted consistent with customary practices.

There is a danger that these aspects of the system whereby rights to land are allocated and perpetuated receive too little attention in native title claims. Indeed, it is perhaps a commonplace observation that many of the disputes that develop between native title claimants are the result of too many people making a claim over too few countries. In a number of areas where I have worked there is a common (and to my mind misplaced) assumption on the part of some claimants that all that has to be proved for a person to be a native title holder is descent from an ancestor. This may be sourced to Tindale, some other early genealogy, or simply be a product of the oral account. The claim is made regardless of the network of social relationships, acquisition of knowledge and the gaining of qualifications that I show below to be an essential part of the social process of gaining rights to country. One Native Title Representative Body with which I am familiar adopted the rule that a person could only be a claimant on one claim – thus attempting to obviate potential conflicts. However, the fact is that in customary arrangements, as far as we are able to discover, there were robust systems in place that yielded a relatively stable system of land tenure. This must have been sustained by the observance of rules that rendered what is evidently quite a flexible system stable, reliable and predictable. It is important, then, for the native title anthropologist to understand how the system operated in customary terms to ensure that everyone knew whose country was whose.

It is to the ways that rights could be used in customary systems to articulate relationships between people and the control and use of resources that I now turn. In the following sections I examine some of the more common ways whereby relationships between people and country are characterised in customary systems. These may be used to assert a right in a particular country or give an avowed right greater weight than, say, those of others who also press rights to the same country.

Cognation plus?

An eminent Australian anthropologist coined the term 'cognation plus'[11] with respect to the descent of rights in his review for a respondent party of an expert report I had written for a native title application. By this I took him to mean that the system of gaining rights to country (in the particular ethnography that we had both been commissioned to study) was cognatic, but it required an additional dimension. This was that a person's relationship to country was embedded within a totemic or spiritual environment that rendered the person a spiritual representation of the country and its metaphysical characteristics and potentialities. The implication of this was that descent (whether through matrifiliation or patrifiliation) was insufficient of itself to yield rights to country. Rather, there had to be evidence that there continued to be a spiritual correspondence between the person and that country, articulated by reference to a totemic principle, which had been documented, in this case, by the early ethnographer Daisy Bates, who had undertaken fieldwork in a neighbouring area (Palmer 2010a, 81–86). The argument put by the expert for the state in this matter was that there was an absence of the 'plus' factor, and consequently the descent of rights could not be considered to be based on customary principles. While 'cognation plus' was not a term used by the trial judge in his judgment,[12] he concluded

---

11   I acknowledge Professor Basil Sansom as the originator of this term.
12   *Graham on behalf of the Ngadju People v State of Western Australia* [2012] FCA 1455 [47–48].

that there was evidence that there continued to be a spiritual relationship between the claimants of the application area[13], and he found in favour of the applicants.

Establishing a spiritual link between people and country provides the basis for asserting a correspondence between a person and the land. This is a noumenal phenomenon but provides legitimation for the belief in the immanence of land-based spirituality inherent in those who assert rights to country. This has been a theme in the writings of Australian anthropology. T.G.H. Strehlow wrote in this regard:

> The religious and totemic ties that united not merely whole groups with their group areas, but the individuals constituting each group with one or more defined mythological centres with each group area, were of the utmost importance. … The depth of this emotional attachment was a result of the identification of the human beings born or conceived in a certain totemic landscape with the supernatural beings who were believed to have created that landscape. (Strehlow 1965, 127)

R.M. Berndt wrote of Arnhem Land:

> Where land was concerned, man's relationship with it was not merely social, but socio-religious. In other words, while relationships between persons belonging to a particular stretch of country or to a site were expressed genealogically or otherwise, there was believed to be an additional *quality* which the bare social relationship itself did not define. Or, to put in another way, the social relationship was *underpinned* by a spiritual association which defined all relationships of that kind and no others. (Berndt 1970, 1; emphasis in original)

This spiritual dimension may not only be expressed in terms of a totemic link of the sort referred to by writers like Strehlow and Berndt and documented by Bates as noted above. Where it is believed that ancestors were autochthonous – that is, they originated from the very land that is subject to claim – their spirituality is believed to be a part of the same spirituality that informed the landscape. This metaphysical quality is believed to have been transmitted through the blood to subsequent generations and thus to the present-day claimants. While the belief in the spirituality derived from ancestors is not commonly asserted in my experience, it is usual for claimants to express a strong and abiding spiritual relationship with the country they claim as their own. The task

---

13   ibid., [94].

for the native title anthropologist is to provide a view, based on sound data, that such a belief has customary content. It is probably not likely to be argued that such spiritual connection was not a part of customary systems.[14]

Realising rights and dangerous places

In common with many other legal systems, Australian law requires that many rights must be realised before they can be acted upon. By this I mean that while the right exists, it cannot be exercised until certain conditions are met. For example, the right to drive a motor car in Australia is conditional upon the acquisition of a licence, itself dependent upon age and demonstrated competence and the payment of a fee. In Aboriginal Australia the exercise of the right to use country is dependent upon detailed knowledge of that country. Such knowledge is not to be understood merely in terms of the geography, although that is important from a practical point of view. In my experience, the greater emphasis is placed amongst those with whom I have mostly worked on the metaphysical dimensions of the landscape. Some places are believed to be spiritually potent and thus actually physically dangerous.[15] Examples include ritual grounds that may contain places forbidden to women or areas where sacred objects are stored. Generally, places where it is known that rituals were practised in times past are avoided since the details of the forbidden places (some for men and some for women) are no longer known. Consequently, it is judged wisest to avoid the area altogether rather than run the risk of inadvertent trespass on dangerous ground. Other examples of dangerous places are areas associated with malevolent or negative spirituality, including sites that are believed to cause sickness or a natural disaster. The presence of a mythic water snake in certain pools and reaches of rivers and creeks mandates particular attention, observance of protocols and ritual greetings. Without this knowledge practical use of the country remains impossible. Country that is redolent with powerful spirituality, some of it potentially dangerous, is like a minefield. Lack of knowledge of the location of danger might result in fatal consequences. Knowledge of country, whether it be practical, economic or spiritual is

---

14 However, see *Akiba on behalf of the Torres Strait Islanders of the Regional Seas Claim Group v State of Queensland* (No. 2) [2010] FCA 643 [655]. It was submitted that 'the absence of the spiritual element … is almost probably unique to this case' (ibid., [172]).

15 To my mind, the classic Australian article written about safe and dangerous places is by Biernoff (1978). Kaberry also noted the significance of spiritual danger in country for different areas of Aboriginal Australia (e.g. 1939, 138–139, 203–204).

then an essential component for the exercise of rights to country. The continuity of rights to country, however legitimated, requires possession of this qualification. Without it, so it might be argued, the exercise of rights remains potential. In those cases where there is now no longer anyone to teach and pass on this esoteric information, it would never be possible to achieve the exercise of rights to country according to customary principles, although the rights may remain all the same.

Given cases where ego has potential claim to several countries, there is likely to be a limit to his or her knowledge of the range of estates involved. This may be considered to be a reflection of place of residence, since familiarity with country implies at least a degree of physical presence. Thus, one or two (maybe more) countries may be privileged in that person's dealings with country by virtue of the knowledge of the land concerned. Thus, country claimed via filiative links with a distant forebear that is little known might be classed as country wherein ego would choose to exercise rights to a very limited extent, perhaps under the guidance of a kinsman who knew the country better. To do otherwise would be to risk spiritual danger in unknown and potentially fatal country.

Ranking rights

In native title research the pressing of rights to a particular country by members of different groups may be an issue that gives rise to dispute or controversy. Typically perhaps members of one group might claim that their rights to the country should prevail over the rights asserted by another group to the same area. This may be argued on the basis that their rights are superior (stronger) or have greater customary legitimacy than the competing claims of others. The former argument gives rise to the question as to whether in customary systems some rights had greater weight within the community of rights holders than others. If so, what was the system that regulated and legitimated the ranking of rights to country? In my experience, this is a complex and fraught matter. There is a small literature on the distinction between a primary and a secondary right that developed from the *Aboriginal Land Rights Act* where such a distinction was implicit in the legislation (see Peterson, Keen and Sansom 1977; Stanner 2001, 113–114). As I noted in the previous chapter, Radcliffe-Brown also differentiated rights in this manner. This distinction typically rests on the manner whereby the right in question was acquired (cf. Peterson 1983, 137–139). Kolig, writing of the central Kimberley region, distinguishes what he terms 'secondary rights' of access and usufruct from 'ownership', by which, presumably, he meant a spiritually legitimated absolute connection with the country in question (1988, 83). He considered that members of the patriline had rights in the intellectual (or religious) knowledge of the patri-lodge (1978, 57; 1981, 31). This included the rights to use (or sanction the use of) knowledge of sites, narratives, songs and ritual performances associated with the lodge and its Dreaming attributes (1980c, 281). For Kolig, by my reading, the rights of the members of the patriline were superior to those who only had rights of access and usufruct.

In a native title inquiry, then, it may be helpful to examine the field data collected to see if there is a clear system in evidence that stipulates that, say, rights gained via descent are somehow regarded as superior to those gained via totemic attachment occasioned through birth or conception. A difficulty is likely to be that rights that are articulated through social relationships and concomitant interaction are pressed in complex ways according to the manner whereby the relationship is negotiated. While some writers have suggested a dyadic distinction between primary and secondary rights (Kolig 1980b, 42; Peterson, Keen and Sansom 1977; Peterson 1983, 137–139; Stanner 2001, 113–114), my own view is that this does not adequately represent the social processes involved or the range of choices exercised in the assertion of rights to country. A distinction between 'primary' and 'secondary' rights, neat dyad though it may be, is unlikely to be evidenced in social practice. Understanding how rights are pressed and so ranked requires examination of the social process involved.

I have already set out what I regard as some of the important qualities and qualifications that may be required for rights to be realised through their exercise. The manner of this exercise and the rules that regulate it are important to an understanding of the process involved. For example, the degree to which the rights may be pressed in the face of competition for recognition of rights within social interplay that characterises contested environments will depend upon an individual's status and eminence. This is consistent with a system that generally honours the senior members of the community, placing value on age, experience and knowledge. In Aboriginal Australia, as a general rule, it is senior members who command respect and who through their command of sacred as well as mundane knowledge are regarded as decision-makers, the source of information, sage advice, comprehension and understanding, qualities that are highly esteemed (Berndt 1965). Being of a certain age is insufficient to obtain this status on its own since it must be accompanied by the qualities enumerated above. Attainment of this status I call 'standing', recognising that it is a relative attribute so that one man may have greater standing than another depending on the accumulated knowledge and its manner of disposition. The category of person so qualified is often today referred to generically as 'elders'. In areas of Aboriginal Australia where ritual practice continues, such men and women are sometimes referred to as 'Law Bosses' in recognition of their eminence in ritual matters.

According to customary systems in matters related to the pressing of rights to specific country, standing is recognised with respect to that country through the legitimating pathways discussed above, including knowledge of the country in question. According to this process standing is achieved through social and ritual maturity, as well as through the nature of the connection claimed to a specific area of country. In terms of personal predilection, it is a matter for an individual to negotiate the degree of standing claimed with respect to a particular country. A person with standing with respect to country that is not the subject in question would likely make clear that his or her interests lay elsewhere and that they had no intention of pressing a right to the country being discussed. In these cases, where a person decides that the country at issue is one in which they have filiative attachment but no standing, they can defer to another or others, saying, typically, that they 'come behind', 'help them out' or act as 'back stop' to those whose rights they judged (and are judged by others) to be superior. This facilitates an exercise of choice in which area or areas of country rights will be pressed. The discriminations relating to the pressing of rights in country that develop from 'standing' operate as a means whereby individuals effectively exercise a choice over the articulation of rights. Given that there are multiple ways to attain rights, this exercise of choice is an important means of regulating the geographic extent of the effective exercise of rights to country.

Permission, trespass and licence

Owning a right requires that those who do not own that right ask permission before seeking to share in the benefits derived from the exercise of the right. Acts of seeking or giving permission with respect to property signal the existence of a proprietary system where some own rights in a particular property while others do not. In native title inquiries, then, field data relating to a requirement that some seek permission with respect to the use of country, while others have the power to grant it, is an important means whereby the normative system governing the allocation of rights to country is to be understood. The act of infringing a right in property is known as trespass and may incur censure or penalty and, in extreme cases, was punishable by death. Nancy Williams has written extensively about the nature of permission in Aboriginal Australia (1982, 1986 and 1999) and her work provides a detailed examination of the topic.

Lawyers in particular are attracted to this aspect of a normative system and often seek out examples of permission when eliciting evidence. This is not always as straightforward as one might expect. Take the following examples from the transcripts of a native title hearing.

Example 1

Counsel: Now, what about if something happens on … Yanturi country … who, according to law way, who's got to be asked about that?

Claimant:[16] Me.

Counsel: And just you?

Claimant: Me and my brother, because we're the eldest, and then we're going to call up the other Nungali mob.[17]

Example 2

Counsel: What about if it's your father's mother's country? Can you give permission for that one, your father's mother's country?

Claimant: Yes, I can give permission if old people not around here. They come to me and I'll go there, and I'll look around with them, and I'll call a meeting, ask R H or D to come along to talk up.

Counsel: And why are R and D the ones who should be talking up?

Claimant: Because it's their Kakung country.[18]

In the first exchange the female claimant told the court that she had the right to be asked in relation to any proposed action within a named area of country. However, she quickly added that this was not solely her responsibility. Permission would require participation of her brother

---

16 I have removed the names of claimant and counsel.
17 *Griffiths v Northern Territory & Anor. D6012*, transcript of evidence, 335.
18 Father's father's country; ibid., 336.

(because he and she were 'the oldest') but additionally members of a named language group would be called together as well. The evidence does not tell us what might happen if there was disagreement between the variously defined participants in this process. Permission is evidently the product of a group rather than an individual.

In the second exchange, which features the same claimant as witness, the rules for granting permission in ego's father's mother's country are more circumspect. The witness considered she could give permission 'if old people not around here', implying, by my reading, that these unnamed 'old people' had precedence in this matter. She then adds that she would accompany the prospective visitors and 'look around with them', presumably in the country, which I take to mean that she would escort them on their visit for reasons not there explained. Finally, she adds that she'd 'call a meeting', naming two individuals who she regarded as significant in relation to the granting of permission for this country. These two people had filiative links to the country in question through their father and father's father.

These accounts are entirely consistent with a system where rights to country are not singular but are rather the product of a network of relationships and socially endorsed protocols and rule-based referents. These relationships may include an arrangement whereby a right of access is provided to another by some form of agreement or understanding. This has sometimes been called 'standing permission'. Standing permission is not a right but a licence and may be revoked. In native title research it is important to distinguish rights (determinative or contingent) from access or use offered on licence since the two are easily confused and can give rise to misunderstandings amongst claimants. One example, in some areas, is the privilege provided to a spouse over her husband's (or his wife's) country. Spousal unions seldom give rise to absolute rights to country in Aboriginal Australia, but there may be recognition that a wife gains a licence in her husband's country (and vice versa). These arrangements, where evident in the ethnography, need to be carefully probed and subject to close scrutiny in terms of their likely antiquity.

In my experience, the complexity of the way whereby rights to country are distributed throughout a given population means that answers to questions of permission are seldom simple. There is also another aspect to the 'permission' question, apparent from a close reading of the second extract set out above. It relates to duty and danger in country.

Working with a group of senior male claimants when undertaking an inquiry for a native title claim, I sought to gain ethnography relevant to the different sorts of rights claimants might consider they could freely exercise in the land over which they sought recognition of native title. My success in this regard was limited because I found that these senior men found the concept of listing rights alien – it was, after all, in their view their country in which they could do what they pleased, consistent with customary practice. The qualifier is important. It was their exclusive property (their right) but nevertheless subject to rules that governed how this right was to be exercised. One principal consideration was the nature of the spiritual potentialities of the country and the danger inherent in access gained in ignorance of the totemic geography of the country. This reflected the complexity of the spiritual hazards of the country that I have outlined above (see 'Realising rights and dangerous places') and the need to possess knowledge of places and to know where it was safe to go and where it was wise to avoid. But the minefield that is spiritual country also imposes an obligation upon those who know in relation to those who are ignorant but who seek permission for access. These people who are ignorant of spiritual danger must be protected from spiritual harm. The best way to do this and ensure that nothing untoward occurs is to accompany them and 'look around with them'. Given spiritual danger in country, trespass acquires a rather different complexion to that common in mainstream Australian thinking, where to trespass is simply to enter someone else's land or property without permission. Trespass in customary Aboriginal dealings is an act of great folly and has potentially fatal consequences. There would, then, need to be good reason to take such risks. Owners of the country who also know its spiritual particularities have a duty to protect strangers and feel responsible if something untoward happens to them.[19] Given the nature of country and entry upon it by the ignorant it is understandable that the senior men with whom I worked provided me with data relating to conditions of access and duty of care, rather than an enumeration of rights such as might be found in a native title application.

---

19   A well-known example of this duty of care is the request, issued by the traditional owners of Uluru, that visitors to the Rock do not climb it. 'Anangu have a duty to safeguard visitors to their land. They feel great sadness if visitors to their land are killed or injured. As such, traditional owners would prefer that as guests to their land, visitors will respect Anangu law and culture by not climbing.' www.ayersrockresort.com.au/uluru-and-kata-tjuta/uluru-and-kata-tjuta-national-park/can-i-climb-uluru accessed 25 January 2017.

This does not mean that trespass was unknown in times past. The early ethnographic literature indicates that trespass occurred, presumably by those who felt confident in their knowledge of country and perhaps their spiritual status to enter another's country for gain or murderous intent (e.g. Radcliffe-Brown 1913, 146; Roth 1906, 8; see Sutton 2003, 23–24 for a review). The lesson for native title work is to present a complete picture of how rights to country worked in practice, about how they are possessed and how rules govern their exercise, without confusing the two. The account will include consideration of the requirement to ask permission when seeking access to another person's country and its resources. Permission and trespass need to be explained within the matrix of the complex set of relationships between people whose links to country are variously articulated. These relationships must be understood in terms of the special spiritual characteristics which are believed to inform country – land is fundamentally imbued with spiritual potency such that it can provide potentially fatal consequences if crossed.

A common manifestation of the duty of the owner of country to others who lacks rights in his estate is the act of welcoming or greeting country. I have come across many manifestations of this small ritual, ranging from simple 'calling out' to country to more elaborate head wetting, spraying water from the mouth across a pool or the use of body sweat. In areas where language remains more or less intact, there is often a requirement for the use of the local language in rituals of greeting on the ground that the spirits of a place will only understand the language of the country. Speaking in any other language, including English, will cause the greeting to fail. Words typically introduce the visitors (as well as the owners) and seek protection of the sprits, who are often characterised as the spirits of 'the old people' – that is, those who lived generations ago but whose presence continues to inform the spiritual environment of the place. Good luck may also be sought for fishing, hunting and gathering expeditions that are the occasion of the visit to country. In some instances, specific mythic beings may need to be placated – the water snake being notable in this regard. Water taken from a pool may be poured over the heads of visitors as a kind of ritual induction – a task which is usually done by one who exercises rights within the country. Sometimes, owners take water from a pool and blow it in a fine spray across a pool. One explanation for this given to me was that the spirit of a mythic being[20] in the pool

---

20   The term 'mythic' is discussed in Chapter 5 of this book – see footnote 5.

recognises the saliva of the visiting countryman and so accepts their presence along with those who accompany him. Much the same applies to the use of body sweat; the smell from an owner being transferred to the visitor as a form of assimilation, so spirits and mythic beings are not offended or disturbed by exotic sweat.

Native title research that yields examples of these ritual greetings provides good evidence of customary behaviour since rituals of greeting have been recorded in the early literature and are likely to have been a part of past practice (Biernoff 1978, 103–104; Roth 1897, 160; Williams 1986, 85). While they demonstrate that owners of country have the right to bring others into their estates, they also show that there is a duty to protect visitors which, as I have noted above, is in my experience more often in evidence in the ethnography than a preoccupation with actual trespass.

Rights and process

Applications for the recognition of native title must necessarily be supported by strong ethnographic evidence that there is a customary system whereby the title to country is sustained. Appreciating how this continuity is substantiated to the present cannot be found solely in an account of the system that was likely to have been in place at sovereignty. What is required is data that supports the contemporary observance of the laws and customs that sustain rights to country and their orderly exercise. In this chapter I have set out a number of topics that I consider may be helpful when attempting to accomplish this. While rights may be understood to reside in proof of descent from apical ancestors (or other customary system), the complex of rules about how they are to be exercised (and so realised in action) requires much more. The exercise of rights is subject to social process where group status, standing and seniority are essential markers of an ability to command rights before others. Within this complex social process, an understanding of which I argue is needful in any native title report, lies the fundamental relationship between a person and country. This is a relationship that attributes sentience to country. It consequently prescribes the manner whereby engagement is had with the country: the laws, customs and normative values that define customary dealings with the land. Thus, the exercise of rights, the granting of permission, the idea of trespass and the exercise of duty are best understood in this ethnography in terms of the management of the relationship between people and sentient country. These are all important matters for anthropological consideration in any native title inquiry.

This discussion about the exercise of rights also provides a useful analytical distinction between the possession of a right itself and the rules and normative referents evoked to govern their exercise. Native title law, as I understand it, seeks to inquire whether there are rights that are possessed under traditional laws and customs. The manner of their exercise is a separate but obviously related issue – although one that had undoubted relevance to the continuity of the observance of laws and customs since sovereignty and to the present.

5

Aboriginal religion and native title

A popular and sustained view of Aboriginal society and culture has been and remains that it is essentially spiritual. Concepts like the 'Dreaming' or 'Dreamtime', stories relating to localised supernatural beings (the Wagurl in Western Australia, the bunyip in eastern or south-eastern Australia and the Djanggawul of northeast Arnhem Land to mention just a few) are known and appreciated by informed Australians. Indigenous relationships to land are commonly represented in spiritual terms. For example, until recently, the official Australian Government website, informed the world that 'For Indigenous Australians, the land is the core of all spirituality and this relationship and the spirit of "country" is [sic] central to the issues that are important to Indigenous people today'.[1] Accounts of Aboriginal religion, beliefs and practices are common in the anthropological literature, both as classic ethnographies as well as shorter accounts in edited volumes and academic journals. Tourist bookstalls carry popular accounts of 'Aboriginal Dreamtime stories', children's picture books and illustrated narratives, many of which are authored by Indigenous Australians. In short, across the spectrum of popular and academic publication (digital, as well as hard copy)

---

1   The quotation came from the Australian Government's website (www.australia.gov.au/about-australia/australian-story/austn-indigenous-cultural-heritage, accessed 9 December 2016), which has since been removed and replaced by a short catalogue of services and general information about 'Indigenous culture and history' (see www.australia.gov.au/information-and-services/culture-and-arts/indigenous-culture-and-history). The website of the Australian Human Rights Commission, on the other hand, states that 'Native title is a property right which reflects a relationship to land which is the very foundation of Indigenous religion, culture and well-being' (see www.humanrights.gov.au/our-work/aboriginal-and-torres-strait-islander-social-justice/projects/native-title, accessed 13 March 2018).

Aboriginal religious beliefs and practices are as much in evidence as the koala and the kangaroo, while the iconic Uluru is commonly represented as the embodiment of Indigenous spirituality and belief.[2]

This apparent privileging of Aboriginal belief and practice has its downsides. Beyond the academic work produced by both Aboriginal and non-Aboriginal scholars, popular culture has commoditised Aboriginal spirituality and has often shown a scant regard for authenticity or accuracy. This has led to misunderstandings and even trivialisation of some aspects of belief and practice. In turn, the classic ethnographies of Aboriginal ritual practices[3] provide ready examples of the richness and diversity of ritual practices in some remote areas of Aboriginal Australia. This wealth of ritual and belief is not reflected in the ethnography of many native title claimant groups whose ritual practices are either substantially diminished or, as is the case in many rural and urban areas, no longer a part of contemporary practice. In a native title business that requires proof of traditionality, such comparisons are odious.

Given the centrality of religious belief and practice to Indigenous Australian culture, it is self-evident that the subject should be discussed in any report written in relation to a native title application. However, as with all other ethnography discussed in this book, the account has to be relevant to native title questions. In writing a native title report, an account of the claimants' religious beliefs and practices will not, of itself, provide a basis for the provision of an expert view as to the continuity of law and customs that relate to rights to country. Moreover, the prominence afforded to Aboriginal spirituality and the manner of its representation, particularly in the popular media, may require that the account clarifies issues and that it provides a corrective to popular misconceptions. Treatment of the field data may also require accepting and admitting that the ethnography relied upon reveals a religious life somewhat diminished in scope and content when compared with the earlier accounts of customary mytho-ritual performance as witnessed and recounted by mid-century anthropologists. This may have the potential to weaken the claims of right, but is a matter that cannot be neglected.

---

2   See, for example, uluru-australia.com/about-uluru/uluru-and-aboriginal-culture – along with advertisements for Kangaroo Island, Broome's Cable Beach and women's fashion garments. Accessed 9 December 2016.
3   For example, Berndt's *Kunapipi* (1951), *Djanggawul* (1952); and Meggitt's *Gadjari* (1966). Many other examples could be cited.

Making it relevant

Some dos and don'ts

The content of an expert or connection report will, of course, depend upon the ethnography available. No two reports, then, will be the same. The comparative process, whereby present practice and belief is compared with documented past practice will also be determined by the availability of materials in the early literature. In some cases such accounts will be very limited or perhaps altogether absent. In these cases the writer will have to rely on early accounts from a neighbouring area (if available) or from the scholarly literature for comparable areas of Aboriginal Australia. Claimant testimony that beliefs and practices have been a part of their culture 'for ever' may have some value in supporting the continuity argument. However, a discerning critic of the application is likely to evoke views relating to the shallowness of the oral tradition and its potential for transmutation, as I discuss in the next chapter of this book (see Chapter 6, 'Native title research and oral testimony'). As with other aspects of the laws and customs of the claimants, an expert view supporting their continuity through time really does need to rely, at least in part, on independent archival or ethnographic data. This process may attract its own problems. When reviewing the early literature in relation to a practice or belief that is known now to be entirely absent, there is little point in providing a detailed account of the practice if the conclusion will be that it is no longer a part of the contemporary account. Better to note its past occurrence and then state that its absence today is an evident loss of customary practice. I have read reports that detail past practices at length, only to conclude that the ritual is long gone, so rendering the historical account redundant. In native title writing, cultural losses require neither explanation nor excuse, but should, nonetheless, be openly and clearly admitted without requiring the reader to labour through descriptions of practices long abandoned.

The Dreaming, the secret, the sacred and the Law

Given the comments I have set down in the preceding paragraphs, it is essential that the writer of a native title report makes clear exactly what is meant by words or phrases that may commonly occur in the popular literature or might otherwise be subject to uncertainty or possible misunderstanding. This serves to anchor the ensuing account to key concepts evident in the ethnography, as well as helping to demonstrate that the beliefs and practices constitute a system with normative content and a structured form and process. This may also serve to counter the perception common in early accounts that Aboriginal belief and practice did not constitute a proper religion, but was magic or superstition – a perception that is not altogether absent in some circles today.

Australian Indigenous languages often have a term that roughly translates to 'the creative period of the Dreaming'. *Jukurpa* is common in areas of the Western Desert, but *bugarigara, ngaranggani* and *munguny* are common further west. I have recorded the term *mura* in northeast South Australia and southwest Queensland and *ularaka* from the Lake Eyre Basin.[4] In the Yindjibarndi language (central Pilbara region of Western Australia) a phrase is employed that can be translated as 'when the world was soft', being descriptive of the state of the country as it was believed to have been in this creative time. These terms (and many others besides) carry a range of meanings depending on the context of their use but all provide a foundation concept for Aboriginal religious belief that underpin a range of spiritual beliefs, practices and concepts. Dreaming, as represented by the Indigenous term is, in part, regarded as a period of time in the far distant past. During this time extraordinary events took place at certain locations typically effected by mythic[5] beings with extraordinary capabilities. These events fashioned aspects of the claimants' physical, social and cultural world, providing an explanation and mandate for a particular cultural practice (like a ritual, prescribed behaviour between classes of kin or way of gutting an animal) or natural phenomenon (like a hill, rock, river or plain) today. Anyone who has worked with Aboriginal people in Australia in remote as well as rural and urban areas is likely to be familiar with these aspects of belief as they are found commonly in daily discourse. Notable in this regard is the idea that country was first allocated to human groups in the Dreaming and has subsequently been 'handed down' through the generations to the present Indigenous owners.

---

4   Cf. Elkin 1934, 176, 181.
5   As far as I know, the term 'mythic' was introduced into the literature by Ronald and Catherine Berndt (see, for example, R.M. Berndt 1970, 218, 219; Berndt and Berndt 1993, 223ff.) but was not used in their earlier work where 'mythical' seems to have been preferred (e.g. Berndt and Berndt 1964, 189). While 'mythic' suffers from the same imperfections as 'myth', its substitution for the more common 'mythical' may serve to alleviate the pejorative connotations of the latter. In lectures Ronald Berndt used to speak of 'my-thick' beings, so the word had little resemblance to the cognate 'mythical'.

Dreaming is dynamically manifest in the present and its spirituality traverses the temporal dimension such that it is neither solely of the past nor the present. As a reference to potent spirituality, the term may be used to denote a manifestation of contemporary sanctity derived from the creative era. Spirituality evident within place is attributed to events of the distant past but is elementally contemporary and a part of present experience. Consistent with this concept, Dreaming (or its Indigenous equivalent) can also be used to denote a particular relationship between a person and the natural world (a place or a natural species), which is readily understood as a totemic association.

These preliminary comments relating to the concept of 'the Dreaming' should serve to illustrate that the popular view of the Dreaming as some quasi-romantic period steeped in myth and legend and being the stuff of children's stories egregiously misrepresents the ethnographic reality. I have worked with some claimants who refuse to use the term 'Dreamtime' for this very reason. The word Dreaming is probably the better choice than 'Dreamtime' as the former at least represents the sense of the recent and continuous aspects of the belief. Terms from the claimants' own language may also have advantages when used in native title discourse, but if this choice is adopted the word chosen must be accurately defined.

The spiritual power of the Dreaming is neither passive nor benevolent. Common to all Aboriginal groups with which I have worked is the belief that there is a potent spiritual force present within the countryside or evoked in ritual practice. Things of the Dreaming are sacred and their substance sacrosanct. A place, then, that is believed to have been created in the Dreaming and has continuing Dreaming characteristics is sacred and is generally subject to rules that govern visitation or use. In writing of such things, care needs to be taken to distinguish the idea of sanctity from the ideal of the secret as the two terms are sometimes conflated in popular use, yielding a sort of hybrid 'secret–sacred' notion that obfuscates the system of belief and action that characterises Aboriginal religious belief in this regard. While all aspects of the Dreaming are 'sacred', not all are 'secret'.

Terms from the claimants' own language are helpful in any analysis of these concepts. In parts of the northwest of Western Australia and east into the desert areas, potent Dreaming spirituality is identified by the term *ngurlu*, a term used to refer to phenomena that are potentially spiritually dangerous to those not qualified to encounter them. In parts of the Western

Desert, the concept is expressed by use of the term *milmilpa* while other languages have their own terms. Such words carry the meaning of being restricted and not open to some people (usually women and children), and content so characterised is thus esoteric. Spiritual danger within country (a manifestation of the Dreaming) is a determinant of how country can be accessed, exploited and managed. The term for spiritual danger is also used to refer to a place associated with esoteric and restricted activities like a ritual ground where gender-specific activities are known to take place and it is also used to refer to ritual items, knowledge of which is restricted to senior ritually qualified men. The term is thus a means of referring to such items without making a direct reference to them and so functions as a euphemism. Since these matters are so sensitive, however, no mention is made of *ngurlu* (meaning objects) in the presence of women. Esoteric and highly restricted objects are manifestations of Dreaming and may also articulate a spiritual relationship between a person and a place.

The usefulness of such data in the native title context may be limited by the need for strict confidentiality when discussing such material. It is essential that the management of these data be discussed at the outset of the research with senior male claimants (or senior female claimants if the material is restricted to women) and a decision made as to whether it will be collected and included in some form in the anthropologist's report. One possible solution is to place these restricted materials into a separate report and have the court make orders as to its subsequent distribution and use. This is not uncommon and the court may also choose to hold certain sessions *in camera*, limiting attendance to males or females and imposing restrictions on the subsequent dissemination of the transcript. However, this may result in procedural difficulties. In a recent case that was appealed to the Full Bench of the Federal Court, restricted materials were demanded by the appellant to be discovered since the appeal court needed to review all the evidence considered by the trial judge. The question then arose as to what would be the outcome if one of the appeal judges was a woman. Court orders are only secure for as long as they endure: they can be overturned.

In some areas the original Aboriginal language words for such concepts as Dreaming, 'sacred' and 'secret' are now not remembered. However, it has been my experience that beliefs in these concepts endures and can provide helpful insights to any native title inquiry. Dreaming and the related aspects of potent spirituality within the countryside comprise a significant reference within customary Aboriginal belief. Manifestation within place potentially makes it a part of any daily encounter with the countryside. This is significant in the native title context as it is a belief that serves to link people with country through the conviction that Dreaming spirituality imbues the country and so is a part of the contemporary relationship a person has with their country. The affiliation a person has with his (or her) land is one that comprises a relationship constructed of spiritual interconnectedness, mediated by places and the spiritually potent attributes of those places. Consequently, rights to country are legitimated by reference to the supernatural ordination of the creative period of the Dreaming that continues to the present. The identification of the location of sacred ritual items reflects the belief that the spirituality of the country is immanent in paraphernalia. These beliefs and concepts are pertinent to any native title report that seeks to explore the contemporary relationship between people and country. The rules that are believed to have been set down in the Dreaming and that are now cited as comprising expected and regulating behaviour are important to native title analyses as they serve to demonstrate the existence of a normative system that underpins the claimants' relationship to country. Native title reports generally require careful consideration and analyses of these beliefs, concepts and social dealings in order to show the customary relationship between the claimants and their asserted rights to country.

Both the period of the Dreaming and its principal actors are believed to be responsible for the institution of laws and customs. 'The Law', commonly a term for customary practices and ritual observances, is believed to have its origins within the Dreaming. In many Aboriginal groups, the term 'law' is used with a range of meanings depending on the context. A common use of the term 'law' is to refer to rules of social behaviour, particularly those governing marriage and kin obligations as well as rules that determine access to country and the asking of permission. So, for example, visiting places that are regarded as prohibited to certain categories of person is also a matter of the exercise of law. The term 'law' is also used in context to refer to any one of several of ritual activities, each having its own particular signature or style (songs, body markings) as well as associated paraphernalia and teaching. Used in this sense and in part to distinguish its use from the more general 'law', meaning rules, axioms and required behaviour, some writers represent it with initial upper case ('Law'). Commonly, a person who has submitted to the ritual of induction (commonly 'initiation') is referred to as having 'been through the Law'. The time when rituals are performed may be known as 'Law time', the ground where ritual action takes place as the 'Law ground' and a man who is regarded as having status and authority in ritual matters referred to as a 'Law man' and a woman as 'Law woman' or 'Law boss'. Collection of these vernacular (Aboriginal English terms) helps define the structure and underlying system of Aboriginal belief and practice. Credible exegesis of this sort does, however, require that the terms are carefully and accurately explained at the outset.

Religious beliefs

It may be helpful in writing for a native title audience to separate out the claimants' religious beliefs from practices. This is a pragmatic choice that may assist in the presentation of data for what is ultimately a legal readership where an assessment of data is made in relation to specific criteria – for example, the continuity of customary belief relating to the application area. Care needs to be taken when following what might be understood as a reductionist process that belief and practice are not dissociated, for the two are a part of the whole. The dichotomising that characterises this discourse highlights the problem of writing about complex spiritual and metaphysical matters in a native title report. Data must be applied to the native title questions, otherwise it will be redundant. While beliefs and practices are two sides of the same coin, clarification of beliefs and significant concepts (see previous section) paves the way for an account of practice since the latter can be understood to be the manifestation and realisation of the former.

Each ethnography will yield examples of different religious convictions so the content of the text will vary on a case-by-case basis. In what follows I set down some of the beliefs I have found to occur widely across Aboriginal Australia in my native title research, noting that they are not restricted to remote or northern areas, but with patient and thorough inquiry may be recorded within rural and urban groups as well.

Totemism

The early literature on Aboriginal religion instructs that totemism was a significant feature of belief and practice in times gone by. Consideration of this aspect of belief is, then, a necessary part of any contemporary account of the claimants' religious beliefs. The terms 'totem' and 'totemism' are not without their problems. They have a long history in anthropological writing that is well beyond the scope of this book to review. Spencer and Gillen wrote at the end of the nineteenth century that every person belonging to the groups they studied in Central Australia was:

> born into some totem – that is, he or she belongs to a group of persons each one of whom bears the name of, and is especially associated with, some natural object. The latter is usually an animal or plant; but in addition to those of living things, there are also such totem names as wind, sun, water, or cloud. (Spencer and Gillen 1899, 112)

R.M. and C.H. Berndt (1988, 231) cite Durkheim (1915), Spencer and Gillen (1899), Radcliffe-Brown (1945 and 1952), Warner (1937), Elkin (1933 and 1945), Strehlow (1947), Stanner (1958 and 1959–61) as well as R.M. Berndt (1951 and 1952) as examples of those who have provided comprehensive accounts of totemism in Aboriginal belief. They remark that, 'all have suggested … that a major focus was on totemism. In fact, Aboriginal religion has been labelled as totemic, and a great deal has been written, at second hand, on this subject' (ibid.). The 'second hand' nature of so many of these early accounts is identified by R.M. and C.H. Berndt as a principal problem with the early anthropological literature, observing that 'Totemism is a confusing term, because it has been used in so many different ways' (ibid.). Nevertheless, they conclude that the term is now so 'well-entrenched' that adoption of a different term would 'only add to the confusion' and counsel that it be used with careful attention to what is meant by the writer. They cite Elkin as providing the 'best' description in this regard:

> a view of nature and life, of the universe and man, which colours and influences the Aborigines' social groupings and unites them with nature's activities and species in a bond of mutual life-giving and imparts confidence amidst the vicissitudes of life. (Elkin 1945, 126, cited in Berndt and Berndt 1988, 231)

Elsewhere, and earlier, Elkin defined 'totemism' as:

> a relationship between an individual or group of individuals on the one hand and a natural object or species on the other – a relationship which is denoted by the application of the name of the latter, the totem, to the human individual or group concerned. (Elkin 1933, 257)

Elkin went on to caution against applying the definition without a proper understanding of the implications and consequences of the relationship between totem and person or group, since he understood this relationship to influence and perhaps even determine social action (ibid.).

R.M. and C.H. Berndt echo these definitions by adding that they understand totemism to be, very broadly, about:

> a view of the world in which man is an integral part of nature, not sharply distinct or differing in quality from other natural species, but sharing with them the same life essence. (Berndt and Berndt 1988, 231)

Elkin sought to bring clarity to his analyses by dividing totemism into seven different types that he called 'forms' (individual, sex, moiety, section/subsection, clan, local and multiple) (1945, 129–133). This categorisation is expanded by R.M. and C.H. Berndt into 10 (individual, sex, moiety, section/subsection, clan, local, conception, birth, dream and multiple). They also identified two classes of totemism (social totemism and ritual or cult totemism), all categories belonging to one or other of the classes (1988, 231). Elkin's further classification, however, was based on 'function and meaning' (1945, 133–148), identifying types of totemism that R.M. and C.H. Berndt included as categories. While this may be represented as sound analysis and certainly explores different manifestations of totemism, it may prove of limited assistance in a native title report because of its evident rigidity and conspicuous complexity.

The lists furnished by Elkin and the Berndts may provide a useful checklist for native title researchers to explore with claimants regarding their totemic beliefs. While I do not for one minute suggest that researchers list these categories as a kind of questionnaire ('Do you have birth totemism? Do you have subsection totemism?'), exploration of the concepts that inform the categories may provide a basis for the collection of helpful data. That said, totemism, as the term might best be employed in native title writing, is better understood as a relationship. Classification is not as important as developing an understanding of how the relationship is articulated and how it works to link a person to the natural world through a spiritual correspondence that renders a person correlative with the natural world, either a place or a species or both. Understanding totemism as a relationship rather than a thing, which is sometimes a consequence of categorisation, positions and so helps define the belief within social action and personal credo. Typically, the relationship is manifest as a personal bond between an individual and a place or between an individual and a natural species, many cultures exhibiting examples of both. In a native title account, such an understanding may assist the reader in gaining an appreciation of how people relate to country through spiritual affiliations that are a part of their day-to-day lived experience and their social interactions with others.[6]

In my own experience, I have found that discovering terms from the language of the claimants that identify spiritual relationships between an individual and the natural world is a helpful first step. For example, in areas of the central and western Kimberley I have recorded the terms *ray* and *jarin* that identify the existence of a relationship between an individual and a place and an individual and a natural species respectively. *Ray* is a term used for a spirit that enlivens the foetus of the unborn child. It is identified by an adult (not always the father) through the dream of natural sleep or through a metaphysical experience. Its revelation is rehearsed as a subsequent narrative in which the particulars of the imbuement are told and the place whence the *ray* originated identified (Glaskin 2017, 64–65). In many cultures (although not invariably), the totemic link between the resultant individual and the *ray* and its place of origin (sometimes referred to as *ungurr*) yields rights for the individual within the locale of the *ray* – the locale being known as that person's 'ungurr place'. Such place-specific links between people and country provide data that is helpful when developing expert views on the existence of contemporary links between a person and an application area.[7]

Jarin is a word used to identify an animal or natural species associated with an individual in areas of north-western Australia. Typically, this is explained through the reporting of an incident that occurred immediately prior to a mother's realisation that she was pregnant. The details of a person's *jarin* are generally explained by means of a short narrative that describes the relevant circumstances. Subsequently, the person is understood to have a particular relationship with that animal or natural species, such that the *jarin* is 'special for them' or that they feel a particular affinity toward it. In some cases, the *jarin* is forbidden food, although this is not always so. The *jarin* may also be identified with an individual through some physical mark or distinguishing feature. This characteristic is understood by claimants to be the result of the circumstances that led to the spiritual relationship being created. Thus, if the *jarin* was an animal that was hunted or a fish that was speared, the individual is shown to have

---

6   See Palmer 2016, 130–132 for totemic data drawn from a rural and urban population.
7   See Kaberry 1936, 1938; Kolig 1981, 31–35; Palmer 1981, 336–342 for examples of how a totemic relationship endorses rights to country.

a birthmark or other physical blemish that represents the act of capture or killing. Totemic beliefs of the *jarin* type are widespread across Aboriginal Australia and are not usually linked to a place or locale, although the location where the *jarin* originated may be regarded as significant to the individual.

These two examples serve to illustrate common aspects of totemic belief that may be found in native title ethnographies. There are, of course, others, as the texts I discussed above clearly illustrate. Totems may be passed down through filiation, from either mother or father, or may be associated with a social category (moiety, section, or subsection). A totemic relationship may also develop through ritual practice where an individual (usually a man) experiences induction into an esoteric mytho-ritual tradition such that he is believed to have gained a spiritual affiliation with a particular Dreaming being identified with a place or string of places across the countryside. This belief, or variations of it, has been called 'cult totemism' (Berndt and Berndt 1988, 238–239; Elkin 1945, 136–144; Kolig 1981, 158–176). One difficulty with consideration of such data, should it be available for a native title researcher, is that much of the content may be restricted in its allowable dissemination. This raises difficulties for its use in a native title report that is most usefully an open account available to all parties who have an interest in the application. As I have noted above, restricted materials need to be discussed at the outset of the research and a policy adopted as to how such ethnography will be used, if at all (cf. Glaskin 2017, 132–134).

Myth and narrative

A native title report should include examples of the claimants' oral literature. Some of those with whom I have worked dislike the term 'myth', regarding it as pejorative as it may be understood to imply falsehood or untruth. Notwithstanding that the term 'myth' has a technical anthropological meaning (a sacred tale held to be true), the word is open to misunderstanding, particularly when used for a non-specialist readership. The more neutral term 'narrative' may be the wiser choice. Some oral literature comprises narratives that tell of domestic and social events situated within the context of the Dreaming. These are generally narratives of place and are often publically rehearsed while some are regarded as mostly suitable for children. This should not diminish their importance to an ethnography that seeks to demonstrate the continuing nature of cultural traditions and, provided they are a part of the field data, they have a place in a native title report. Care should be taken, however, to ensure that narratives have been passed on in an oral tradition as there are undoubtedly examples where narratives have been lost to the oral account while being preserved in print as 'Dreamtime stories' only to re-emerge again as an oral account that has been learnt from the printed version. Over a generation or two the interruption to the oral account is not remembered. Asking claimants where they learnt the narrative is sometimes helpful and is an essential part of the research process. Becoming acquainted with materials that have been produced by the relevant community over the last few decades at schools and resource centres is also important as this may provide an indication of the likely history and origins of an oral account. Given that narratives were only ever oral accounts in customary arrangements, an absence of the oral account for a period of time would signal a lack of continuity of this aspect of Aboriginal culture. Its resurrection would not alleviate this loss – although this is a legal matter that might find support from other arguments that are not my concern here.

Narratives of the Dreaming that tell of the actions of mythic beings at known locations across the countryside and particularly within the application area provide useful data for those who seek to provide a view as to the claimants' continuing connections with the countryside. Consistent with the discussion above relating to the inherent spirituality of the Dreaming, such narratives serve to show how claimants continue to esteem and value the country and particular places and areas within it. Narratives can attest to the belief that there is a manifest deep spirituality that is the continuing and contemporary representation of the actions of the Dreaming being or beings. Accompanying song as well as artistic representations may be of assistance to an understanding of how place and narratives enshrine spirituality that is linked to people through a perceived equivalence between a person and his or her country – yet another form of totemism. Travels of mythic beings also lend themselves well to graphic representation as lines across a map (see, for example, Cane 2002, 84; Hawke and Gallagher 1989, 114). Many narratives of this sort are restricted in their dissemination – or have confidential segments or versions. Again, proper management of such data, and indeed whether it be collected at all, is a matter that needs to be discussed with senior claimants, who are themselves privy to these materials, before the research is undertaken.

The reproduction of narratives in a native title report can be helpful in demonstrating the continuity of the oral tradition. This counsels that the accounts be summary rather than effusive, providing only such detail as is necessary for the subsequent provision of an opinion as to the likely continuity of the tradition since times prior to sovereignty. Some narratives in the oral tradition are quite lengthy and have performative aspects that are best omitted from the field data as presented. However engaging the narrative, if it has no bearing on the native title questions its telling will be at best redundant, at worst irritating.

Sites, locales and place

Many narratives relate to country and named places that were typically spiritually ordained and modified or transformed during the Dreaming. The idea of the 'sacred site' has a long and troubled history in the latter part of the twentieth century in Australia that continues to this day. The phrase was brought to academic prominence by R.M. Berndt in the early 1970s in his monograph, *The sacred site: the western Arnhem Land example* (1970). State legislation to protect 'sites' was enacted about this time.[8] Difficulties developed in Western Australia when the local community at Noonkanbah on the Fitzroy River (west Kimberley) sought to prevent drilling on country they regarded as spiritually significant. The state government took the view that the area concerned was not a 'sacred site' as it lay well beyond the compass of the geographic feature that had, apparently, previously signified the site and so could, according to this logic, be drilled with impunity (Hawke and Gallagher 1989). This raised a fundamental problem with legislation that regarded land-based spirituality as essentially contained within the parameters of a definable 'site'. Beyond the boundary, the spirituality and associated cultural and religious significance was absent.

The *Native Title Act* is not sites-based legislation but seeks to recognise rights to country as a whole. However, in writing of 'sites' in a native title report, the researcher needs to be mindful of the baggage the term carries. Indeed, it might be better to avoid the word altogether and substitute a word like 'area' or 'locale' (as I have done above). To avoid subsequent misunderstanding, some discussion of the nature of land-based spirituality and its pervasiveness and absence of evident and convenient containment

---

8   See Williams and McGrath 2014 for multiple references.

is required. Generally, according to Aboriginal customary understandings and belief, named places are not 'sites' in the sense that they can be readily bounded. Typically when mapping country on the ground it is evident that there is a zone of transition between one named area and another with an intermediate region separating them. The spirituality believed to reside at a place is not contained within a bounded site. Rather, it is pervasive and sometimes extensive. Individual named places ('sites') may comprise a complex of significant places that in aggregate constitute an area of spiritual significance having component parts that cannot be separated since they rely on and express common spirituality. In the Pilbara region of the northwest of Western Australia, I recorded a totemic association of an area as being fog. The spirituality of the area was understood to be no more contained as a bounded site as is the very fog that constituted its visual manifestation. A question along the lines of, 'Well, how far does the Fog Dreaming site go?' is, then, incontrovertibly foolish. The same understanding could be applied to any area wherein spirituality is believed to reside.

Sites and areas of importance should be identified by a unique number and listed with summary details, including approximate geographic location, the Indigenous name, the map name, an indication of the type of site (artefacts, ritual, historical and so on) along with a brief description of the place and the source of the information and field note reference. Sites gathered from earlier researchers or extracted from state sites' databases, if presented in the report, should be clearly differentiated from the field data collected in preparation for writing the native title report as the former may not represent contemporary knowledge. Sites should also be shown on a large format map by number so they can be identified by the reader or, should the matter go to trial, by the court and other interested parties. I have found that by sorting the UTM grid references of the sites I can order the sites roughly top to bottom and left to right across the map. While this is unsophisticated, it aids identification of sites when there are many dozens of them. An alternative is to provide an index like a street directory with the map divided into sectors ('A1', 'A2' and so on) so any site can be found on the map. A 'site map' provides a ready and graphic representation of the claimants' knowledge of their country and can be a telling if crude indicator of the continuity of connection.

Beliefs and practices of daily living

Aboriginal religious beliefs penetrate the surrounding natural environment, bringing the metaphysical to the physical world with which Aboriginal people interact in the course of their daily lives. This results in a complex system of belief that circumscribes many aspects of the claimants' quotidian activities through observance of customary ways of dealing with the spiritual world that readily translates to a normative system of laws that prescribe correct action. These aspects of customary observance and the rules that underpin them are founded upon spiritual beliefs but are not set apart like major ritual action or indeed evidently separate from daily life. They are, then, sacred in the sense that they belong to the spiritual world but mundane in the sense that they are a part of the routine of the commonplace and humdrum everyday tasks. For this reason, too, they may be missed in a native title inquiry or considered by the claimants to be of no consequence. However, what might be called beliefs and practices of daily living are an important part of Aboriginal religious belief and should be included in any account of the continuity of those beliefs over time and examined to determine what they can tell us about the claimants' relationship with country. They may also reflect rules about the rights exercised by the claimants within the application area.

Spirits figure prominently in Indigenous cultures. These are manifest as a pantheon of different forms and characteristics. Some are mischievous, some benign and helpful, some elementally dangerous. Spirits are typically present within the countryside and so must be managed when the places they are known to inhabit are visited – reflecting ritual practices of greeting country that I have considered in the previous chapter of this book (see 'Realising rights and dangerous places', and 'Permission, trespass and licence'). In many instances I have found that claimants consider that only those with customary rights to the country can manage these spiritual encounters. This is because it is believed that it is the owners of the land who hold a spiritual commonality with both the country and its metaphysical manifestations. In similar vein, the spirits of deceased ancestors (another important aspect of Aboriginal religious belief) recognise their descendants as those who are, like them, of the country.

Another example of beliefs and practices of daily living are protocols that govern the taking and processing of food. Goannas may have to be gutted in a particular way, kangaroo, turtle and dugong prepared according to normative prescriptions while some meat is forbidden to certain categories of person while others are privileged in its distribution. These customary ways of doing things are well reported in the general Aboriginal studies literature, as any student of the subject will know. Understood as an expression of the abiding relationship that an Aboriginal person has with the natural world through supernatural agency, they may serve to illustrate the continuity of customary action and the deep correlation believed to exist between people and country and much that is within it.

Domestic encounters with birds, dogs and other animals may also carry with them a range of beliefs. Common to many ethnographies with which I have worked is the belief in messenger birds – omens of good (or more often bad) news, visitors and death. The countryside as observed by a keen and knowing eye may also provide information about the availability of natural species, the weather or the wind. While these examples of the beliefs of daily living are more in the nature of a natural history than of a credo, on being pressed claimants are likely to explain that the relationship of one part of the natural world with another is a product of the spirituality of the Dreaming. During this creative time, so is the widely held belief, all things were ordained and the present order and the rules that regulate interaction with the natural world were set in place. Such data is helpful to any native title account since it goes to both normative values and continuity and should not be overlooked in the research process.

Religious practices

Accounts of ritual in a native title report need to be presented in the context of their relationship to the possession of rights by the claimants. If the data available in this regard is either not evident or cannot be provided in a convenient and accessible form, care must be exercised to ensure that the account is not irrelevant. That stated, ritual performance generally signals a vibrant continuity of laws and customs and so finds a rightful place in the ethnography. Ritual is a complex and challenging area to write about in any native title report. Ritual action can be both the most public and spectacular of a researcher's fieldwork data as well as the most private and sensitive. Before lifting the lid on the claimants' ritual lives, great thought, planning and close consultation needs to be undertaken, while the practicalities and resources required to record properly events that occur only periodically and may last for many days will have substantial resource implications for the organisation funding the research. Those of us who have been lucky and privileged to take part in one or more of the major mytho-ritual practices of Aboriginal Australia understand the intensity and all-consuming emotional commitment required of ritual practitioners. This is not an undertaking that should be embarked upon lightly, nor should the velocity of the moment obscure the end goal of the research. To be helpful to the court and others who assess native title applications, ritual data need to be accessible and available. Much ritual action is gender restricted while some claimants may consider that practices that are not so restricted are, nevertheless, not matters that should be made public, even within the limited audience of a native title claim.

While the practicalities of providing a first-hand account of ritual activities may not be possible given the severe restraints imposed by court deadlines and the commissioning agency's budgets, other means can be utilised to provide data on ritual practices where these are a continuing part of the claimants' laws and customs. Anthropologists who have worked at least quite recently with the claimants may have published their own independent accounts of ritual to which the native title research can refer. Obviously, such accounts need to be verified by the claimants and confirmation provided that such accounts continue to reflect current practice. Claimant accounts of their ritual practices may also serve to provide useful field data, again with the proviso that it is evident that what is related refers to contemporary practice. As with all field data, lawyers who manage and finally present the case at trial (if that is the outcome) will wish to lead claimant testimony to support the anthropologist's data.

Major rituals of induction are not practised in many areas of settled and southern Australia. Relevant early literature may attest to this absence in the contemporary account or reveal that the rituals that are practised are either substantially changed or diminished. I have been asked on a number of occasions by prospective claimants whether people can gain recognition of their native title rights if the major life-stage rituals are no longer practised. Based on my knowledge of claims that have been determined, it is evident that ritual, like language, can be lost without jeopardising recognition of native title[9] – although its continued practice

---

9   Examples that come to mind are the Single Noongar Claim in southwest Western Australia (*Bennell v State of WA*), *Dempsey on behalf of the Bularnu, Waluwarra and Wangkayujuru People* and the Juru People (Parts A and B (*Prior on behalf of the Juru People* and *Lampton on behalf of the Juru People*)), but there are any number of other examples that could be drawn from the determined claims listed on the NNTT website: www.nntt.gov.au/searchRegApps/NativeTitleClaims/Pages/default.aspx.

undoubtedly makes claims stronger. While historically anthropologists have made the focus of their research and recording the great initiatory or life-stage rituals as well as the post-initiatory ceremonies that inform classic texts of the sort I have cited at the beginning of this chapter, ritual practice may also be in evidence in less spectacular forms, such as greeting country, hunting evocations and increase rituals. Such practices, particularly when performed in what might seem to the uninformed to be in a rather perfunctory or low-key manner, are easily overlooked in the research process. In my experience rituals that show the continuing relationships between people and their country may sometimes be performed in a disarmingly 'modern' manner, all too easily overlooked during the research process.

Kinds of ritual practice

Studies of ritual have long been a significant topic for anthropological inquiry and it has been subject to extensive review, analysis and theoretical constructs. Trained anthropologists learn of these things during their courses of study and should bring this knowledge to their subsequent presentation and analyses of their data. In this regard the classic work of Arnold van Gennep (1960) and later work by Victor Turner (1968, 1974) are important points of departure. Lloyd Warner's classic *A black civilisation* reveals the complexity and detail of recording ritual practice and furnishing exegesis (1937, 234–401). The challenge for anyone undertaking a native title inquiry is that of relevance. Rituals are often by their very nature protracted affairs, containing complex and sometimes intricate details while ceremonial activity invites a range of possible interpretations, some of which have been in times past speculative and farfetched.[10] To be helpful to those who adjudicate on an application for the recognition of native title, ritual data needs to bear on the question of the continuity of law and custom, particularly as that relates to people's relationship to country and the perdurance of their rights within it.

Ritual practice in Aboriginal Australia is generally directed toward a specific goal and is characterised by unique form, style and content. Different sorts of ritual are named and are not conflated in practice – indeed, to do so would be to break the ordaining rules that are believed

---

10   For a review of some of the problems of interpretation of narrative and ritual, see John Morton's introduction to Geza Roheim's *Children of the desert II* (Morton 1988, vii–xxx).

to have been set down by mythic beings of the Dreaming who first established the way a ritual should be conducted. Emic classifications of ritual practice are useful in any presentation of data since they allow for an orderly presentation of materials that reflects the claimants' beliefs and understandings. In what follows I consider just some of the principal types of ritual that might inform a native title inquiry.

Initiation

Common in ethnographies of northern and remote Aboriginal Australia is the practice of rituals of induction for youths, typically males. This usually (although not invariably) involves the physical operation of circumcision, although an alternative in some areas may include ritual arm tying.[11] The practice is often referred to generally as 'the Law' or 'Law time' and the process as 'going through the Law'. The ritual often involves not only members of the initiates' own community but members of others across the region as well, while several boys may be initiated at the same time, together involving several hundred participants. These rituals are major regional community events, having substantial non-restricted segments, may continue for a week or more and are a significant event in the Indigenous calendar. In some places where I have worked, dedicated ritual grounds have been set up complete with ablution facilities and semi-permanent bough sheds to cater for those attending. European Australians are often invited and welcome to attend, take photographs and participate in the dancing and ritual adornment ('dressing up'). There are, however, restricted episodes, including the actual circumcision, from which women, children and generally European Australians are excluded.

'Going through the Law' by ritual induction and circumcision is a necessary first step for the social transition from youth to manhood. However, while it makes 'a man of a boy', senior men with whom I have worked all agree that it is merely a first stage of a social and ritual education, rather like completing primary school. Being a man (*wati* in many Western Desert languages) requires much more than this. A fundamental feature of Aboriginal religious practice is that it is progressively revelatory. Knowledge of the Dreaming, the narratives and associated beliefs, customs and practices, evocation of spirituality and its renewal and comprehension

11   A number of other male initiatory rites are recorded across Aboriginal Australia by R.M. and C.H. Berndt (1988, 166–175). Initiation rites for girls are also recorded in the literature (e.g. ibid., 180–185), but this is a matter that I feel unqualified to comment upon. It has been explored by other writers – see Bell 1983 and 2005 for a discussion, review and additional references.

of the sacra that may link people to country are sequences in a life-long ritual journey. While the juvenile initiate may hear songs and observe dances and performance that relate to the countryside, he is unlikely to gain much knowledge of them. Moreover, a boy can be circumcised at a community quite far removed from his own ancestral country, so the relationship between the ritual practice and activating rights to ancestral country may not be evident. The observation of the ritual is likely to demonstrate that there is a continuity of laws and customs in this regard. However, the relevance of this practice to the assertion of rights to the country of the application may not be evident.

Higher rituals

Post-circumcision rituals are, in my experience, often replete with restricted episodes, furnishing significant challenges as to how such material might be managed in a native title application. These revelatory ritual practices are sometimes euphemistically referred to as 'higher Law', 'bush business' or simply 'men's business', although they have specific names that are often themselves restricted. For obvious reasons I can write very little about these rituals except to observe that it is these that often relate to what might broadly be called the totemic relationship between people and their country. In those communities where such rituals continue to form a part of customary practice, lifetime exposure to the rituals yields status and a depth of arcane knowledge that legitimates eminence and standing and so are an important feature of the social organisation of the claimant group and its governance. Progressive revelation and rehearsals of ritual, narrative, song and performance is also a means to ensure the continuity of this knowledge through time and facilitates the preservation of its content. These matters go to the normative system whereby claimants manage their social relationships, structure their quotidian exchanges, manage disputes and impose discipline. Consequently, they are relevant to any native title inquiry. In this sense it may be sufficient simply to note that such higher rituals are a part of contemporary practice, without any need to go into any detail beyond the sort I have provided here. However, in an open report at least it will not be possible to provide a fine-grained explanation of how higher rituals function to link people to country through spiritual evocations.

Entertainment and 'corroborees'

Native title research may reveal a genre of oral literature that comprises single songs believed to have been composed by a named individual. Such songs are generally believed to have come to the composer in the dream of natural sleep and may be associated with a particular place within that person's country, either because of the content of the song or because it was conceived at a particular location.[12] These songs are sung informally for entertainment or for the edification of the researcher and some individuals may have a repertoire of several dozen pieces. These songs are the property of the composer and pass to his or her heirs on the originator's death. They can be helpful in a native title inquiry in so far as they demonstrate a continuing relationship between a person and country.

Some groups retain knowledge of more complex song sequences, sometimes with dance and ritual paraphernalia, including some restricted intervals. These 'corroborees'[13] may also serve to demonstrate continuity of customary practice – and may also articulate a relationship, born of the Dreaming whence the song poetry originates, with the country of the claim.

Some other rituals that might come to notice

Mortuary rituals were a notable feature of the early ethnographies.[14] However, for one reason or another these complex rituals have now been largely replaced by Christian services and interment.[15] Nevertheless, funerals are significant events across Aboriginal Australia and native title research should not neglect these sad but important events that demonstrate the magnitude of social relationships, kin ties and concomitant duties and responsibilities. I have found burial practices to include the use of grave goods, steps taken to avoid the escape of the deceased's spirit and post-mortuary smoking rites. There is often a declared preference for being buried in one's ancestral country, based on the belief that the spirit of the deceased returns to the land whence it is believed to have also originated.

---

12   Common terms from the north of Western Australia are *jawi, jabi* and *nurlu*. In South Australia they are commonly referred to as *yinma*.

13   From *garaabara*, a word of the Dharuk language of the Sydney area, first recorded by Europeans in about 1790 (*The Australian National Dictionary*, 'corroboree'). While the term is not much used in standard English now, its use by Aboriginal people to identify particular forms of public entertainments is common.

14   For example, Dawson 1881, 62–67; Howitt 1904, 426–508; Roth 1907; Spencer and Gillen 1899, 497–511; Warner 1937, 402–440.

15   But mortuary rituals remain a significant part of ritual practices in parts of Arnhem Land.

In one area of north Queensland, where return to ancestral country for burial was impractical, I recorded that sand taken from that remote location was buried with the deceased so the spirit would be able to be absorbed by the elements of ancestral country within the grave. I have also observed how the news of a death is disseminated according to custom, ritualised visits to the deceased family and communal weeping. All of these are likely to have had parallels in customary practice and can be used to demonstrate to the respondents of an application for the recognition of native title that aspects of customary belief and practice endure to this day.

I have noted above that rituals of greeting the country are helpful in a native title context since they demonstrate the spiritual relationship between a person and their land occasioned by physical visitation. While rituals of increase (again well documented in the literature[16]) may now be uncommon as rites, I have noted how claimants sometimes speak out to the country when visiting to fish or hunt, expecting that such an exhortation will facilitate their success at securing a good catch. If such observations are a part of the researcher's field data, they are helpful to a native title report and should not be overlooked.

Bringing the data to a proof of native title

In writing about Aboriginal religion in the native title context the anthropologist faces two challenges. The first is common to all native title writing: the requirement that the data provided brings to a focus the nature of the relationship a claimant has with his or her land and how this may serve to perpetuate and legitimate rights to that country. The continuity of laws and customs that are otherwise a part of the claimants' cultural experiences are not without a place in a native title report as these serve to demonstrate that there is a continuance of a society whose members share commonalities. However, aspects of these laws and customs need to have a bearing on the core business of native title: how rights to country were held pre-sovereignty and how they have endured to the present. Graham Hiley, then a native title lawyer, wrote:

---

16   For example, Elkin 1933, 284–296; Piddington 1932; Spencer and Gillen 1899, 167–211.

> The relevant laws and customs ... are those that, inter alia, define and regulate rights and interests in land (and or waters). Thus, the relevant 'society' for the purposes of native title jurisprudence is the society that gives rise to and is defined by the body of laws and customs which includes that important element.
>
> It is not sufficient just to identify any body of laws and customs. For example the identification of a body of laws and customs regarding matters totally unrelated to rights and interests in land – for example, regarding social discourse or behaviour -- will not without more identify the relevant society for native title purposes. (Hiley 2008, 146)

Given the essentially land-based spirituality that informs Aboriginal religious belief and practice, consideration of this aspect of Indigenous culture should provide fertile ground to further an understanding of the intense and enduring relationship which Aboriginal Australians have with their country and their age-old proprietorship of it. However, the problem of relevance and focus is exacerbated in any account of Aboriginal religious belief and practices. This is a result of the richness, complexity, diversity and multidimensional nature of the subject that comprises in a very real sense the totality of Aboriginal cultural space. The temptation is to become absorbed in presenting ritual descriptions, enumerating beliefs and then embarking on lengthy explanation or exegesis. In this extravaganza the application of the data to the native title questions is easily overlooked. Native title writing seeks not to provide the definitive account of the claimants' beliefs and ritual practices, but rather to articulate how they encompass relationships to country and articulate the exercise of customary rights within it.

The second problem relates to secrecy and sacrilege. Writing well before the native title era, Eric Kolig commenced his study of the 'modernisation' of Aboriginal religion in the central Kimberley region by writing:

> An enormous stumbling block faces anyone who wants to write about traditional Aboriginal religion – the strict secrecy of its most sacred aspects. ... the most treasured parts are shrouded in deep secrecy and access to them requires special and formal training not readily granted ... and any breach of secrecy has traditionally been considered a heinous crime, the gravest possible sacrilege, for which nothing but the most severe punishment is adequate response. (Kolig 1981, vii)

I have watched senior Aboriginal men agonise about whether or not to disclose restricted materials to the court, sometimes (but not always) encouraged by their lawyers or enthused by the researcher who want the best case made without perhaps paying enough attention to the longer-term consequences for the claimants. Fatal car accidents have been blamed on the perceived betrayal of sacred lore, terminal cases of cancer linked to statements made in court – albeit during a restricted session. The fear of supernatural consequences and of social opprobrium for betraying a sacred trust is a very real and present one. Researchers and lawyers need to consider such matters with great care before exhorting claimants to tell all, particularly if such matters are not critical to an understanding of the possession of rights. It should be evident from the content of this chapter that there is much that can be written that relates to Aboriginal religious belief that does not compromise the secrecy of the esoteric. My opening position has always been that there should be no restricted materials included either in my field note book or in the evidence: my report, the *viva voce* evidence or the claimant affidavits. The case for the recognition of native title can with skill and industry be put without the need to reveal the most personal and secret aspects of an Indigenous culture. It seems to me that Aboriginal people are asked to subject enough of their cultural heritage to close scrutiny in the process of making a native title claim without having to give away their deepest secrets and feel themselves potentially at least to be liable to suffer direly as a consequence.

This said, I have been involved in a number of claims that have seen the presentation of restricted materials. In some cases this has been as a result of the inextricable nature of esoteric belief and practice and the articulation of rights to country. Sometimes, a proper understanding of these matters must include the restricted dimensions of belief and practice, otherwise it cannot be fully comprehended – which is why, of course, it is senior ritual leaders who take the lead in matters relating to the use and management of country. In other cases I have witnessed the claimants taking action on their own account to reveal restricted materials to the court because they have felt that this will serve their interests best in the long run. In such circumstances one can but hope that the outcome is one that makes the revelation worthwhile.

6

Native title research and oral testimony[1]

Do we tell it like it is?

In applying ourselves to native title inquiries, we face two methodological obstacles. The first relates to resources, including time. The second relates to the type of data that is required for the proof of native title. Both have implications for how we do our fieldwork, assemble our data and the reliance that may need to be placed on oral testimony rather than first-hand observation.

Time, money and the oral account

What might best be called 'classical anthropology' involved long periods of time in the field – perhaps a year or more – during which knowledge of the language was acquired, familiarity with the people gained, trust and respect earned and often deeply forged personal relationships developed with informants who became, in time, life-long friends, confidants and perhaps colleagues. This participant observation, bred from many months in the field, living with those studied, had the advantage of yielding insights and knowledge impossible to gain over shorter, more intense periods of

---

1   This chapter builds on my paper, 'Piety, fact and the oral account in native title claims' (Palmer 2011a). In order to contextualise my account, I have included some short pieces from this paper in this chapter to facilitate presentation of additional materials relevant to the uses of oral tradition in native title anthropology.

fieldwork. It also had the advantage of providing a ready testing ground to evaluate statements made by informants. So developed the important distinction for anthropology between what people actually do and what they say they do. Recording the former requires observation, often over a prolonged period of time. Recording of the latter requires only the right questions and the opportunity to ask them.

The reality of the situation for native title research is that time and resources are unlikely to stretch to permit prolonged periods of time in the field. The Native Title Representative Bodies have limited funding available for claims. Research has to be focused, intensive and strategically organised so as to maximise opportunities for participant observation, particularly during visits to the claim area. Other techniques are also employed including in-depth interviews and group discussions that may produce good field data and, on occasions, copious ethnography. Properly documented fieldwork undertaken over a period of several weeks that includes return visits and trips to the country of the claim can provide a reliable and detailed account of relevant aspects of the claimants' customary laws, customs, beliefs and practices. This fieldwork method relies to at least some considerable extent on oral testimony. It is not possible to observe at first hand every reported activity. For anthropologists researching a native title claim, then, substantial reliance must then be placed on the oral account.

The type of data – establishing continuity

Proof of native title relies upon a relationship being established between past customary practice and present practice. The evaluation can then be made as to whether there is continuity of laws and custom over time and, ideally, since the time of sovereignty. As a consequence, native title anthropologists need to ascertain from those with whom they work whether a practice or a belief is of some antiquity. Questions that relate to identity or the language of a forebear, their place of birth or country and the family genealogy are all significant in this process. For an anthropologist researching a native title claim it is not possible to observe past events, interrogate the asserted identities or genealogical relationships of those now long dead. Primary data, in the absence of any archival record, must be derived solely from the oral testimony of those who advance the propositions today.

The anthropologist who seeks to provide an expert view as to the continuity of customary beliefs, practices, identities and relationships for a native title claim has little choice but to place substantial reliance on the oral account of claimants. Given the limits imposed on undertaking extensive empirical fieldwork, this reliance is somewhat increased. On both counts, then, the use of oral tradition in native title proceedings is a significant factor in the research process when undertaking a native title inquiry. The native title anthropologist needs both to appreciate this fact and ensure that his or her use and analyses of oral materials is based on a proper appreciation of the nature of the data considered.

Oral tradition, reliability, anthropology and the courts

Oral testimony and the court

The bulk of the evidence in any native title claim that goes to trial is the oral evidence of the claimants. In addition, affidavits and witness statements may be provided to the court as part of the evidentiary process and they too usually rely on the oral testimony of the claimants. The use of oral testimony is commonplace in many legal proceedings. However, witnesses in, say, a criminal or a road traffic accident trial, usually only give evidence about the events they actually witnessed (otherwise, it may be disallowed). Further, the events witnessed are likely to have occurred not long before the trial. This may not be so in a native title trial where people are asked about relationships to forebears, language identity and places of birth and residence that they have only been told about. Evidence may also be given about the antiquity of practices and beliefs based on what the witness recalls being told about the matter by parents or grandparents, sometimes decades ago. My observation in trials is that counsel for the respondent parties may object to some evidence of this sort.[2] I also think it reasonable to assume that judges make up their own minds as to the

---

2   For example, 'The State discounted the Aboriginal testimony about societal unity at the second trial with the broad proposition that "… in the absence of traditional methods of recording social history, Aboriginal historical memory is notoriously shallow, infrequently extending beyond two generations". The basis for this contention was not stated and I do not accept it as a global proposition which has any part to play in my decision. My assessment of the Aboriginal evidence is based upon ordinary processes of inference and assessment of probabilities and credibility that apply to the testimony of any witness.' *Sampi v State of Western Australia* [2005] FCA 777 [981].

reliability or weight of the evidence they hear.[3] However, the fact remains that the proof of native title requires consideration of some issues that cannot have been observed by the witness and may rely on an oral recall extending back many decades.

The legal problem develops from the jurisprudential principle that some forms of testimony may be what is called 'hearsay' and cannot be afforded the same weight as other evidence and, indeed, may be ruled out of consideration altogether by a judge. The 'hearsay rule'[4] prohibits most statements made outside a courtroom from being used as evidence in court. Thus, oral accounts that rely on statements that report what others have said may be judged as constituting hearsay. Oral traditions are, by their very nature, dependent upon a verbal transmission over time where authority for a belief or practice is usually cited as an ancestor or deceased forebear, neither of whom would be available to give evidence. Customary Aboriginal systems place heavy reliance on the oral account, imputing a gravitas and authority that stems from the very aspect that European Australian law finds at fault. According to customary Aboriginal principles, the past enunciates authority. Traditional values and beliefs transmitted through the oral account are afforded the quality of unchallengeable inviolable Law and are often regarded as having a sacred quality. Yet, in an Australian courtroom such pronouncements may potentially be categorised as 'hearsay' and may be challenged.[5]

This is a thorny legal issue that has exercised the courts and jurists for many years now. Peter Gray[6] is a distinguished former judge of the Federal Court with a long interest in cross-cultural communication, particularly in the legal system as it has impacted on Indigenous Australians. Gray has provided some helpful insights into the legal background to this

---

3   See, for example, 'However, Mr Nathan's oral evidence in this proceeding has cast some doubt on the reliability of what he recounted to Dr Palmer and, indeed, the reliability of his recollections generally. By saying this I mean no disrespect to Mr Nathan: he is clearly held in affectionate and important regard by many people inside and outside the claim area and is a Pitta Pitta elder. However, his evidence was somewhat confused and contradictory'. In fact, I (Dr Palmer) did not work with Mr Nathan but relied on the research conducted by another expert who did. *Dempsey on behalf of the Bularnu, Waluwarra and Wangkayujuru People v State of Queensland* (No. 2) [2014] FCA 528 [261]. See also *Aplin on behalf of the Waanyi Peoples v State of Queensland* [2010] FCA 625 [234].

4   *Evidence Act 1995*, section 59.

5   There are provisions in the *Evidence Act* that provide exceptions to the rule against hearsay evidence with respect to traditional laws and customs (section 72). Robert Blowes SC, pers. comm.

6   Hon. Professor Peter R.A. Gray AM. Now Adjunct Professor, Monash Law School. See www.monash.edu/law/current-students/resources/course-unit-information/postgraduate/sess-peter-gray accessed 26 January 2016.

issue (2000). Gray noted that the reliability (perhaps 'truthfulness') of oral accounts was a matter of debate amongst social scientists (ibid., 6). In relation to claims made by Indigenous Australians to have rights to country, this matter was first examined by Blackburn J in the Gove case.[7] Gray (ibid., 8) cites his Honour as ruling that 'No question of hearsay is at this stage involved; what is in question is only the personal experience and recollection of individuals. The substance of this evidence had to be proved, in some manner, as an indispensable preliminary to the exposition and understanding of the system of "native title" asserted by the plaintiffs'.[8] Evidence of a witness was then admissible provided he (or she) 'spoke from his own recollection and experience'. Gray notes that the difficulty of some oral accounts being regarded as 'hearsay' and potentially not admissible was a feature of the Mabo trial.[9] The evidence included testimony based on what Torres Strait Islanders had been told by their forebears and this evidence gave rise to hundreds of objections (ibid., 8). Gray observed:

> Moynihan J admitted much of this evidence, such as statements made by Eddie Mabo's grandfather relating to boundaries of land, but stated that further evidence would be needed for it to be accepted as truth. His Honour said:

> 'I have little difficulty in accepting that the fact of assertions being made by persons other than a witness may be relevant and hence admissible. The evidence is not, without more, however necessarily admissible as to the truth of the matters asserted.' (ibid., 8)[10]

Gray reports that other jurisdictions, notably the Supreme Court of Canada, have shown more acceptance of the importance of oral tradition as evidence in cases relating to indigenous rights to land (ibid., 6). Gray cites Lee J of the Australian Federal Court in *Ward v Western Australia*,[11] who himself cited a Canadian case. Lee J identified the disadvantage faced by Aboriginal people should they not be able to 'depend upon oral histories and accounts, often localised in nature' and found there to be 'no suggestion of unfairness in a trial process in which Aboriginal applicants are permitted to present their case through use of oral histories

---

7   *Milirrpum v Nabalco Pty Ltd* (1971) 17 FLR 141.
8   *Milirrpum v Nabalco Pty Ltd* (1971) 17 FLR 141 [153].
9   *Mabo v Queensland* [No. 2] (1992) 175 CLR 1.
10 *Mabo v Queensland* [1992] 1 Qd R 78, per Moynihan J [87].
11 *Ward on behalf of the Miriuwung and Gajerrong People v Western Australia* (1998) 159 ALR 483.

and by reference to received knowledge'.[12] Gray considered that Lee J's comments might 'lay the foundation for a more liberal attitude by Australian courts to the admissibility of oral records of Aboriginal people' (ibid., 7).

Some trial judges have shown themselves willing to accommodate oral testimony based on what witnesses were told by their grandparents. Weinberg J stated in this regard:

> Of course what they were told will be hearsay, but it is hearsay of a kind that has been readily admitted in native title cases. In *Gumana*,[13] the relevant date for sovereignty was 1788, and not 1825. Selway J concluded that the evidence tendered by the applicants of genealogies and linguistics was sufficient to establish that some of the ancestors of persons who were currently claimants were members of Yolngu society in 1788 and, indeed, well before then.

His Honour wrote (at [194]):

> 'Ultimately the evidence of the existence of the relevant Aboriginal tradition and custom as at 1788, and of the rights held by the particular clans in 1788 and thereafter pursuant to that tradition and custom, is based upon evidence derived from what the Yolngu claimants currently do and from what they have observed their parents and elders do and from what they were told by their parents and elders ...'

His Honour continued (at [195]):

> 'As already discussed, there is nothing peculiar or unique about this sort of evidence. It is oral evidence of a custom. It is evidence of fact, not opinion. To the extent that it consists of what Mr Gumana was told by his father and by other old people it constitutes a recognised exception to the rule against hearsay.'[14]

Gray was also cognisant of substantial changes to the *Native Title Act* that did not auger well for the adoption of a more liberal attitude:

> The resolution of the relationship between the rules of evidence and Aboriginal traditions in Australia will be particularly important now that amendments to the *Native Title Act 1993* (Cth) have come into operation.

---

12   *Ward on behalf of the Miriuwung and Gajerrong People v Western Australia* (1998) 159 ALR 483 [504].
13   *Gawirrin Gumana v Northern Territory of Australia* [No. 2] [2005] FCA 1425.
14   *Griffiths v Northern Territory of Australia* [2006] FCA 903 [574] to [576].

These amendments make the rules of evidence applicable to the hearing of applications for determination of native title, unless the Court otherwise orders. The rules of evidence, so far as applications for determination of native title are concerned, are now to be found in the *Evidence Act 1995* (Cth). An introductory note to Chapter 1 of that Act states 'This Act sets out the federal rules of evidence'. The provisions of that Act with respect to hearsay are more liberal than the common law rules, but are potentially restrictive of any attempt to create new exceptions. Perhaps the solution lies in a recognition of oral traditions as a category of real evidence, not hearsay at all. (Gray 2000, 9)[15]

The admissibility or otherwise of evidence is firstly a matter for the lawyers who must consider the proper form of the evidence, both of the Aboriginal and expert witnesses. Ultimately, the matter if challenged is a question for the courts. It is also a matter for the court to decide what weight (creditable proof) to place on the oral evidence. However, the questions raised by an evaluation of the reliability of oral tradition, recall and evidence based on non-witnessed events are not confined to legal proceedings. Anthropologists are also aware of the limitations of the oral account and some of the difficulties it raises for understanding and making sense of past action.

Professor Sansom and Timber Creek

In the Timber Creek native title determination, Weinberg J[16] had cause to consider the evidence provided by claimants as oral testimony, as this had been the subject of debate between the experts – the author (Dr Palmer, called by the applicant) and Professor Sansom (called by a respondent, the Northern Territory Government). As I have noted above, his Honour was sympathetic to the oral accounts provided by the applicant and concluded that reliance on an oral account was not unique to native title law. He also found that there was evidence from claims under the *Aboriginal Land Rights Act* (NT) that supported genealogical connection with the application area to a period at or about the time of sovereignty. His Honour stated that there was 'Evidence given in the Timber Creek Land Claim in 1985, and also in the other land claims involving adjacent areas' (Griffiths FCA 903 [572]) that established 'a direct connection between the claimants, and their direct ancestors' in relation to the claim

---

15 Footnotes excluded.
16 *Griffiths v Northern Territory of Australia* [2006] FCA 903 (Griffiths).

area (Griffiths FCA 903 [572]). By this logic, then, the oral account was not without support from independent legal findings, notwithstanding the fact that these very findings had themselves been founded on oral testimony. In addition, based upon the same reasoning, his Honour was prepared to accept that there was evidence of a continuity of laws and customs (Griffiths FCA 903 [572] to [583]). He therefore concluded that 'It would be wrong, in my view, to approach the issue of connection by turning a blind eye to these historical realities' (Griffiths FCA 903 [583]). He was able to determine that 'the rights and interests' that were enjoyed by the forebears of the claimants had 'passed on through this system of descent'. They were rights and interests that were 'in my view, recognised by the common law of Australia, and are therefore properly to be characterised as native title' (Griffiths FCA 903 [584]).

The judge's comments were in part a response to Professor Sansom's assertion that 'In the absence of total and reliable outside documentation of the history of a local group since sovereignty, it is not possible to say of any contemporary local group that it was represented by the antecedents of present members in 1825' (cited in Griffiths FCA 903 [431]). His Honour's comment was, 'Of course, if this statement were taken literally, no native title claim could ever succeed in the Northern Territory, or perhaps in any other part of Australia' (Griffiths FCA 903 [432]). His Honour did accept, however, that Sansom's opinions regarding some 'particular dangers associated with historical recall' were perhaps relevant to the understanding of oral testimony. He cited, by way of example, the customary ban on calling the names of the dead, the shallowness of oral recall and the practice that 'proscribes the telling of stories about a person or persons that one has never met' (Griffiths FCA 903 [433]).

These apparent impediments to the free flow of an oral account were, I think, not quite what Professor Sansom had in mind when, as the judge wrote, Sansom consigned 'oral history to the periphery' (Griffiths FCA 903 [431]). Subsequently, Professor Sansom developed his views regarding oral testimony at Timber Creek and elsewhere (2006). In this paper, Professor Sansom noted the propensity for judges to place substantial reliance on the evidence of the Aboriginal claimants.[17] He was of the view that such reliance showed a misunderstanding of the nature of the oral account. He argued:

---

17   Citing Sackville in Yulara (FCA [288]) and other related references.

Of itself, widespread Aboriginal tradition limits recall of traditional practice. Emplaced traditions work, furthermore, to eliminate all memory of any historical departures from once-established norms. The consequence is that credible information about anything but the personally witnessed past cannot be rendered up by the Aboriginal testator who has not had recourse to records. If proof of the continuity or discontinuity of tradition from the time of sovereignty is to be supplied, the court has no choice but to rely on those devices for the remembering, preserving or retrieving the past that have been imported into Australia since settlement. Proof (if any proof there be) is to be gained by recourse to records and/or expert opinion. (ibid., 150–151)

Sansom is not alone in his views regarding the shallowness of historical recall. Morphy (1993, 236) is of the view that, in Yolngu ontology, 'landscape and myth are … machines for the suppression of history' (see also Samson 2006, 153–154). A lack of written history means that changes in the groups that occupied country were 'masked' (Morphy 1993, 236). On Groote Eylandt, I collected narratives about migration and settlement. These purport to identify members of a third ascending generation (for example, a great grandfather), but in fact evoke individuals who belong to higher generations, a truth that can be recovered by the use of names in the genealogies collected some decades ago, supporting the view that the oral account can work to truncate or telescope historical events. Chronology is not, however, entirely absent. My experience in other areas of Aboriginal Australia supports the view that Aboriginal history does reveal some sense of limited depth. I have collected stories of Captain Cook in the Victoria River District of the Northern Territory, as has Rose (1992, 187–191). These narratives place him in the distant past, but not in the primordial Dreaming. Stories of Noah's Ark, which I have collected from the Kimberley, are narratives synthesising customary content with Biblical content (Kolig 1980a) while the events related are assigned to the Dreaming and an indefinite period in the past. Rose (1992, 206–207) writes that events within the Dreaming had a chronology, again something that I have encountered many times in my own fieldwork.

While the case for concluding that Aboriginal history is lacking chronology is not altogether made out, from an anthropological point of view oral accounts are shown sometimes to lack depth and may be unreliable. Given that native title requires a demonstration of a continuity of social formation, laws, customs and ancestral connection to land that spans more than the compass of witnesses' lived experience, the uses and reliability of oral traditions is a significant consideration for native title anthropology. Consequently, for both the court considering a native title application as well as for the native title anthropologist, the reliability of oral tradition is an important issue.

In a paper I published in 2011 I have set out a detailed critique of Sansom's position (Palmer 2011a, 272–285). I was of the view that Sansom, while identifying some important issues relating to oral tradition, had rather thrown 'the baby out with the bath water' (ibid., 269). It is one thing to understand the context of an oral tradition and exercise care and qualification as to how it should be used or interpreted. It is quite another to discard Aboriginal oral tradition altogether on the ground that it is somehow 'untrue', not to be trusted and that sole reliance must be placed on 'records and/or expert opinion' (Sansom 2006, 151). Some sorts of oral tradition that relate to the domain of religious beliefs and practices are innately conservative because they are creatures of a fundamentally conservative culture. I have argued elsewhere that this conservativism works to limit change in oral transmission (Palmer 2011a, 281–284). In assessing the validity and veracity of an oral account, these factors that work to limit change may be relevant and I discuss some aspects of this matter in what follows.

Factors that affect continuity

Conservative societies?

Ronald and Catherine Berndt characterised Aboriginal society prior to European settlement as 'conservative', although they did note exceptions (1988, 492). They considered that this was a consequence of geographic isolation, small populations and limited resource exploitation (ibid.). The social and religious systems were sustained by rules and sanctions that discouraged nonconformity, 'their members emphasising the unchanging quality of life, the importance of tradition, rather than the desirability of change as such' (ibid., 493). The Berndts were writing of pre-contact Aboriginal society in the context of an examination of the impacts of European settlement and invasion. However, these researchers were not alone in understanding Aboriginal society to be innately conservative, a feature that endures to the present in at least some areas where native title research is currently undertaken. Meggitt, writing of the Walbiri of Central Australia, commented that 'regularity, frequency, efficiency, and propriety are all expressions of normality – behaviour is predictable because it should be' (Meggitt 1962, 253). Walbiri belief was then 'inevitably moral, conservative and circular' (ibid.). Nor did this change fundamentally with the innovations that came with European settlement. Rather, while ways of behaving may have changed, the rules that govern these changed circumstances 'have altered little' (ibid., 254). Kolig explains this conservative tendency by reference to what he terms 'mental continuity' (1977, 51), represented in an 'elaborate ideological superstructure' that could 'exist undisturbed in their basically traditional and highly intellectually oriented milieu' despite harsh environmental conditions and, more latterly, the changes wrought by European settlement (ibid.). Morphy sees the beliefs and oral traditions as providing fixed and structured forms, where 'the untrammelled creativity of the ancestral beings is lost precisely because they created the world in a form that could be passed on from generation to generation as the order of the world' (1995, 189). Theirs were 'frozen experiences', left behind to be significant to the lives of others (ibid.). For the Yolngu, Morphy was of the view that 'the most conservative part of the system is the totemic division of the landscape and certainly in the case of place names there is remarkable continuity at least since the 1880s when we first have evidence' (1993, 236).

Myers, writing of the Pintupi of Central Australia, remarked that part of the idea of the Dreaming for the Pintupi is that it 'implies continuity and permanence' (1986, 52). According to this understanding and belief, 'the cosmos has always been as it is and that, indeed, it cannot be different' (ibid., 52–53). Change and alteration is not absent from Pintupi thinking, for 'the evidence of new customs and new cults is unassailable; life is not static' (ibid., 53). However, the Pintupi apply the concept of the Dreaming in such as way so as to present the changes as though the experiences of them '*appears* to be continuous and permanent' (ibid., 53). This resonates with Morphy's observation of the Yolngu that while change is all apparent, 'the mythic screen that covers landscape makes the relationship appear unchanging' (1995, 204).

These writers were not arguing for an unchanging society, far less one that was incapable of adaptation. The common theme is an appreciation of the conservative nature of Aboriginal societies and their inherent stability and adherence to the forces of tradition. So, where changes did occur, as indeed they must, it was on the understanding that the fundamentals of the system had remained intact and only the circumstances or relationships had become modified. The ideology of stasis and a fixedness of rules and their determining progenitors could not have been sustained in the face of blatant alteration – the 'mythic screen' and the *appearance* of an unchanging world had to be based on the conservative and change-resistant structures that the Berndts first identified. These provided for a stability and continuity of belief and practice such as Sutton noted for the Western Desert:

> In fact as a basis of tenure interests such knowledge perhaps reaches its greatest prominence in that region. The Dreamings (*Tjukurrpa*) and their sites and tracks seem to be the most stable elements of the system, one that was demographically porous as individuals came and went over long periods. (Sutton 2003, 159)

The Law and the Dreaming

In an earlier chapter of this book, I discussed the Aboriginal metaphysical construct of the Dreaming (see Chapter 5). The Dreaming unites past and present. It is believed to be the source of all spirituality and supplies an explanation and justification for present action, ritual belief and practice. The customary way to do things is believed to have been ordained in the Dreaming, which is considered to be the spiritual originator and perpetuator of consuetudinary practice that comprises the normative system. The Dreaming and its constructs are important to native title as they provide the legitimation and justification for the view that these ways of doing things are unchanging and unchangeable.[18] The codification of these principles is often enunciated by the use of the English term 'Law', reflecting the jural and mandatory nature of the rules, which are understood to be evoked by the use of the term. The choice of the Aboriginal English term 'Law' reflects the authority of its precepts and the imperative that its tenets be obeyed – just as European Australians respect and observe Australian law, showing deference for the gravitas that its institutions represent and understanding that penalties may apply to acts that contravene its regulations and edicts. The Dreaming, and the Law it is believed to have engendered and continues to sustain, is a matter of high seriousness in customary dealings. These concepts are implicit in any understanding of how Aboriginal belief systems operate and both, in their separate ways, are a means to emphasise the stability, unchanging character and thus the authority of customary belief and practice.

---

18   Meggitt 1962, 251–252; Myers 1986, 53; Sutton 2003, 83.

In the Aboriginal cultures with which I am familiar, a key aspect of belief and dogma articulated though beliefs in the Dreaming and its mandated rules for action is that a person does not meddle with a Dreaming or willingly contravene a Law without fear of dire consequences. This is not only a matter of fear of human physical reprisal or opprobrium. Contravention of Law is a matter for the spirit world. Grave consequences will follow, so it is believed, whether there is a human prosecutor or not. These strictures apply to accounts of the beings of the Dreaming and the names, languages and marks they left behind them and the laws and customs they ordained. One example of this is the canonical lists of place names that a senior ritual leader may rehearse when discussing a narrative string in which a Dreaming protagonist visits numerous places in a traverse of country. Such strings and associated adventures may follow lines of hills, lakes, coast or a river.[19] During the many years I have worked in Aboriginal Australia where oral traditions remain vibrant, I have collected many such accounts that demonstrate the detailed knowledge a person has of country and the activities of the Dreaming beings. I have set out one example of this form of oral tradition in a paper I published (Palmer 2011a, 282) and there are plenty of additional examples to be found in the literature. Narratives, song and ritual performances are all subject to the imperatives of the Dreaming and the demands of the Law. Thus, correctness of word and action in the rehearsal of these traditions is essential. One way whereby people ensure that there can be no suggestion of wrong action relating to oral traditions is to make their performance and commemoration group activities. This works as a kind of insurance, safeguarding practitioners from making mistakes, as well as ensuring that all relevant people knew how a particular business had been conducted. These oral traditions are practised, then, in the company of others who usually have senior status, either in the same country that was being celebrated, or in a neighbouring area.

Individuals are generally unwilling to talk about country without others being present to witness the account. These discussions are often accompanied by an interplay between individuals, which provide a means of ensuring that accounts are correct; that is, consistent with corporate memory. In ritual performance, such commensality is a significant feature of interactions. Without the presence of others, ritual performance could

---

19   See, for example, von Brandenstein (1973, 97) who related such a list collected from the Pilbara region of Western Australia.

not take place. In such an exchange, oral knowledge is not individuated. Its presentation is subject to group correction and validation. Performance and transmission is regulated by a jural public, ensuring continuity of content. Ritual instruction is characterised as vigorous and attention is paid to ensuring that an initiate learns fully and correctly. 'Getting it wrong' is subject to sanction and is not tolerated.

Such a process of oral tradition works toward the maintenance of continuity of accounts and limits the possibility for revisionism or innovation. While oral accounts will, inevitably, suffer transmutation over time, transformation is not facilitated by the process I have outlined here. These examples are, of course, taken from a particular genre of customary belief and are more likely than not to be found in ethnographies where customary beliefs and practices remain quite vibrant.

While the texture of Aboriginal belief and practice in such contexts favours conservativism over radical transmutation in the oral account, a common difficulty arises when oral accounts must provide the basis for claimant family history and the related topic of country and language of origin. In making inquiry into these matters, the anthropologist may need to seek independent verification from other sources, should these be available.

Using oral accounts in native title claims

The task for the native title anthropologist is to comprehend oral tradition as a social exchange replete with meaning and bring these understandings to both the method employed and the subsequent analysis from which expert opinion is derived. For my present purpose I focus on two subjects that recur in native title research. The first is oral family histories which include genealogical knowledge. The second is what can be broadly called 'oral tradition', being the compendium of oral accounts relating to a forebear's place of origin, country of affiliation or language group identity. These two aspects of the oral account have in common a reliance on recall and often involve comments or statements regarding relationships, events or customary belief and practice that are remembered as a part of a continuing oral tradition. What I seek to explore here is how these data can be comprehended in anthropological analysis, making allowance for transmutation or other changes to the original. In this way we can admit oral accounts to our analysis based on a proper understanding of the materials we present and upon which we ultimately rely.

Genealogies and family history

The fact that genealogies are typically limited in generational depth is well documented in Aboriginal Australia (see Barnes 1967, 119; Sansom 2006, 157–59). Given sole reliance on the oral account, a person generally commands knowledge of two or occasionally three ascending generations from his or her own. Rarely, unless documentary and archival materials are relied upon, will oral recall extend to the great great grandparental generation (that is, ego's FFFF or mmmm[20]). In some cultures learned canonical listings of genealogies are themselves a part of oral tradition[21] but this is nowhere a feature of Indigenous Australian cultures where genealogical knowledge generally extends only as far as ego's own lived experience or that of his or her parents, passed down through the oral account.

Most of those with whom I have worked in native title inquiries have genealogical recall of two ascending generations. If ego is a man or woman of middle to late middle age, then it is also likely that they will have knowledge of two descending generations. Thus, typically, genealogical recall covers five generations, including ego's own. This means that if ego was, say, 70 years old in 2015, and allowing for a gap of between 20 and 25 years per generation,[22] then ego's grandfather is likely to have been born between 1895 and 1900.[23] While it may be possible to find claimants older than this, it is an unfortunate fact that this is unusual and many are younger.

In terms of continuity of ancestral connection, a date of 1895 (allowing for the older of the calculated dates) does not match sovereignty anywhere on mainland Australia.[24] However, in many remote places the frontier did not advance much more than two or three decades before this date. Prior to this, it might be reasonably inferred, customary systems would have remained intact.[25] Thus, the date of what I call 'effective sovereignty'

---

20 Kinship abbreviations are explained in Chapter 9 under the subheading, 'Some methodological and procedural issues'.

21 For example, the Maori *whakapapa*, recited as part of an oral tradition describing a line of descent from ancestors down to the present day.

22 Peterson and Long have calculated an average generation gap for Aboriginal women as 15 years minimum and for men 30 years, as men traditionally married later (1986, 149–150).

23 Ego was born in 1945, his father in 1920–25 and his grandfather in 1895–1900.

24 Parts of the Torres Strait have a date of sovereignty as late as 1879 (Queensland Government 2003, 23).

25 This is accepted by the Queensland Government 'for the purposes of mediation' (2003, 5) and has been used in a number of native title cases.

will often be some decades after actual sovereignty. In this reasoning, genealogical recall to two ascending generations is useful, if not conclusive, to supporting arguments about ancestral connection.

One way to remedy this shortfall in attaining the date of effective sovereignty is to rely on archival genealogical materials in order to trace the family tree back several additional generations to the required date. I examine some of the practical matters that develop from the use of archival materials generally in native title work and the problems and difficulties attendant upon this task in Chapter 7 of this book. In Chapter 9 I examine the uses of genealogies including aspects of what I there term 'genealogical truth'. Here I am concerned to explore how genealogical accounts recorded by earlier researchers may be brought to bear on the oral account of the claimants, which may serve to bring credibility to the latter. Alternatively, bringing the oral account to bear on the archival account may render the latter more meaningful to the native title inquiry.

There is a range of archival genealogical materials available to researchers in native title claims. Two of the most commonly referred to are genealogies collected by Daisy Bates and Norman Tindale, although there are many others available depending on the location of the research, including Radcliffe-Brown, Elkin and Kaberry. Bates's genealogies were collected comparatively early, generally dating to the first decade of the last century, although some are later. Radcliffe-Brown collected some of his genealogies in company with Daisy Bates and others from the Pilbara region in 1911. I have also used Elkin's genealogies collected from the Dampier Peninsula, western Kimberley region, which date from the period 1927–28, and Kaberry's Kimberley genealogies collected in the period 1934–36. Norman Tindale's work is a common source for genealogical material. He collected his data somewhat later than Bates, although he did take some genealogies as early as 1928 in South Australia (at Koonibba Mission) and carried on this work in many places round Australia until the 1960s. Some of Tindale's genealogies are complex, tracing back three generations from ego with multiple co-lateral branches that can make them difficult to follow. Tindale sometimes complemented his genealogical data with social information entered onto cards, as well as anthropomorphic measurements.

The archival account may itself present challenges for interpretation and should not be uncritically regarded. In this respect, both Bates and Tindale present some difficulties. Bates's genealogies are sometimes hard to follow and the meanings of her many annotations are often unexplained while actual relationships are not always apparent (see Palmer 2011a, 273–274). Bates used Aboriginal personal names for the most part so it is difficult, if not impossible, to trace English names to her account without the knowledge of claimants who recall those Aboriginal names. Tindale's 'tribal' ascriptions make assumptions about how these identities were formed and the implications of their use (see Palmer 2009). These reservations must be borne in mind when attempting to interpret the archival record. While the written account may command a certain authority by virtue of its being rendered as text, documentation does not mean that it is either unambiguously intelligible or factually correct. Such a qualification should be applied to all archival sources. Thus, reliance on the archival record is no magic cure for the inaccuracies of reported history.[26]

These archival sources are of no assistance to a native title inquiry unless they can be convincingly identified as being the record of a claimant family. The archival record will generally cease at the date of its collection and without the oral account of the claimants there is often no way of linking the written record with claimants today. European names, Aboriginal names and sometimes nicknames may all be helpful in identifying the forebears of a claimant family in a genealogy. Names of offspring and other family members may be helpful in providing some evidence that the genealogy in question does indeed have as its subject the claimant family being discussed. However, care has to be exercised when common names occur in the genealogy, such as 'Polly' or 'Topsy', lest the name is the sole basis for identification and, in fact, the genealogy has no relationship with the subject family. Given consistency between the archival document and the oral account, the latter, limited though it may be to several ascending generations, provides the means to make sense of the archival account. Without the informants' knowledge of their forebears, contained in the oral histories, the archival documents would be of no relevance since there would be no way to link claimants with those represented in the genealogies.

Archival accounts, then, complement and supplement the Aboriginal evidence and provide a useful source when trying to reconstruct genealogical connection. The data they contain may provide ground for interpretations

---

26   See Rose's (2002) analysis of the use of European texts such as Curr (1883), which she argues must be read with caution. I discuss the problems of the use of archival materials elsewhere (see Palmer 2010a) and examine the issue in greater detail in the following Chapter 7.

as to people's country of origin and language-group affiliations, which may assist a native title inquiry. The archival evidence supports the oral evidence. This does not render the oral account compromised through processes of its transmission, but rather recommends it as the logical starting point for any genealogical account. The two sources complement each other and resolve the problem for native title work which requires genealogical knowledge that extends beyond the range of oral recall.

From the point of view of anthropology, the implications of this understanding are important as they instruct that identifying native title ancestors back as far as the date of sovereignty or even effective sovereignty through oral tradition alone is limited to the shallow depth of oral genealogical recall. Consequently, it is desirable to subject to analysis archival genealogical data where these are available. Consequently, the use of genealogical materials collected by earlier researchers provides confirmatory data that will support the oral account and may also provide a corrective.

History

An oral history account is of the present, notwithstanding the fact that it details past events. Since it is of the here and now, it is possible (perhaps likely) that it will be influenced by the present, including the context of its performance and the objectives of the teller. In a contested environment, oral accounts may provide legitimation for pressing a particular suit or point of view so their substance is shaped by contemporary aspiration. This inherent flexibility of an oral history may eventually result in the transmutation of the original 'fact'. Historian Patrick O'Farrell, in an attack on the privileging of oral sources over other data in his discipline, was scathing in his criticism of such singular reliance:

> The basic problem with oral testimony about the past is that its truth (when it *is* true) is not primarily about what happened or how things were, but about how the past has been recollected. That being said – hardly a startling revelation – at once all the claims made for oral history – accuracy, immediacy, reality – come under most serious suspicion, and we move straight away into the world of image, selective memory, later overlays and utter subjectivity. (O'Farrell 1979, 4)

O'Farrell does not suggest that the oral account of history has no place – only that it requires other sources to bolster its incompleteness or provide a corrective to the oral testimony, which, being a recollection, is vulnerable to inaccuracy (ibid., 4). This is not to say that such flexibility is conscious manipulation or eventual transmutation is deliberate on the part of the teller. Views of past events may be held with almost religious conviction by claimants in native title claims and expounded to the court with passion.[27] The challenge for a native title anthropologist is how to evaluate the field data collected from claimants, taking into account the nature of oral tradition. In tackling the likely nature and extent of such, the anthropologist is faced with a forensic task, which is commonplace enough. It is reasonable to expect the researcher to apply checks and balances to the field data. Typically, these may be in the form of archival references, prior accounts or other independent contemporary versions of the same set of incidents. However, these may not always be available and a good deal of the data we collect in the course of our research into native title matters relies on the oral account of the claimants, based on their recollections of what they were told. This means that at times oral history must stand as the field data and the sole basis for an expert view. In these cases the degree of concordance in oral accounts may be significant. Unanimity amongst those who relate events through an oral history account is an important pointer to its possible verity because there is a commonality of recall in the oral memory. Methodologically, then, the absence of a dispute relating to an account of oral history, provided the field has been thoroughly canvassed, places less demand on a need for verification, although where this can be supplied the oral account will have greater weight. This does not mean that uncontested oral histories are uncritically accepted, but it does mean that they should be subject to different methodological procedures than those that are clearly in contention between claimants or claimants and respondents. In cases where there is a contest between Aboriginal parties, inconsistent accounts may flag changes or ruptures to the oral history. Disagreement may be a sign of error in one of the accounts. Assessing which is most probably wrong can only be done in conjunction with the other tools outlined here – archival documents and prior statements.

In practice the application of these methodological principles may be accompanied by some pain when there is contestation between Indigenous participants. Potentially, then, the anthropologist will be required to give an opinion as to the validity or otherwise of an oral history, which may be

---

27   See Sutton 2017 for examples and analyses of innovation in an oral account.

uncomfortable in a public hearing. Discomfort will not only develop from those whose views are brought into question, but may also be subject to criticism by the courts if the process followed is not properly understood.

Commonly in native title matters the question at issue will relate to avowed facts given as oral history that might provide evidence of connection to the claim area or rights in it of a particular person. Such facts might relate to the asserted place of birth of an individual, typically an ancestor of a set of claimants or those represented by an Indigenous respondent. More generally they might relate to an individual's country or place of origin or affiliation. Common, too, are claims relating to an ancestor's language group identity, which in turn is identified with particular parts of an application area. Evidence relating to such matters is often adduced in court in the form of statements like 'I was always told this was so by the old people' or 'I've always known this was so. It was just something we were always brought up to know'. This is common in field data too – there being no authority greater than the oral tradition carried by remembered forebears. Where these assertions are advocated by the applicant, the anthropologist may be asked whether there is documentary evidence to support the contention, this usually being done in the expert report. Where these assertions are challenged, the means to support such a challenge is also likely to rely on one or more independent evidentiary items that can be argued to call the oral account into question. In short it is not uncommon in my experience for an assertion that relies on oral history to be subject to scrutiny by the anthropologist whether supported or brought into question, so permitting the court to evaluate the weight that might be placed on the oral evidence.

While documentary evidence that might illuminate the validity of oral history is not always available, where it is it is likely to comprise three broad categories of materials: archival documents; prior statements made in previous native title or land rights claims; and the comments, views and perhaps testimony of others. Each brings its own particular problems, and the path to validation or testing oral history is strewn with obstacles and potholes for the unwary.

Archival documents typically include birth, marriage and death certificates, Native Welfare reports or records and the genealogies collected by earlier researchers where these included comments or annotations relevant to the matter in question. With respect to the last-named source, Tindale is of particular note since he was in the habit of annotating his personal names with a language group designation and sometimes a place name.

The specific problems relating to the use of these documents is a matter I address in the following chapter of this book, so I will not dwell on it here. I note only that interpreting these documents is often a challenge and while they have the authority of the written word, this does not mean they are necessarily accurate.

The surrounding noise

It is sometimes the case that Indigenous claimants or respondents have been involved in court hearings relating to land claims made under state or territory Acts. These include claims heard under the *Aboriginal Land Rights Act* (NT) or state Acts like the *Queensland Aboriginal Land Act* (1991). There are also cases where claimants or Indigenous respondents have featured in earlier native title claims. The transcripts of these and the reports of commissioners and the determinations of judges may contain evidence relevant to an oral account offered up in a later case. The Bularnu, Waluwarra and Wangkayujuru native title claim in which I was involved[28] illustrates the use of evidence and findings of a prior court case, as well as the role that the competing claims of Indigenous testators may have in the evaluation of the oral traditions upon which the evidence is based.

In the Bularnu, Waluwarra and Wangkayujuru claim, the applicant had rejected the inclusion of the descendants of a woman known as Bunny or Bonny. The family in question, descendants of Bunny, sought and were granted leave to be joined as respondent to the claim. The Indigenous respondent, who was self-represented, asserted that her ancestor held rights to and affiliations with country and language identified with the application area. The experts in the case had identified for the court that the same ancestor had featured in an earlier claim made under the *Queensland Aboriginal Land Act*.[29] The commissioners who adjudicated the claim determined both the language group name and the country of affiliation of Bunny and her descendants (Land Tribunal, Queensland 1994, para 380). This was different to that now pressed by the respondent. The findings of this prior inquiry were a significant factor in the experts' evaluation of the conflicting oral accounts gained from the claimants and the Indigenous respondent.

---

28 *Dempsey on behalf of the Bularnu, Waluwarra and Wangkayujuru People v State of Queensland* (No. 2) [2014] FCA 528 (Dempsey).
29 Dempsey, [311].

The native title trial judge, Mortimer J, noted the findings of the commissioners at some length.[30] Her Honour went on to rule that she was not 'satisfied on the balance of probabilities that Bunny Craigie [the ancestor in question] had rights and interests acquired through traditional law and custom in the land around Roxborough within the claim area'.[31] Her Honour was of the view that the 'most likely hypothesis on the evidence as it is before the Court' was that the ancestor in question belonged to a language group and had affiliation to country well to the south of the claim area, but that lack of evidence meant that her place of birth could not be determined.[32] The 'hypothesis' was drawn from the findings of the hearing held under the *Queensland Aboriginal Land Act* and the reports of the experts who had evaluated these and other archival materials. The 'hypothesis' was in accord with the opinions advanced by the experts and was also based on the evidence provided to a former land claim hearing that had been subject to analysis by these experts.[33]

During the trial the Indigenous respondent's witnesses had given evidence that Bunny was born in or came from the claim area[34] while some additional evidence was either unclear or contradictory.[35] The applicant submitted that Bunny 'was not a person who was, under traditional law and custom, capable of transmitting rights in Wangkayujuru country'.[36] The applicant argued that her country was likely to have been south of the claim area, although its location was, according to the experts' views, uncertain.[37] The state submitted that Bunny probably did not have traditional country in the claim area,[38] noting 'the general absence of any evidence by the claimants about Bunny's connection to the claim area'.[39]

My assessment of the oral tradition that supported these contradictory propositions had situated them in the context of other materials I had considered as relevant, including the findings under the *Aboriginal*

---

30   Dempsey, [311], [319] to [336].
31   ibid., [844].
32   ibid., [848].
33   ibid., [849].
34   For example, QUD6115/98 24.10.13 p. 405 Rhonda Pagura, xxn Mr Blowes SC; p. 457 Ms Bogdanek, xn Ms Bogdanek; 29.10.13, p. 885, Alfred Nathan, fxxn Mr Blowes SC.
35   Dempsey, [266], [778].
36   ibid., [776].
37   ibid., [778] to [780].
38   ibid., [786].
39   ibid., [787].

Land Act and the family's former espousing of a language identity at odds with that advanced in this trial. I called this (too cryptically perhaps) 'surrounding noise'. I told the court:

> So, assessing the data as best I can in relation to these disciplinary notions which flow from my understanding of how the world works as an anthropologist, I then have to look around me at the surrounding noise, if you like, that's been generated about the Craigie family over the years. And there's no doubt that within the evidence, or the data which has been presented, there are points of variation about the origin of – of the ancestor including from the family itself who has strongly in the past espoused a Wangkamadhla language identity. [40]

My consideration of the oral account was then informed by the land claim case. My conclusions, like that of the judge, admitted prior documentation to my conclusion that Bunny was probably not in command of any part of the claim area according to the customary system in operation. Despite this consensus, I was criticised by the judge for my evaluation of the oral account that was advanced by the Indigenous respondent. I had found that presented by the applicants more convincing. The judge wrote that in weighing the data available to me I was demanding that the respondent and her witnesses should be 'held to a higher standard' than, presumably (although this is not made clear), the other witnesses, particularly those for the applicant. Moreover, with respect to my apparent non-acceptance of the evidence from the respondents that Bunny was born at Roxborough (as opposed to 'information sourced to the applicant's witnesses') that this was 'difficult to explain other than by some kind of unstated preference' for it as being 'inherently more reliable'. [41] My 'inexplicable reluctance on this issue' and my unwillingness to accept the verity of the oral histories presented by the respondent and her witness, so her Honour concluded, 'undermine[d] the weight I am prepared to give to his opinion about where Bunny may have been "from", or, indeed, where she may have been born. I give more weight to other sources.' [42]

40   *Dempsey on behalf of the Bularnu, Waluwarra and Wangkayujuru People v State of Queensland* (No. 2) [2014] FCA 528 [819].
41   Dempsey, [820].
42   ibid., [821].

The lesson to be drawn from this less than mild rebuke is to make it clear how we evaluate differing and contradicting oral accounts. The conclusions I had drawn were not those that favoured one sort of field data over another, nor was I egregiously inclined to doubt the sincerity of the statements made by the respondent, as her Honour suggested.[43] Rather, they were conclusions that evaluated the oral account within the context of prior materials and (in this case) evidence given before a judicial body. This was not a matter of any appraisal of individual witnesses and their characters. I was speaking of an assessment of oral history in relation to the additional materials considered which threw doubt on the reliability of the oral history of the respondent. It was a matter of anthropological analysis of these materials taken together, rather than some unstated preference to believe one set of persons rather than another. Evidently, I did not explain this process with sufficient clarity at the time. It highlights a fundamental difference between the legal and anthropological process: the former deals with proofs and standards of proof; the latter with the comprehension of social process and how this is represented by protagonists. As I noted above, Mortimer J found against the claims of the respondent, a judgment that was consistent with my expert evidence and the other materials I and the other experts had considered.

Native title research and oral tradition

In this chapter I have shown that the conservativeness and continuity in customary Aboriginal belief and practice, encapsulated in the Law and the Dreaming, works to limit change through oral tradition. The innate conservative nature of Aboriginal societies is a quality found across many areas of Aboriginal Australia. This includes those that are sometimes regarded as being situated in 'settled Australia' – parts of southeast Queensland, the southwest of Western Australia, to name but two. Consequently, oral traditions can be argued to exhibit in their telling compliance with a system of belief and action that militates against too much change. In native title this understanding may prove helpful when considering the degree to which contemporary beliefs and practices represent past observance and credo. When claimants have told me that a belief or practice has 'always' been a part of their culture, or that

---

43   ibid., [819].

a connection to land can be traced to ancestors beyond reckoning because that is what the 'old people' told them, I think these comments should be given some credibility, unless, of course, there are grounds for concluding otherwise.

Oral testimony is central to any native title case, whether it be the oral evidence of the claimants as given to the court or their written affidavits. When provided to the court, these accounts can be subjected to mechanisms to test their reliability. During a trial this generally takes the form of cross-examination, questions from the judge and an assessment of the consistency of accounts across the witnesses. Given that an anthropologist relies on data provided by claimants as oral accounts when writing his or her report, they, too, should assess the reliability of the spoken account. An appreciation of the limitations of Aboriginal oral tradition is an important quality of good native title research. Oral accounts relating to genealogical relationships or an ancestor's identity and country can be tested against archival materials or the findings of prior claims, where these are available. Claims that 'this is our country, from the old people, that's what we were always told' or that a particular observance was 'always' a part of customary practice because this is what 'the old people' had said, which are common in native title research, can be tested against early ethnographic accounts – again, where these are available. However, in those instances where authenticating materials are unavailable or their usefulness is limited by the circumstances, methodologies or prejudices of their collection, an oral account constitutes the data upon which we must found our anthropological view. This may not be a problem for the court, given consistency in the accounts and general agreement between Indigenous witnesses. The issues that develop from unsubstantiated oral accounts are exacerbated and become extremely vexed in circumstances when there is a dispute between Indigenous parties to a native title claim, resulting in a stark difference of opinion and contradictory testimony. It seems to me very likely that such disputes will not lessen in time and the difficulties of competing oral histories will exercise the anthropologists as well as the court with increasing frequency. This argues for a more rigorous application of testing and verification of the oral account and, perhaps, less ready acceptance by all involved of the unqualified oral testimony of an Indigenous witness.

7

Early texts and other sources

Introduction

In order to demonstrate that native title has survived, the court will require that the laws and customs of the claimant society be shown not only to have survived substantially uninterrupted but also to have remained 'traditional'[1] in their content. What exactly is to be understood by the use of the term 'traditional' has been subject to extensive debate.[2] Most, if not all, of the ethnography relevant to a native title inquiry will demonstrate the fact of some form of change. This is unsurprising since few anthropologists would argue for an unchanging society. It is the degree and measure of the change against customary systems that is subject to contestation. In short,

---

1   'A traditional law or custom is one which has been passed from generation to generation of a society, usually by word of mouth and common practice. But in the context of the *Native Title Act*, "traditional" carries with it two other elements in its meaning. First, it conveys an understanding of the age of the traditions: the origins of the content of the law or custom concerned are to be found in the normative rules of the Aboriginal and Torres Strait Islander societies that existed before the assertion of sovereignty by the British Crown. It is only those normative rules that are "traditional" laws and customs.

Second, and no less important, the reference to rights or interests in land or waters being possessed under traditional laws acknowledged and traditional customs observed by the peoples concerned, requires that the normative system under which the rights and interests are possessed (the traditional laws and customs) is a system that has had a continuous existence and vitality since sovereignty. If that normative system has not existed throughout that period, the rights and interests which owe their existence to that system will have ceased to exist. And any later attempt to revive adherence to the tenets of that former system cannot and will not reconstitute the traditional laws and customs out of which rights and interests must spring if they are to fall within the definition of native title.' *Members of the Yorta Yorta Aboriginal Community v Victoria* (2002) 214 CLR 422 [46–47].

2   *Members of the Yorta Yorta Aboriginal Community v Victoria* (2002) 214 CLR 422 [63–65, 78–86].

How much change is too much change for the court to decide that the law or custom in question is still 'traditional'? Setting this thorny issue to one side, generally, the anthropologist's task is to provide an opinion as to whether the laws and customs of the claimant society can be shown to have endured mostly intact or at least clearly developed from those customary practices likely to have characterised the society at the time of sovereignty. The duration of this continuity is that period from the date of sovereignty by the British Crown over the application area to the present. The date of sovereignty varies across Australia but can be as far back as 1788. One state at least has accepted that laws and customs are likely to have changed little between the date of legal sovereignty and the date of the settlement of the land by Europeans (Queensland Government 2003, 5). Such acceptance of a difference between legal sovereignty and what I term 'effective sovereignty' is helpful in that it advances the date, sometimes by many decades, of that time judged to be the benchmark of the incidence of a customary system.

Early texts and later difficulties

Reconstruction of an ethnography from early texts (sometimes labelled as a 'sovereignty report') can provide a basis for assessing how much the contemporary claimant society has changed. Thus, contemporary laws and customs can be compared with those recorded at some earlier time – perhaps relatively close to sovereignty. If the accounts are congruent, at least to some extent or in relation to some laws and practices, this may provide support for the conclusion that enough of the society's laws and customs have survived to enable the court to recognise the existence of native title. The laws and customs can then be said to be 'radicular'; that is, they are rooted in or founded upon consuetude or the customary ways that things were done or beliefs held at or about sovereignty.[3] This 'before and after' equation and the legal calculations and judgments made in this regard are complex and sometimes obscure and are not a matter for anthropology or anthropologists. But, however regarded, the examination of the foundation ethnography remains a central component in the native title process.

---

3   'For the reasons given earlier, "traditional" does not mean only that which is transferred by word of mouth from generation to generation, it reflects the fundamental nature of the native title rights and interests with which the Act deals as rights and interests rooted in pre-sovereignty traditional laws and customs.' *Members of the Yorta Yorta Aboriginal Community v Victoria* [2002] HCA 58 [79].

Establishing the likely system of laws and customs relevant to claimants is hedged about with many difficulties. One of the reasons for this is that the quality and reliability of the early accounts is immensely variable. The manner whereby the data were collected, the selectivity exercised by those who did so, their preoccupations, predilections and perhaps, most importantly, their prejudices and assumptions, make the data difficult to judge in terms of its overall reliability. Many of the early accounts are impossible to assess with respect to specific issues that might affect their reliability because there is no account of the collectors, or of their preoccupations, assumptions and prejudices.

Generally, there are no ethnographic records dating from a time prior to the date of effective sovereignty. Consequently, the only way to proceed is to extrapolate and make an inference back in time from the records of early colonial writers. These include diarists and settlers or correspondents who provided data from the frontier to collectors such as Curr and Howitt. The reports from the Cambridge expedition to the Torres Strait (1898–99) provide one of the earliest sources of ethnography, although Haddon first undertook scientific research in the region in 1888 (Haddon 1901–35; also Haddon 1890). In the absence of early writers, later writers have to be relied upon. These may comprise representatives of some of the first professional anthropologists who collected ethnographic accounts in Australia, often dating from the late 1920s on. However, there are earlier accounts by professional researchers. Radcliffe-Brown, for example, collected Australian materials at the very beginning of the second decade of the twentieth century.

The materials drawn from Radcliffe-Brown, Kaberry and others reviewed in Chapter 3 serve two purposes. First, they demonstrate how early texts may be used to characterise customary systems. These can then be used for comparative purposes as a basis for expert opinions as to the continuity of systems of title to property. Data sourced from early texts have evident limitations, as the discussion in Chapter 3 illustrates. The material drawn from Radcliffe-Brown shows that his account lacked detail, was evidently incomplete and relied upon assumptions that have subsequently been shown to be defective. Consequently, the use of comparative ethnography must be a process subject to qualification and extrapolated by reference to other ethnographies that might provide a corrective to what (in terms of customary tenure) might now be regarded as the anthropological orthodoxy. A further limitation relates to applicability. Early, reliable, professional and relevant fieldwork was carried out in relatively few locations. For areas where pertinent early ethnography is lacking, reliance must be placed on materials drawn from elsewhere to provide the basis for the expert view as to the perdurance of customary systems. Aboriginal societies were not all the same across the continent, although there were many similarities and commonalities. Given that there is likely to have been some variation across Aboriginal Australia, selection of material for comparison has to be undertaken with a view as to its defensibility on grounds of relevance to the area of the inquiry. For example, ethnographies of desert areas (e.g. Cane 2002; Myers 1986) are probably less defensible if applied to areas of coastal tropical country than if they are used for native title inquiries that relate to the more arid parts of Australia. The same would hold true for ethnographies of tropical or coastal areas that were used for comparative purposes for claims made in arid Australia. However, the researcher may have little choice if material is not readily available for the study area.

Earliest is best?

Joseph Birdsell, whose collaboration with Norman Tindale extended from 1938 for nearly 50 years, was of the view that after 1930 there were only two small areas of Australia that were untouched by 'the expanding frontier of colonial occupancy' that converted 'the Aborigines into dependent, second class human beings' (1970, 115). Consequently, he dismissed the accounts of anthropologists studying Aboriginal Australian local organisation whose data were collected after 1930. A similar argument was made by Basil Sansom who argued that at least some later texts reflected post-sovereignty changes and no longer mirrored the system likely to have been found at the time of either sovereignty or effective sovereignty (2007, 74). He argued in relation to the Yulara case[4] that when judging early texts the rule was 'earliest sources are best' (ibid., 79). He then catalogued what he judged to be a 'formidable' list of 'authorities' who were 'pioneer scholars of Western Desert ethnography' whose findings allegedly contradicted the applicants' position, as advanced by their expert anthropologist Peter Sutton (ibid., 74). It seems the judge preferred the 'formidable authorities' rather than the applicant's evidence, a fact that Sansom suggests may have been a determining factor in the failure of the claim.[5]

---

4   A claim made for compensation under the *Native Title Act* in relation to the Yulara area (Ayres Rock) of Central Australia. The case is often referred to as 'Yulara' after the area involved or 'Jango' after the name of the application. See *Jango v Northern Territory of Australia* (2006) 152 FCR 150.
5   *Jango v Northern Territory of Australia* [2006] FCA 318, [11(2)]; [223] to [224]; [258] to [259] and [499].

The ensuing anthropological debate (e.g. Burke 2007, 164; Glaskin 2007; Sackett 2007) showed that the interpretation of the pioneer scholars was not quite as straightforward as has been suggested (e.g. Glaskin 2007, 167; Sackett 2007, 173–175; Sutton 2015). It was argued that earlier writers were not answering native title questions or necessarily addressing issues that are now of significance to an adjudication of native title. While earlier accounts were written closer in time to the way things were at sovereignty, their authors may have been at some distance from the culture and world view of those they studied. As time has passed, the accumulated findings of scholars of Aboriginal Australia has added enormously to our understanding of laws, cultural practices and systems. Comprehension of systems of land ownership, for example, has become more sophisticated as concepts have broadened and research data has become more comprehensive. Judging early texts must, then, be undertaken with due regard not only to their relative position in the time-line between sovereignty and the present, but also in terms of the then prevailing orthodoxy these authors then embraced (perhaps quite uncritically), the inconsistencies in their accounts and the amount of field data they actually collected. Overall, applying these and other qualifiers to ethnography renders simple rules like 'earliest sources are best' particularly unhelpful and subverts the fundamental methodological rules: exercise caution, recognise context and take due account of the likely paradigms, assumptions and preconceptions of the author.

Using early texts

In a paper I wrote that examined aspects and associated problems in relation to the use of early texts, I provided three examples of ethnography used in native title contexts (Palmer 2010a). I showed through my examination of these examples some of the difficulties and considerations that needed to be kept in mind when reconstructing foundation ethnography for native title reports. These case studies were drawn from a range of materials: accounts of the early settlers in the Swan Valley in Western Australia, Daisy Bates's materials collected from Eucla on the Western Australian–South Australian border and Elkin's account of totemism that was the product of his fieldwork in the west Kimberley. I found that it was the preconceptions of the writers that were largely determinative of their analyses, rather than the quality of their data or the collectors' proximity to effective sovereignty. So, while the earliest account was in fact the most helpful in outlining aspects of the foundation ethnography, this was largely due to the fact that the recorder and author called it as he saw it (Palmer 2010a, 89–90). Most importantly, I was also of the view that the lesson to be learnt from any reconstruction founded on early texts is that it is best understood as provisional, interpretative and in some circumstances speculative. It is usually not possible to render an account of the foundation ethnography as an unqualified representation of the laws and customs of the claimant society at sovereignty.

In order to explore these issues further, I now examine the work of two researchers whose writing and field data are sometimes used in native title research. The first is the anthropologist Phyllis Kaberry, who was one of Elkin's students and who worked in the Kimberley region of Western Australia in the period 1934 to 1936. The second is Norman Tindale, who is frequently cited in native title research as a consequence of his extensive fieldwork in many different areas of Australia over a period of many decades. Tindale has provided extensive genealogical accounts relevant to many areas of Australia, as well as ethnographic observations on a wide range of customary practices. As I will show in the latter part of this chapter, Tindale's 'tribal' legacy is not always easy to accommodate in native title matters. I delay a consideration of Tindale's genealogical records and their attendant problems for a later chapter of this book (see Chapter 9).

It is important to remember that when researching a native title claim it would be unusual to rely on just one early source. So, for example, in the case of the Kaberry materials considered below, a number of other researchers also produced data relevant to the central and south-eastern Kimberley region, including R.H. Mathews, Daisy Bates, Elkin, Tindale as well as the linguists Arthur Capell and more recently Tasaku Tsunoda. A good native title report would consult all the sources available and provide an indication of the likely foundation ethnography based on a synthesis of the materials considered. Moreover, in cases where there was an apparent inconsistency between the accounts of different authorities, these would need to be fully canvassed and, to the extent that it was possible, reconciled.[6]

---

6   In Jango this was an important point as the applicant's anthropologist, Professor Sutton, advanced a different model of land ownership than Tindale had done based in part on his fieldwork undertaken in 1933. *Jango v Northern Territory of Australia* [2006] FCA 318 [476]. See also Sutton 2015.

Phyllis Kaberry

Phyllis Kaberry made a significant contribution to the development of modern Australian Aboriginal anthropology. She carried out in-depth research over a period of many months as a participant with, and observer of, those with whom she worked. She subjected her data to the theoretical lens that developed a view as to the role of women in Aboriginal society, their relationships to men and their status as individuals. In this she sought to provide a corrective to male scholars, including Malinowski, Roheim and Warner, who had argued that women were excluded from the religious life (Toussaint 2004, xiii). In this, then, Kaberry advanced our understandings of Aboriginal society in general and of the role of women in it in particular.

Kaberry carried out her fieldwork in the Kimberley region in 1934 and then again in 1935 to 1936 (Kaberry 1939, xix).[7] Her first field trip included visits to Forrest River (four months), Wyndham and Beagle Bay in the west Kimberley (ibid.). In the following year she spent six months with a number of different groups in the east and central Kimberley (ibid., xix).

Kaberry observed that those with whom she worked had been in contact with Europeans 'for over forty years' (ibid., xx). However, all the older women with whom she worked would have been born prior to European settlement of the region, and some may have spent periods of their young adulthood in pre-contact conditions. While Kaberry wrote as though the beliefs and customs she recorded were a part of current practice (ibid., 215), she did report that working on pastoral properties had resulted in some changes to 'timetables' (ibid., 246, footnote 1), that European goods had changed the availability of traded items (ibid., 166, 170) and that there was greater freedom of choice over marriage partners than in pre-contact times (ibid., 111). While the impact of European settlement and the imposition of European ways was not a matter that Kaberry specifically addressed, her account stands as the best we have of

---

7   Kaberry's 1939 publication *Aboriginal women: sacred and profane* was republished in 2004. It is, for the most part, a facsimile edition (see Toussaint 2004, xv, footnote 5). However, the page numbering of the Prefaces, Foreword and Introduction are different to the first edition, while the balance of the page numbering appears to be the same. I here cite the work as 'Kaberry 1939', but the page references are to the 2004 edition, which is the one I used.

the likely composition of pre-contact cultural practices for this region. It is, then, a useful and indeed essential starting point for foundation ethnography for the east and central Kimberley.[8]

Reading Kaberry's published and unpublished works allows aspects of the laws and customs of those with whom she worked to be described. The fact that she had worked closely with those who had lived in pre-contact times, as well as her scholarly credentials, provides a sound basis for advancing the argument that her accounts are a reliable source for determining the nature of those laws and customs relevant to a native title inquiry. For the purposes of this account, these can be summarised as comprising data that reveal the significance of language and identity, customary systems of rights to country, social organisation, governance, religious beliefs and practices, and totemism. These may not necessarily be found as individual chapters or papers in Kaberry's corpus as these are headings useful for a native title report and not necessarily a focus of her anthropology. Consequently, it is necessary to work through Kaberry's published and (if available) her unpublished materials to garner data relevant to the topics selected for consideration. In what follows I examine Kaberry's account of the first of these topics ('tribes'; language and identity) in order to provide a working example of the sorts of content that might be useful when drafting foundation ethnography, as well as the conclusions and possible conundrums that might be drawn from it.

Kaberry on 'tribes' and language groups

Kaberry uses the term 'tribe' throughout her writing, apparently regarding it as a term of some utility for the numerous language groups present in the areas wherein she worked: Lunga (or Kidja), Djaru, Walmanjari (Wolmeri), Kunian, Malngin and Nyikina being some of the ones that figure in her accounts. She defined the tribe as 'a territorial, linguistic, and cultural unit' (1939, 184) but qualified the definition by adding that 'affinities with neighbouring people are recognised to exist in language, kinship, totemism and local organisation' (ibid.). Thus, its integrity as a unit was, by this account, limited to matters of territory. Consistent with this view, Kaberry published a 'language map' in an article (1937, 94) showing her understanding of how the speakers of different languages were distributed across the landscape. Kaberry's field data did not reveal

---

8   Toussaint notes that Kaberry has been used in 'several Kimberley native title claims' and has been important as providing a 'contextual threshold on how rights in land existed in the past' (2004, xiv).

that the 'tribe' had any political structure (Kaberry 1939, 178), which calls into question how it was in any sense a corporate land-holding body. Kaberry's anthropology had not at this date benefitted from the work of later writers who understood the local group to be the territorial unit – although members of local groups spoke and identified with a principal language and as a consequence the country wherein they exercised rights was also identified with that language (see discussion in Chapter 2).

Kaberry considered that 'tribal' areas were bounded, but noted that knowledge of these boundaries was the inverse of distance (1937, 92). However, she also found that the names of these 'territorial units' varied and were not exclusive. Names used appeared sometimes to depend upon the identity of the speaker. In this regard she wrote:

> Many of the tribes are known by two or more names. The Wolmeri of Christmas Creek are called Wolmadjer by the Nyul-Nyul and Kunian; the Mulbera are also called Wandjira, and the Waneiga of Tanami are called the Ngambudjugara. The general term for the tribe at Moola Bulla is Lunga, whilst the alternative– Kidja– is more frequently heard at Violet Valley and Bedford, ninety miles to the north. The Punaba on the west, and the Djaru on the east, sometimes refer to the Lunga as Burnana or Baiambal. The Lunga themselves often say: 'We got him Djerag' translated as 'We got him language.'… Finally, the Kidja word 'to talk' is *djerag*. With tribal egoism they identify their own language with language in general. (ibid., 92)

Despite Kaberry's resolution of the origins of the term Djerag, she was unable with confidence to articulate the difference between Djerag, Kidja, Lunga and Kuluwarin (see McGregor 1988, 97), except to imply, perhaps, that they were all dialects of Kidja.

> Now Professor Elkin has referred to the tribe at Turkey Creek and to the north of it as the Djerag, and from evidence I collected I am inclined to think that it is only a dialect of the Lunga. The Kidja at Bedford said that the natives at Violet Valley and Turkey Creek spoke Djerag, and that Djerag, Kidja, and Lunga 'all box up together.' Actually Violet Valley and Turkey Creek are strongholds of the Kidja natives. Again, the Ivanhoe natives to the east told me that at Alice Downs, Lyssadel and at Goose Hill (just out of Wyndham) the natives spoke Djerag or Kuluwarin. I collected genealogies from Kuluwarin men and women at Ivanhoe, and the kinship terms and totems were all Kidja words. (Kaberry 1937, 92)

Kaberry also recorded that sometimes a single name 'embraces a group of tribes' (ibid., 93).

Kaberry was interested to understand how the Aboriginal people with whom she worked understood language difference. While some languages were regarded as being similar or mutually intelligible, in other cases she found there to be a substantial difference between language groups. She thought that this might have been based on the degree of intelligibility (or lack of intelligibility) of their respective languages. In this regard she wrote in a paper:

> The Blacks themselves tend to group certain languages together. The Lunga at Moola Bulla say of the Djaru language: 'We talk-talk him little bit, we "hear" him,' using 'hear' more or less as a synonym for 'understand.' Even when they cannot speak the language, they can sometimes understand the gist of what is being said at an intertribal meeting. Speaking of more distantly situated tribes the Lunga declare with finality: 'We can't hear him.' Probably the chief factors there are contiguity and familiarity, due both to intermarriage and frequent meetings for initiation rites. (ibid., 91)

However, Kaberry found that 'contiguity' (that is, being in contact or proximate) was not always a determinant of mutual intelligibility between members of neighbouring language groups:

> But there are at least two examples of neighbouring tribes who both recognize a complete cleavage between their respective languages. This is true of the Lunga or Kidja tribe which extends from Moola Bulla north to the east side of the Durack Range and of the Wula tribe, whose territory extends from the western side of the Durack Range out towards the coast north of the Leopolds. (ibid., 91)

She remarked that people were proud of their language and country, having some contempt for those who had a different kinship system (1939, 184–185). But while Kaberry found language to provide a basis for recognition of social difference or similarity, she also found that the manner whereby identity was asserted and commonalities pressed to depend on factors other than language and consequently to be complex and at times ambiguous. For example, she notes that the Wula and the Lunga, although having a 'complete cleavage between their respective languages', attended initiation rituals together, while the Lunga were in the process of adopting the Wula subsection system (Kaberry 1937, 91). Yet the Wula were 'formerly linked culturally with the Forrest River tribes; and in fact the more western branch of the Wula still have moieties without subsections' (ibid.). Similarly, Kaberry distinguished the Kunian and Nyikina linguistically and considered their different kinship systems as a basis for their being considered as quite separate (ibid.). In contradistinction she then added that another language group, the Punaba, were considered by members of the Walmanjari group to have commonalities with the Wula, 'though actually the social system differs' (ibid.).

Kaberry also provides a more generalised statement of the relationship between five language groups:

> The Wolmeri, Djaru, Kunian, Lunga and Malngin tribes form a group, where comprehension seems to be due to contiguity and a gradual infiltration of words from one tribe into the other. The Djaru and Lunga hold certain terms in common, and frequently meet in the region of Halls Creek, which is a melting pot for both tribes. (ibid., 91)

Extracted data from Kaberry's writing regarding the social, cultural and linguistic commonalities of 'tribes' are summarised in Table 7.1.

Table 7.1: Kimberley 'tribes' and cultural groups

	'Tribes'	Relationship	Reference
1	Lunga and Djaru	Understand each other's language. Participate in ritual together.	Kaberry 1937, 91
2	Lunga (Kidja) and Wula	Languages quite different. Participate in ritual together. Share aspects of social organisation.	Kaberry 1937, 91
3	Nyikina and Wula	'Stand outside the rest of the group'.	Kaberry 1939, 184
4	Bunaba and Wula	'Associated'. Different social organisation.	Kaberry 1937, 91
5	Forrest River tribes and Wula	'Formerly' linked culturally.	Kaberry 1937, 91
6	Kunian and Nyikina	Different language. Different social organisation.	Kaberry 1937, 91
7	Wolmeri, Kunian, Djaru, Lunga, Djerag and Malngin	'Form a group' through use of shared vocabulary.	Kaberry 1937, 91

This grouping of 'tribes' is reflected in part in the map noted earlier found in her 1937 publication where Kaberry shows the 'Kimberley Division' divided into four areas: Northern, Southern, Eastern Kimberley and Daly River area, numbered I–IV respectively (Figure 7.1). Number III, 'Eastern Kimberley', includes the language groups (or 'tribes') Wolmeri, Kunian, Djaru, Lunga, Djerag and Malngin, which with the exception of the Djerag corresponds to Kaberry's statement cited above from

Kaberry's 1937 account (91). Kaberry's assemblage of language groups or tribes on her map reflected her views that members of some different language groups could be placed together on the basis of commonalities of language, laws, culture, beliefs and practices.

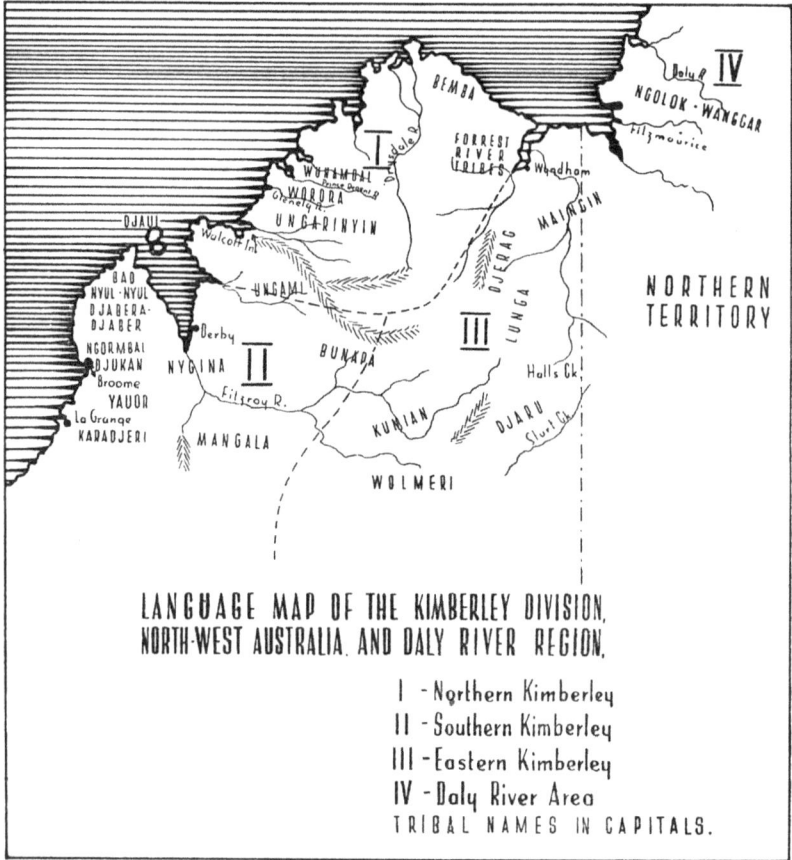

Figure 7.1: Kaberry's language map of the Kimberley

Source: Map reproduced by kind permission of Oceania Publications. *Oceania* 8.1, 1937, 94.

A comparison of the data presented in Table 7.1 with Kaberry's map (1937, 94) shows some inconsistencies in the accounts. Absent from Kaberry's map is Wula, a group she described in her text as occupying territory that 'extends from the western side of the Durack Range out towards the coast north of the Leopolds' (ibid., 91). The Durack Range is just over 60 km northwest of Turkey Creek and the Leopold Range runs some 80 kms north of Fitzroy Crossing. Mapping the Wula on to country given these geographic references yields uncertain results but would appear to place the Wula in Kaberry's division I (North Kimberley) or division II (South Kimberley), or perhaps division III (East Kimberley) and maybe all three. In her writing, Kaberry's division I is reflected in item 5 of Table 7.1, but with the addition of Wula. Constituents of Kaberry's division II are found in items 3, 4 and 6 of Table 7.1 with the addition of Wula in items 3 and 4, while item 6 includes a name found in division III. Kaberry's division III is broadly the same as item 7 in Table 7.1.

Kaberry's 'tribes' and language groups and native title anthropology

The term 'tribe' is common in both the early as well as much later ethnography relating to Aboriginal Australia. The term resonated with colonial notions of the primitive, evoking a small-scale territorial political unit typically with the 'chief'. A 'tribe' was to be found in pre-industrial pre-Christian societies in contrast to the nation states of England, western Europe and later north America. While anthropology, particularly in Africa, sought to render 'tribes' a tool for analysis, it remained (and remains) a troublesome term that evokes more problems than it can ever remedy. It is likely that Kaberry came to the field with the baggage of the term 'tribe', which she employed rather loosely but with some attempt at definition. In the Kimberley region, she found such an entity to have no political structure, no overall leader and to be composed of several different dialects of a single language.

Kaberry accommodated the term 'tribe' to her data by venturing the proposition that the tribe was composed of a community of speakers of a common language (or of dialects of what was understood to be the same language), whose members recognised more or less bounded land associated with that language as well as having cultural practices and beliefs in common. However, Kaberry's data on how these 'tribes' were named served to demonstrate that these language groups were not exclusively or definitively named, but appeared to have had membership and characteristics that shifted though time. Names were sometimes multiple, non-exclusive and variable over time and place. Languages themselves were internally divided, raising the question of the unity of the whole and how dialects were, in practice, differentiated from other mutually intelligible and adjacent languages.

Kaberry's data relating to language use is more satisfactory. Kaberry established that in the area of the Kimberley where she worked there were distinct language-speaking groups whose members sustained substantial mutual intelligibility with proximate and near proximate neighbours, but which generally lessened with distance. But Kaberry understood that language was not the only means whereby social intercourse could be organised and cultural bonds were evoked for the purpose of trade, ritual and finding marriage partners. Cultural similarities and dissimilarities were the stuff that bound or separated groups into those who shared commonalities and could be grouped as divisions on her map, or as different societies whose commonalities could and often did transcend language group boundaries. While Kaberry's field data and her conclusions in this regard are, in my view, not entirely consistent, she does conclude, without ambiguity, that the Walmanjari, Djaru, Kunian, Kidja and Malngin all formed a 'group'. Recognition of commonalities was based in practice on mutual intelligibility of language as well as social interaction and shared understandings. These conclusions leave the baggage and preconceptions of 'tribes' far behind and, freed from such constraints, provides for a sounder analysis.

Working through Kaberry's ethnography is no simple matter and that perhaps is the first lesson to take from this exercise. Foundation ethnography is likely to be complex, data inconsistent and the understandings of the time in which it was written likely to cloud or colour the author's findings. Accepting this, there are some important pointers to the likely nature of the societies Kaberry studied relevant to identity, social formation and commonality.

The first of these relates to the fact that Kaberry recorded numerous language groups in the area in which she worked. Foundation ethnography recovered from Kaberry's writings can serve to show the degree to which modern naming and identity labels have survived and serve to demonstrate the radicular nature of the contemporary account – or otherwise, as the case might be. Kaberry mapped language groups (if somewhat generally) on to country, and this account should find some degree of congruence in the contemporary account of those seeking recognition of native title today over the same areas of country. Some of the names Kaberry recorded may have changed. For example, in the east Kimberley the name Lunga is almost never heard in my experience, the term having been replaced by

Kidja. However, this is consistent with the apparently ephemeral nature of language names noted by Kaberry so is not inimical to the continuity argument.

The second helpful contribution that ethnography of the sort I have reviewed here may make to a native title inquiry relates to the complex issue of the native title society – a matter I discussed in an earlier chapter of this book (see Chapter 2). Kaberry's data on groups and identity reveal that those with different language identities (dialect or different language) who could understand one another perceived themselves to be of a single mind with respect to the practice of customs, rituals, their beliefs and ways of doing things. In some cases members of such a group could very well share the same single language association. However, this need not necessarily be so and group community membership could, given the acceptance of other cultural commonalities, include those who spoke another language. Members of these different language groups can, in consequence, be understood to have formed a society or community.

Again, this is a model that can be applied in native title writing to the contemporary ethnographic account. If it is evident that Kaberry found a certain set of people to share laws and customs in common and this is reflected in the contemporary ethnography, there is a case to be put for a continuity of the society since the time Kaberry worked in the Kimberley – and so, by inference, to the time of effective sovereignty and beyond.

Norman Tindale[9]

Norman Tindale worked in many areas of rural and remote Australia over a period of more than four decades from his base at the South Australian Museum where he held his first post as an assistant entomologist in 1918. During these expeditions he recorded his observations on a wide range of subjects including entomology, botany, geology, archaeology as well as Aboriginal culture. His first trip was in 1921–22 to Groote Eylandt and the Roper River in the Northern Territory. Expeditions soon followed in 1926–27 to Cape York Peninsula and Koonibba (west coast of South

9   Philip Jones's obituary for Norman Tindale provides an excellent account of Tindale's life, professional development and research contribution. See Jones 1995, 9–10 (downloaded from www.anu.edu.au/linguistics/nash/aust/nbt/obituary.html).

Australia) in 1928. During the following decades he made numerous field trips to Central Australia, Western Australia, the Northern Territory and Queensland up until 1966.[10]

Tindale's voluminous and wide-ranging research interest coupled with his scrupulous attention to documenting his research findings has meant that his journals, field notes, genealogies and other published as well as unpublished works are important documents in any native title claim made to country where he worked. The sheer volume of his material and the systematic way he recorded his field data means that it must be taken into account. Moreover, some of his data were collected comparatively early and from those who in some areas at least were born prior to the date of the frontier. As the years passed, he clocked up increasingly impressive fieldwork credentials over many different areas of Aboriginal Australia.

Tindale was interested in genetics and racial characteristics, particularly as they could be related to Aboriginal people of mixed descent. It was this interest that led him to collect the many hundreds of genealogies and accompanying physiological measurements and observations that he gathered from all round Australia and which are now of such interest to researchers undertaking native title work. Tindale's field data, which he often recorded in his journals, included accounts of material culture, kinship, ritual practices, beliefs and, perhaps most significantly, what he came to call 'tribal' data. Tindale's later journals include small maps of tribal boundaries and names of what he judged to be territorial groups. These data provided the basis for his first major work on Australian tribal boundaries published in 1940. He later revised and expanded this work to produce his well-known and monumental work on tribes and boundaries in Australia that was published in 1974. Tindale's journals, in particular, are a useful source of field data relating to a whole range of cultural beliefs and practices; in native title work, it is his genealogies and his 'tribal maps' that are probably the most commonly cited and which can evoke the greatest controversy.

---

10   For a complete list of the journals he wrote of these trips and other materials, see archives. samuseum.sa.gov.au/aa338/AA338-04.htm accessed 8 May 2015. For a comprehensive account of the many places where Tindale undertook his research with Aboriginal Australians, see Jones 1995, 9–10 (downloaded from www.anu.edu.au/linguistics/nash/aust/nbt/obituary.html).

Tribal mapping and ecological determinism[11]

Tindale's interest in Aboriginal culture was apparently spurred by his first extended period of fieldwork to Groote Eylandt in the Northern Territory where, according to one source, he gained an interest in the boundaries that delineated a group's rights to country.[12] Tindale was influenced by a desire to demonstrate that Aboriginal people were not 'nomads' in the sense that they might popularly have been understood to roam at random across tracts of land with no territorial possession (Jones 1995, 3).[13] Boundaries and the tribes that sustained them indicated, in his view, 'that Australian wanderings are at present and have long been restricted within specific territorial limits' (Tindale 1974, 10). Tindale understood tribes as a fundamental and determining unit of social and territorial organisation in Aboriginal Australia and his ideas in this regard appear to have been carried through his extensive periods of fieldwork in Aboriginal Australia and to have informed his data analyses and subsequent writing accordingly.

In his published 1974 account – marking the culmination of his research into 'tribes and boundaries' – Tindale wrote that the tribe was the central feature of Aboriginal social life. He argued that 'tribal' members shared:

> [a] common bond of kinship and claim to a common territory, even though the sharing in it may be the subject of restrictions on the taking of certain foods and the exploitation of some other resources may be limited without prior arrangement or permissible only by reason of the possession of specific kinship ties, for within the tribe there are sometimes distinctions between what a man may do in his own clan country, in that of his mother, and in those of his wife's people ... In Australia this larger unit has a widely recognised name, a bond of common speech, and perhaps a reputation, and even an aura of names – polite, rude, or insulting – given to it by other tribespeople who live in adjoining territories. (Tindale 1974, 30)

---

11 I thank Dr L. Sackett for drawing my attention to some of the materials set out in the following three paragraphs.

12 www.samuseum.sa.gov.au/collections/information-resources/archives/tindale-dr-norman-barnett-aa-338, accessed 11 May 2015.

13 'Edgar Waite [Director, SA Museum] insisted that Tindale remove tribal boundaries from a map of Groote Eylandt and the adjacent mainland being prepared for publication in the Museum's Records, maintaining that nomadic Aborigines could not occupy defined territories. Tindale realised that a new paradigm in ways of regarding and describing Aboriginal Australia was sorely needed' (Jones 1995, 3).

Tindale adopted quite uncritically the idea that boundaries were delineated by the environment. He thus asserted that rivers or hills were boundaries, seemingly with little field data to support his opinions. Based on this assumption he sought ecological distinctions in order to map groups on to country and so place 'tribes' as corporate entities within delineated territorial boundaries. Examples of Tindale's assumptions in this regard illustrate the consequential doubtful conclusions he uncritically advanced as a result.

When travelling in the Pilbara region of Western Australia, Tindale remarked that the Peawah River east of Roebourne which he crossed was 'Of course the Ngaluma-Kariara tribal boundary' (1953a, 573). Tindale wrote of the eastern boundary of the Kariyarra that it was 'At Wodgina …Wodgina Range marks the boundary' (ibid., 249). He wrote that the Kariyarra boundary with the Yindjibarndi was 'at the Yule River' (ibid., 333). Some years later in 1966 Tindale visited the Eastern Goldfields of Western Australia during a trip from Adelaide to the southwest of Western Australia, as far north as Onslow and back via the Goldfields. On the drive from Mt Margaret to Kalgoorlie he noted in his journal:

> Knowing that the boundary between the Ngurlu[14] tribe and the 'Kalgoorlie side' Maduwongga[15] tribe lay just south of Menzies, the Koara being in the mulga country we studied in more detail the relatively quick change from the universal mulga scrub of the country where we have been staying around Laverton and Leonora, to the mallee and salmon gum country to the south. (Tindale 1966, 181 and 183)

Thus changes in vegetation, often corresponding to underlying geological formations, were identified by Tindale as boundary markers. Writing of his observations of the countryside in central eastern Queensland, he wrote:

> The northernmost part of Kabikabi territory south of Bundaberg was surprisingly dry looking as we passed along through low range country. Further south much of it was rainforest but now almost all of it has been replaced by crops. Formerly the whole of Kabikabi territory was said to have been rainforest in which limited areas had been opened up through Aboriginal burning, with consequent conversion to temporary woodlands of *Callitris* and *Eucalyptus*. Thus the dry forested country of their western

---

14 Underneath is written 'Nguludjara ngurlu'.
15 'Maduwongga' is written over 'Kalgoorlie side'.

neighbours, the Wakawaka, was called by them *naran*, literally 'outside', indicating an ecological distinction they were able to make. (Tindale 1976, 24)

I have noted in an earlier chapter of this book (see Chapter 3) that the nature of territorial boundaries in customary arrangements in Aboriginal Australia was likely marked by areas of shared country as the rights of an individual often formed a palimpsest of entitlements across different country group areas. Tindale himself was told on a number of occasions that country was shared,[16] but this does not appear to have caused him to modify his hard-line boundaries or to have accommodated a system that evidently had greater flexibility than the one he represented on his maps. Given that 'boundaries' are innately problematic in this context, assuming *a priori* that they were determined by ecological factors renders the analysis flawed. It is possible that in some cases boundaries did coincide with changes to the ecology, but Tindale does not provide consistent field data to establish that this was the case in the examples cited above.

Tribal mapping: indeterminacy of boundaries and named groups

Tindale's published data also reflect a further complexity of his analysis. In his 1974 work Tindale explained that his aim in mapping tribal boundaries across Australia was to render them as they had been at or before the time of European settlement (Tindale 1974, 5). This attempt at reconstruction adds yet another layer of complexity to his accounts as his attempts to reconstruct boundaries retrospectively by many decades necessarily meant that he had to speculate on the former position of boundaries.

That Tindale failed to understand fundamental truths of the anthropology is illustrated by the interesting case of the Maduwongga and the Kalamayi of the Eastern Goldfields of Western Australia. In 1966, Tindale interviewed a man called Don Roundhead and his wife Nuna Roundhead at Kalgoorlie. He noted in his journal that Don was 'of the Kala:mai tribe' and that 'in language terms he spoke Kabul' so it would appear that the 'tribal' name was not the same as the language name – but the matter is not explained (Tindale 1966, 187). Don gained his country and 'tribal

---

16 For example, see Tindale 1953a, 581 (Kariyarra and Ngarluma boundary); Tindale 1974, 245 (Kukaja and Djaru boundary); Tindale 1974, 247 (Mangala–Nyikina boundary); Tindale 1974, 254 (Nyikina–Mangala boundary).

identity' from his father's father. Tindale reported that Kalamayi country extended from Southern Cross, east to Kalgoorlie and also northwest from Kalgoorlie to include a sweep of country that included places called Kanowna, Broad Arrow, Orabanda, Callion, Davyhurst and Goongarrie. Tindale then noted that 'It is probable therefore that the Kala:mai boundary of my map[17] should be placed a little further to the northeast since it seems to reflect a SW push of the Wa:ljeri or "Wanggai Junggara" to Kalgoorlie in the 1890s' (ibid., 193, 195). Tindale's comment sought to correct his earlier mapping (based on 1939 fieldwork) and to establish the pre-sovereignty arrangement of boundaries that, in this case, had been influenced by the apparent incursions of the 'Wa:ljeri' or 'Wanggai Junggara' from the northeast, so pushing the Kalamayi to the southwest.

Tindale recorded his interview with the Roundheads. A transcript of the interview (Barwick 1999) reveals that Tindale sometimes had trouble hearing Aboriginal names correctly. For example, he was unable to differentiate 'Ngata' (his hearing) from 'Nyatha' which is what Nuna Roundhead is recorded as saying (ibid., 5). Tindale's 'Kabul', which he recorded as being Don's language, was in fact a mishearing of 'Kapurn':

> NBT: [18] and what language was that?
>
> DR: we call it Kapurn, Kapurn.
>
> NBT: Kabul.
>
> DR: Kapurn, that's all my …
>
> NBT: Say it again.
>
> DR: Kapurn.
>
> NBT: Kabul.
>
> DR: Yeah. (Barwick 1999, 1)

Don Roundhead's final gratuitous concurrence allowed Tindale to run with the erroneous 'Kabul', the term that made it into his 1974 publication. The error in reporting 'Kabul' instead of Kapurn, while unfortunate, is understandable. However, in the ensuing conversation, Tindale slips from discussions about language group names (specifically, the Kapurn)

---

17 Presumably his 1940 published map.
18 NBT = Tindale; DR = Don Roundhead; and NR = Nuna Roundhead.

to asking the location of an individual's country. Consequently, it is not apparent whether he was eliciting information about the location of the speakers of a particular language or about their proprietorial rights to country. Moreover, he found himself in possession of an additional two group names (Marlpa and Ngatjunmaya) that threw further complexity and ambiguity on his account which he sought to represent as 'tribal groups' mapped on to country. Tindale elicited place names that Don Roundhead identified as his country that were consistent with those noted above and taken from his 1966 journal (Kanowna, Broad Arrow, Orabanda, Callion and Davyhurst). But Don also told Tindale that his father's country included Norseman and Balladonia (ibid., 8) but then stated that people in these places spoke 'a different lingo altogether'. At Balladonia they spoke Marlpa or Ngatjunmaya (ibid.). Later he stated that his father's 'run' included Fraser Range (between Balladonia and Norseman), commenting, 'yes he worked there when he was a young fella, he growed up there himself, before he met Mum' (ibid., 10). It is, then, unclear from the interview whether rights to country reflect a language group territory or some other arrangement. The territory associated with the language (Kapurn) is similarly unclear as its relationship to a different (perhaps larger?) unit the Kalamayi is nowhere explained. There is confusion as to the meaning and significance of the terms collected in this interview: was the territorial group the Kabul (that is, Kapurn) or the Kalamayi and how were they differentiated? Finally, the language Marlpa or Ngatjunmaya appears to be associated with a separate area of country within which Don's father also exercised customary rights. However, the basis whereby these rights were legitimated is not established.

In his 1939 journal, Tindale wrote of the Maduwongga. He expressed the view that members of this group 'originally came from the spinifex country to the east of their present location. They drifted in at the time of the first gold rush (middle 1890s)' (Tindale 1938–39, 907). In his 1940 map, he shows the group occupying a band of country from Kalgoorlie north (1940a). Wishing to check his earlier account, Tindale asked Don and Nuna Roundhead about the Maduwongga but found that 'neither he nor she recognise Maduwongga and inferred it referred to the Maduitja of Meekatharra' (1966, 195). The discussion ran:

NBT: An old man at Norseman once told me that the Marduwongga lived at Kanowna and Kalgoorlie.

NR: Yes.

NBT: But I don't know whether he meant on the other side of Kalgoorlie, he was talking from Norseman and he was saying you know Marduwongga live north and he pointed up Kalgoorlie way.

NR: No, Martu-itja live what's a name, Wiluna side, Meekatharra side, they call them Martu. (Barwick 1999, 10–11)

Tindale did not admit Don and Nuna's information to his subsequent re-drafting of his map. He reproduced the Maduwongga group and their boundaries in his 1974 book more or less consistent with his 1940 map, apparently ignoring his own later field data both with respect to the Maduwongga and his own journal note to place the boundary of the Kalamayi 'a little further to the north east'. Inexplicably he gives the term 'Kabul (language name)' as an alternative to Maduwongga, implying that Maduwongga, Kabul and Kalamayi were one and the same, although the 1974 map has Maduwongga and Kalamayi as separate groups. Tindale added, 'Statements suggest a protohistoric[19] movement from the east displacing Kalamaia people west beyond Bullabulling. Their language was called ['Kabəl] and was understood as far west as Southern Cross' (1974, 246). This would suggest that the Maduwongga's pre-sovereignty country lay to the east of where Tindale places them on his 1974 map, the exact location depending on where 'spinifex country' is considered to commence but ignores the Roundheads' opinion that the Maduwongga came from further north and in the vicinity of Meekatharra or Menzies.

The basis for Tindale's conclusions about demographic movements is unclear and seemingly speculative. The unhelpful permissive passive 'statements suggest' implies that he was told this by those whom he interviewed. Older informants alive at the time of his 1939 fieldwork would have had first-hand experience as far back as the 1880s or possibly the later 1870s, which accords with the date of effective sovereignty for parts of the area being discussed. However, according to his 1939 data the group that moved southwest was the 'Wa:ljeri' or 'Wanggai Junggara', terms which are not found on his maps. Considered together, Tindale's data from 1939, 1966 and the final production of his tribal map in his 1974 publication are inconsistent and unsatisfactory. His data provide a slim basis upon which to support a conclusion that a whole 'tribe'

---

19   Tindale's use of the term 'protohistoric' is arcane. Mulvaney (1975, 19–49) uses the term for that period prior to permanent European settlement of the continental land mass of Australia but following European and other peoples' discovery of the continent.

relocated from the spinifex to the west,[20] whatever it was called, while the names Maduwongga, Kalamayi and Kabul are ambiguous and their functions as social, territorial or linguistic units are unclear.

Table 7.2: Eastern Goldfields, WA: some 'tribal' names recorded by Tindale

Reference	Term	Standardised term	Comment
Tindale 1938–39, 905–907	Kɑla:mai	Kalamayi	The language of Southern Cross; those in vicinity of Southern Cross.
Tindale 1938–39, 915	Kɑla:mai	Kalamayi	Close relationship with Ngadjunma; shared kin terms.
Tindale 1939 sheet 73	Ka:lamai	Kalamayi	Golden Valley WA near Mt Jackson.
Tindale 1966 transcript, 1	Kalamaia	Kalamayi	Extended south to include Norseman and perhaps Balladonia.
Tindale 1966, 195, 196	Kalamaia	Kalamayi	Language derived from Kala = fire. Informant considered Kala:ko and Kalamaia to be the same or having same meaning.
Tindale 1966, 196	Kalamayi	Kalamayi	Boundary at Widgiemooltha but formerly not as far east.
Tindale 1974, 243	Kalamaia	Kalamayi	Southern Cross; east to Bullabulling etc.
Tindale 1966, 187	Kala:mai, Kabul	Kalamayi; Kapurun	Kala:mai name of tribe; Kabul name of language. Comment about Don Roundhead.
Tindale 1938–39, 904	Kala:ko	Kalarku	Kala:ko is the Southern Cross district. Speak Kɑla:mai.
Tindale 1938–39, 987, 989	Takalako	Kalarku	Takala:ko people.
Tindale 1974, 243	Takalako	Kalarku	Alternative for Kalamaia.
Tindale 1974, 243	Kalaako	Kalarku	'Tribe' with country from Scadden to Coolgardie etc.
Tindale 1974, 243	Kalarku	Kalarku	Malba is alternative term.
Tindale 1938–39, 904	Ka:bu(d)n Tr.	Kapurun	Ka:bu(d)n Tribe called Kɑla:mi.

---

20 Movements of desert groups westward are well documented in the literature. See Christensen 1981, 60, 100–102; Stanton 1984, 60–63.

Reference	Term	Standardised term	Comment
Tindale 1939 sheet 116	Ka:bu(d)n Tr.	Kapurun	Four words in the Ka:bu(d)n language (man = ka:bun).
Tindale 1966 transcript, 1	Kabul mishearing of Kapurun	Kapurun	
Tindale 1966 transcript, 1	Kapurn	Kapurun	Southern Cross to Kalgoorlie.
Tindale 1974, 280	Kapurn	Kapurun	Alternative name for Maduwongga.
Tindale 1966, 196	Kabul	Kapurun	Country from Southern Cross to Kalgoorlie.
Tindale1939, sheet 116	Ka:bu(d)n Tr. and Kαla:mai Tr.'	Kapurun, Kalamayi	Annotation for Nellie Champion.

I have extracted Tindale's data on the Kalamayi, Ngadjunma, Malba, Kabul (i.e. Kapurun), Kala:ko and Maduwongga from Tindale's 1939 journal (1938–39), his genealogical sheets (1939b), his 1966 journal (1966) and his 1974 publication (1974). I have summarised these data in Table 7.2. The table reveals that Tindale's field data show there to be both a diversity of names and a lack of consistency or definition over their employment. This instructs that Tindale's so-called 'tribal' names with clearly delineated territorial boundaries, determined at times by ecological markers, are not a true reflection of his original field data. These names appear to represent other forms of social formation that were neither exclusively applied nor delineable as units of territory.

Tindale's late appearances[21]

Tindale's 'tribal' mapping and the data upon which it was based have been subject to the attention of native title researchers because Tindale characterised these tribal groups as having a proprietary interest in land.[22] This is particularly evidenced by Tindale's maps which show an apparent named group in possession of a bounded country. These maps and accompanying accounts of clearly defined boundaries mask the

---

21   Peter Sutton has shown in a detailed and scholarly analysis the inconsistencies between Tindale's field data and some of his later views with respect to local organisation. See Sutton 2015.

22   See Christensen 1981, 75–82 who provides a critique of both Tindale and Birdsell. Christensen concludes, in part, 'The only substantial evidence supporting the existence of relatively discrete "tribal" groupings in the Western Desert has been provided by Tindale and Birdsell' (ibid., 80).

complexity and variability of group names but dazzle with their rendition in fundamentally European terms of bounded blocks of land such as you might find on a land titles register. These 'tribal' models have a beguiling attraction to both Indigenous claimants and those who advise them and can easily come to inform native title applications and, in time, may be invested with authority. I have seen many instances of claimants turning up at meetings to press their rights to country with photocopied pages of Tindale's map in support of their suit. Clear boundaries lead to a clear division of benefits that may devolve from winning native title rights. They work to both include and to exclude. The passion of modern native title politics is familiar enough to those who have been working with claim groups both prior to and after native title. The essential task for the native title anthropologist is to peel back the postmodern interpretations and reveal the likely nature of the foundation ethnography. This is essentially the focus of the court's attention in seeking to determine whether the laws and customs of the claimants' society are radicular. Satisfying the present political desires, demands and aspirations of claimants is another matter.

The accounts I have provided in the analyses of the examples considered above are not meant to demonise Tindale. There can be little doubt that in some areas Tindale's data better reflected the ethnographic reality than the examples I have subjected to scrutiny. Tindale chose a large canvass, attempting to map all 'tribal' groups across a whole continent. In attempting to paint the larger picture it is understandable that some of the details got lost, were obfuscated or were just plain wrong. Tindale had an idea about local organisation that led him to focus on a particular way of interpreting his data and impose his paradigm on his fieldwork findings. It is easy looking back over his magnificent corpus to judge him too harshly or to minimise his accomplishment and quiet achievements. However, in native title work, winners may be selected on the ground of the court's acceptance or privileging of one early ethnography over another – as was clearly shown in the Jango case[23] and to the detriment of the applicant.[24] Tindale, then, needs to be thoroughly scrutinised and fully evaluated before his ethnographic account is either relied upon or rejected.

23 *Jango v Northern Territory of Australia* [2006] FCA 318.
24 Sutton 2015, 26.

Lessons from the 'tribal' literature

Language names may sometimes be helpful in establishing those who lived in a particular region and who together shared cultural commonalities through the use of a shared language. However, identity names which may evoke referents other than language are sometimes inconstant over time, the groups they identify labile and members may share cultural commonalities across different identity groups. Interpreting data from Kaberry, Tindale and many other early ethnographers on named groups and their members' territorial associations requires identification of the significant research issue that should be addressed when seeking an understanding of customary rights to country. In coming to an understanding of how systems of rights to country worked in Aboriginal Australia, it is not the names of identity groups that are important. These were not landed entities, being rather ephemeral terms derived from language styles, characteristics of speech or geographic location. Their significance is relevant to considerations of how groups shared laws and customs together and how members of different groups interacted and forged and perpetuated commensal relationships that helped sustain their common interests and existence. In summary:

- Different sorts of aggregations of people may be named and a person may belong to more than one named group. Consequently, identity labels may not necessarily be exclusively applied.
- Language groups and other identity units are not corporations whose members are capable together of holding rights to country. In Aboriginal Australia the land-owning group was the local descent group, not the larger language speaking or 'tribal' group.

When it comes to understanding the system whereby rights to country were pressed and sustained, the important task is to identify the ancestors of claimants and the locales within which they are likely to have asserted customary rights as close to the time of effective sovereignty as possible. Where there is a system of the descent of rights, the task is, then, to develop an understanding of how such rights have been transmitted to subsequent generations through a process that is consistent with customary practice.

8

Native title disputes

Introduction

The promise of the *Native Title Act* was that it would deliver 'justice and certainty'. The Act provided a framework whereby Indigenous Australians could make application to the Federal Court for recognition of those rights that had survived the settlement of their continent by (mostly) European peoples. The new settlers had imposed a novel set of laws and asserted a new set of rights in relation to the land. Indigenous – or 'native' – rights had survived, so it was acknowledged in the Preamble to the Act, in certain circumstances. Part 3 of the Act set out in detail the rules for making application for the recognition of native title and so, too, determined the procedures that would be followed. The Federal Court was given the power to hear and decide native title applications. The National Native Title Tribunal (NNTT), established under Part 6 of the Act, had powers to mediate native title and compensation claims referred to it by the Federal Court so the matter could be settled by consent. The Registrar of the NNTT was required to apply the registration test to claims to determine whether they had merit.[1]

I think it true to say that in designing the architecture of the *Native Title Act*, the overall goal of delivering 'justice and certainty' was seen in terms of righting past wrongs and creating certainty for land owners and developers as well as for state and territory governments. The ideal

---

1   The *Native Title Act*, Commentary, 52 and 53.

resolution was to accomplish this through a mediated outcome – between the claimants (the prospective native title holders) and the respondents (the state or territory, pastoralists and developers) through the agency of the NNTT. Disputes between Indigenous Australians who sought justice and certainty were not explicitly factored into the process as proposed. Disputes were to be expected but these were likely to be between the claimants and the miners, pastoralists and state governments (which indeed they were), rather than between competing Indigenous interests, claims and counter claims.

As things have turned out, the reality is rather different. Applications made for the recognition of native title have increasingly been characterised by intra-Indigenous disputes that most commonly have as their focus disagreements as to who are the individuals or groups with customary rights to the country of the claim.[2] This contested field is manifest in many different ways. It may be that one particular family or an individual feels aggrieved that they are not included in the application. On a larger scale the dispute may develop from the complaints of members of a language group who argue that the land claimed belongs to their own language group rather than that identified in the application. In whatever way the battle lines are drawn, the result is a dispute between competing Indigenous parties that is often acrimonious and evokes strong emotions.

My own experience has been that the NNTT originally operated to mediate intra-Indigenous disputes.[3] The NNTT has the function to mediate disputes on its own account (*Native Title Act* section 108) or, originally, at the direction of the Federal Court (*Native Title Act* section 72; repealed 1998). At the time of writing, the Tribunal's website advertised its function as mediator as a service that could be requested through a Tribunal office.[4] However, the Australian Law Reform Commission's *Connection to country: review of the Native Title Act (1993)* noted in 2015 that 'from 2007, the NNTT has sole responsibility for mediation, but in 2010, the mediation function was transferred from the NNTT

---

2   See Burnside 2012 for a discussion of the problem from a legal perspective. The problem was subject to comment early in the native title era by Edmunds (1995).

3   'The primary purpose of the Tribunal was conciliation and mediation. A proposal in 1995 that the Tribunal be redesignated as "The National Native Title Mediation Service" fell on deaf ears' (French 2003, 8). Article downloaded from www.austlii.edu.au/au/journals/MelbULawRw/2003/18.html, accessed 12 October 2016, pp. 1–29.

4   www.nntt.gov.au/assistance/Pages/Assistance-with-indigenous-dispute-resolution.aspx, accessed 11 October 2016. See also ibid., 10, 15–16.

to the Federal Court'.[5] While the Federal Court advocates mediation in intra-Indigenous disputes, it lacks the resources of the original NNTT. Moreover, given the intransigent nature of many disputes mediation has often been an unrewarding experience. The upshot is that disputes between Indigenous groups frequently result in the disputing party seeking to be joined as a respondent to the application. This effectively means that a mediated outcome reflective of some compromises on both sides is discarded in favour of a court ruling. In this it is the judge who must decide on the merits of the disputing Indigenous parties and their various claims and counter-claims.

This has resulted in a function for the Federal Court and its judges that requires that it make decisions relating to disputes between Indigenous Australians with respect to property rights founded upon customary principles but adjudicated in terms of postcolonial legislation. In applications that go to trial where there are Indigenous respondents, an issue before the court is whether the granting of native title will damage or reduce the rights of that respondent.[6] The question then before the court is more complex than was originally envisaged: whether native title has survived more or less intact through demonstrated continuity of laws and customs. Rather, the court has to decide whether the granting of the application might be detrimental to the Indigenous respondent. Presumably, a part of this assessment would be to determine whether the respondent could rightly be regarded as a native title holder – either as a part of the application or on their own. In cases where there are overlapping claims (that is, two applications are made over the same land, either in whole or in part) the claims may be heard together or the matters delayed pending some ultimate resolution through mediation. In such cases the question before the court must be not simply whether native title rights have survived but rather, if this is so, which set of claimants are the 'correct' set for the country of the application or applications.

While this seems to me to raise some difficult questions about processes and outcomes, it is a significant feature of native title claims and one into which anthropologists are likely to be willingly or unwillingly drawn. My own view is that in the post-native title era challenges to the integrity

---

5   Australian Law Reform Commission (ALRC) 2015, 3.41.

6   'The Federal Court may at any time join any person as a party to the proceedings, if the Court is satisfied that the person's interests may be affected by a determination in the proceedings and it is in the interests of justice to do so' (*Native Title Act* section 84(5)).

of native title bodies, claim group membership and authorisation will become increasingly matters brought to the attention of the Federal Court for determination. I think that there is a good case to re-evaluate the role of the Federal Court in this regard and consider providing a special division within the court to deal with such native title matters, as has been suggested by two eminent jurists (Hiley and Levy 2006). The Australian Law Reform Commission noted the lack of mediation services (ALRC 2015, 10.117–10.123) and suggested that the Australian Government consider establishing a national Indigenous dispute management service (ibid., 10.124).

Given this background, native title anthropologists must be prepared for a contested field of action and understand the complex and often uncomfortable nature of these disputes and their contribution in bringing them to some sort of a resolution in the court. This raises significant questions about our practice, ethics and methodology. Anthropologists as experts are likely to play a role in these disputes so it is important that we understand both the potential of the discipline of anthropology to assist the court in these matters, as well as the limitations of our social science. In this chapter I consider the processes and difficulties that face anthropologists when asked to provide an opinion based on their research when rights are contested between Indigenous groups. I examine likely scenarios that illustrate the complexities of a process that seeks to engage anthropology in dispute management and settlement. I define the limits of useful anthropological involvement in these circumstances. I set down a practice guide to what is possible and likely to be helpful for use by both anthropologists and those who seek to use their services.

Native title disputes and anthropological evidence

In native title claims disputes arise when one person or group holds a view about their customary rights to country that is not shared by another. The truth of an assertion made by one party is then contested by another. Subject to the Federal Court process this translates to an adversarial relationship between the applicant (the claimants) and an Indigenous respondent or competing (overlapping) claim group. In seeking to convince the court (that is, in the first instance a single judge) of the veracity of their claim, each seeks to rely on evidence. This is likely to include the testimony of the individuals involved. However, contradictory oral accounts are the hallmark of overlap or membership disputes and provide a neutralising and often irreconcilable dialogue that invites appeal to other data – a matter I have considered in Chapter 6. Moreover, the use of oral accounts with respect to the reconstruction of a system as it might have been over 200 years ago raises issues as to the reliability of the oral account, which has been questioned elsewhere (Sansom 2007) and defended to some extent by me (Palmer 2011a). Typically in a native title claim, rights to country are understood to derive from filiative relationships and associations that are at some historical distance from the present. Given that such a time depth may be well beyond oral recall, reliance cannot be placed on the recollections or present-day opinions of the individuals involved, but rather on documentary materials like genealogies or early ethnography which shed light on the legitimacy or otherwise of claims and counter-claims of rights to country.

In the previous chapter of this book, I discussed the use of what I term 'foundation ethnography' in the native title research process to provide a reconstruction of a pre-sovereignty society for comparative purposes (see Chapter 7). This is one means to tackle the continuity issue in native title: is the society and its laws and customs one that has continuity with the past? By comparing the way the society may have been understood at or about the time of sovereignty or effective sovereignty and the way it is now, it is possible to provide a view as to the nature of the changes that are evidenced in the contemporary ethnography. The degree or quality of change that might be understood to accommodate the continuation of a system of law and custom consistent with the case law of the *Native Title Act* is a principal matter for consideration by the court. However, the use of early texts is not restricted to the formulation of foundation ethnography. It may also be called upon to serve a related purpose. Early texts may assist in illuminating past genealogical relationships or an individual's country of association or his or her language identity. As such, they can be used to posit language group affiliations of an ancestor from whom a party to the dispute traces descent. Genealogical particulars or language group identities collected some many decades ago and prior to the advent of native title disputes may provide a basis upon which a disputed matter can be adjudicated by the court. Alternatively, they may provide information about the ancestor's place of birth or country identity. Application of this methodology finds particular utility in cases where there is a dispute between Indigenous parties to a native title claim.

Rights contested by Indigenous parties in native title applications may then be subject to inquiry in the context of early texts. A proficiently trained anthropologist has competence in the interpretation of early texts and their comparison with contemporary ethnography. We can provide an understanding according to the paradigms of our discipline of such things as the nature and structure of society, land-owning groups and how people are recruited to them and how rights of its members are articulated, perpetuated and transmitted through time. In this the requirement to answer questions as to the continuity of these social processes and meanings by comparison with the foundation ethnographies is critical. Thus a question as to whether this group or that occupied the claim area at the time of sovereignty becomes a matter of the interpretation of early texts with all the inherent difficulties, problems and qualifications attendant upon the process – such as are illustrated in my earlier chapter. It is appropriate for the anthropologist to provide an expert view in this regard – and, indeed, providing such an expert view should be the basis of much of the work we do.

As an analytical exercise, however, this cannot be undertaken without due consideration of the difficulties inherent in the interpretation of early texts – as I have discussed them in Chapter 7. Accounts provided by early ethnographers need to be understood in the context of the intellectual environment within which they were produced. This may be a product of the proclivities of the individual writers themselves, or, more broadly, within the context of the prevailing intellectual thinking of the time that was brought to bear by the authors on the materials they considered. In addition, the extent of the account is also of considerable relevance to its usefulness today. Much early ethnography was partial, incomplete and covered only certain and sometimes rather esoteric aspects of the culture described. Thus, reliance on some accounts yields a limited reconstructed ethnography with many gaps and omissions. Early records, such as government registers or birth, marriage or death certificates may contain errors or misapprehensions and need to be critically appraised. Finally, and perhaps most importantly, these ethnographies were not collected with native title questions in mind and it may be tempting to assume data are relevant to the contemporary dispute when, in fact, they are not.

Contested truths in native title

In native title applications, contemporary disagreements amongst claimants regarding the legitimacy or otherwise of the claims of others primarily focus on one or the other of two contested truths. The first relates to a dispute over which is the 'right' group for an area of country. This may be manifest as overlapping claims (that is, a claim lodged over another in whole or in part). Data on the number of overlapping claims rapidly becomes out of date. In December 2007, 45 per cent of claims were overlapped, some with as many as five or more overlaps (Neate 2010, 207). More recent figures are elusive but the Australian Law Reform Commission identified overlaps as one of the factors that leads to delay and increased costs (ALRC 2015, 3.4, 3.79). In South Australia, as in most jurisdictions, overlapping claims 'have been a significant issue' while 'in recent years there have been more overlapping claims and more intra-Indigenous disputes' (ibid., 3.27).[7] Figures provided to me by the NNTT in March 2017 identified 227 'registered claims' of which 128 were 'subject to overlap'. Figures from the NNTT website set out in Table 1.1 show there to be 316 applications at that date, so presumably the difference is made up by non-registered claims.[8] Such data as there are, then, indicate that a little over 56 per cent of registered claims are overlapped.

This is consistent with my own experience where overlapping claims are now common and the majority of the applications I have worked on over the last decade have exhibited one or more overlaps. The second contested truth I look at in this chapter relates to an individual's right to be included in a claim group. My sense of this is that the profile of this area of contestation has increased over the last few years – perhaps as individuals become more aware of their rights, have gained access to pro bono legal advice and have gained a better understanding of the potential benefits

---

7   Despite this the same report states that, 'Overlapping claims, while still an issue, have significantly reduced since the 1998 amendments that introduced both the authorisation provisions and the registration test' (ALRC 2015, 10.19, footnote omitted).

8   The data provided was accompanied by the following qualification: 'Please note: Genuine overlaps are as listed in native title determination application compliances. There may be claims that have not had compliances completed as at today's date and overlaps that may be determined as genuine following compliance may not be represented in these results. The National Native Title Tribunal accepts no liability for reliance placed on enclosed information. The enclosed information has been provided in good faith. Use of this information is at your sole risk. The National Native Title Tribunal makes no representation, either express or implied, as to the accuracy or suitability of the information enclosed for any particular purpose and accepts no liability for use of the information or reliance placed on it.' (Data provided by the NNTT to the author, 9 March 2017.)

of being an unambiguous member of the claimant group. While not invariably so, excluded persons are often manifest in the claims process as respondents.

Overlapping claims and Indigenous respondents remain a significant impediment to the successful resolution of many applications. Both overlapped claims and the joining of an Indigenous respondent renders the application almost impossible to resolve via consent with the state. At trial overlapped claims may result in the representation of Indigenous respondents (or applicants, if the claims are heard together) adding to the legion of difficulties in proving the applicant's case while furnishing distracting or (worse still) substantive issues that can be pursued by other respondents. At the community level intra-Indigenous disputes fuel lateral violence and cause social, emotional and economic damage.[9] Given what is at stake both in terms of community relationships and potential benefits or losses resulting from the court's final decision, being involved in intra-Indigenous disputes is likely to be an uncomfortable and probably unforgettable experience for the anthropologist.

While every dispute is different, I noted above that most fall into one of two classes. The first is typified by a disagreement over the language group identity of the claimed area and the constituent language group membership that comprises the claimants. I identify this as 'right people for country' and it frequently results in an overlapping claim or the contesting of the registered application. The second relates to membership exclusion. Typically this happens when the members of a particular family are not accepted as being claimants because their ancestor is not accepted by the claim group as being of the country of the claim. Simply put, this is a dispute about claim group membership.

Contested truths: right people for country

The fundamentals of the dispute

It is not unusual for a claim group to be identified by reference to a language group name. Members of the group make application to the court for recognition of native title by authorising the application (and thereafter

---

9   See Mick Gooda, *Koori Mail* 2011, issue 513, 13, aiatsis.gov.au/collections/collections-online/digitised-collections/koori-mail/koori-mail-issues, accessed 15 March 2018.

subsequent action) and together can be called 'the applicant'.[10] The claim and its proponents, then, easily adopt a language group identity and act as a legal entity with an apparent corporate structure. I wrote in a preceding chapter that language groups (or 'tribes' as they are sometimes called) are identity groups and, in customary arrangements at least, lacked such corporate characterisation. Native title law has the effect, then, of transforming a customary formation that is amorphous but whose members share cultural commonalities into a corporation with a structure, a decision-making process and the capability of legal recognition. In short, the 'tribe' becomes the thing that purports to hold native title rights to the country of the claim. The morphing of one type of formation into another for the purposes of a native title application is not, of itself, a problem. The difficulty is that it leads to misapprehensions that have the potential to be particularly damaging in intra-Indigenous disputes. This is because the dispute over who are the right people for the country in question is understood in 'tribal' terms. The argument is put that the country of the claim (or a portion of it) 'belongs to' the such and such 'tribe', rather than understanding that the members of the language group named in the application were and continue to be commonly associated with it but did not in a customary manner constitute a corporation exercising rights as owners. The discourse typically runs as follows:

- That country always belonged to the X tribe. This is what we were always told by the old people.
- Now members of the Y tribe are saying it is their country and they've put a claim over it.
- I am a member of the X tribe. I have always known this.
- Those Y tribe people are trying to steal my country.

Members of the 'Y tribe' can be understood for their part to assert much the same thing and 'Y' and 'X' are transposed according to their argument. The contested truth is, then, whether the country in question belonged to the Y tribe or the X tribe. In pursuit of the ethnographic truth both the proponents and respondents evoke a plethora of maps purporting to show 'tribal' boundaries, of which portions of Tindale's 1974 publication often figure prominently, along with those produced by linguists and others, many of whom based their maps on Tindale's work and his accompanying texts. Even in so far as the maps and associated

---

10   *Native Title Act* subsection 61(2).

texts can be regarded as providing a rough indication of where speakers of particular language or dialect were to have been found, such mapping, generally done remotely and without regard for multilingualism, shared country and the vagaries and fluidity and flexibility of identity formation, are inherently unreliable and unsatisfactory.

In my view such debates reflect only the legal arrangements occasioned by compliance with the native title application process. They do not and indeed cannot reflect customary process or reflect the land-owning units of customary formations – a matter I have discussed in some detail above (see Chapter 2). The error is aided and abetted by the native title process that comprehends identity groups as corporations. In customary arrangements rights to country are held by the country or estate group. Members of several such groups together in aggregation comprise a language group although membership is not fixed and descent group members may espouse more than one language group affiliation.

For the anthropologist involved in disputes over 'right people for right country', the first and essential step is then to appreciate the science – however the matter is represented through the courts, mediation or by the proponents and respondents. Searching for 'tribal owners' is not only naive but it is likely to be futile at least in terms of attempting to resolve the dispute. What is required is a thorough examination of the question: who was in command of the disputed area at the time of effective sovereignty? Their language group association is only of importance if its discovery or establishment assists in responding to this question.

Identifying the ancestors who commanded rights within a particular area many decades ago is no simple task and such data may well be absent from the ethnographic records. This is not always the case. Some reliance can be placed on early genealogies including Bates, Radcliffe-Brown, Elkin, Kaberry and more recently Tindale and Birdsell – if they are available for the area in question. However, such accounts are sometimes incomplete, unclear or simply lack the sort of data required to establish ancestral country. In these cases it is important that the anthropologist be clear about the limitations of the materials available. While there may be some pressure on the researcher to 'come up with' the facts that will settle the matter, the reality is that this may simply not be possible. In the end, all that can be provided is an informed opinion based on the materials available with the limitations clearly enunciated for the court.

Other archival materials may also be of assistance. Generally, the official records (various registers, government departmental files, birth, marriage and death certificates) are of little assistance in determining country of affiliation as this was not a matter of interest to the official record. Some registers from the Northern Territory are an exception, while the official record may assist in identifying where a person was at a particular date. This does not, of course, mean that this was their traditional country but it may add to other material and so enable the researcher slowly to build a case. Birth, marriage and death certificates often include the name of parents as well as location of the event, so may help in establishing family relationships. None of these materials is likely to provide a swift, unambiguous or definitive answer to the question before the researcher – 'Who was in command of the disputed area at the time of effective sovereignty?' In my own experience, trawling through archival materials is as time-consuming as it is often unrewarding, at least in terms of answering the question. However, by careful and conservative examination and by amalgamating indications derived from several data sources, it may be possible to provide an expert view that will be afforded some weight by the court. This relatively optimistic view should be balanced by the reality of working with early texts. The difficulties with their interpretation are often a major impediment to the formulating of an unambiguous expert view on the part of any of the anthropologists involved. It is important that these limitations are clearly acknowledged to the court by all the anthropologists involved as experts.

Contested truths: claim group membership

A common source of dispute in a native title application relates to the legitimacy of membership of the claim group. A typical example of this is when a family or individual presses to be included in a claim and the members of the claim group reject the request. The rejection is often based on the ground that it is not evident that the apical ancestor for the family originated within the claim area and exercised customary rights within it. Alternatively, or in addition, it may be argued that the petitioning individual or family are unknown to the claim group, as a whole, and were never known to be a part of the claimant community in times past.

Separating group acceptance from findings of fact

Issues of community recognition were highlighted in a Queensland case[11] where the judge held that the *Native Title Act* stipulated certain requirements for claim group membership:

> Inevitably, these requirements lead to the conclusion that for the purposes of the Native Title Act, it is the claim group which must determine its own composition. … A claim group cannot arrogate to itself the right arbitrarily to determine who is, and who is not a member. As to substantive matters concerning membership, the claim group must act in accordance with traditional laws and customs. As to matters of process the claim group must act in accordance with traditional laws and customs or, in the absence of relevant laws and customs, pursuant to such process as it may adopt.[12]

His Honour continued that the jurisprudence:

> clearly demonstrate that membership must be based on group acceptance. That requirement is inherent in the nature of a society. However the society may accept the views of particular persons as sufficient to establish group acceptance.[13]

His Honour accepted that while 'the test is community acceptance … such acceptance may be demonstrated by the absence of opposition from senior people' (ibid., 262). He found that, in relation to the female ancestor Minnie:

> the claim group must determine that question. To date they have refused so to recognize her. I cannot take that decision for them. Nor can I find that during her lifetime, the Waanyi people, as a whole, accepted her as being Waanyi.[14]

These findings as to the nature of claim group membership under the *Native Title Act* are in contrast to the judge's 'factual findings'. Based on the evidence of the expert anthropologists (there were three) and the lay evidence reviewed at some length in the judgment (ibid., [226] to [249]), the Judge found in part that:

> On the balance of probabilities, I make the following factual findings:

---

11 *Aplin on behalf of the Waanyi Peoples v Queensland* [2010] FCA 625 (*Aplin*).
12 ibid., [256].
13 ibid., [260].
14 ibid., [267].

during her life, Minnie identified herself as a Waanyi woman and asserted such affiliation;

such self-identification was based on her belief that she had at least one Waanyi parent.[15]

My lay reading of these findings is that the question for the anthropologist in relation to native title and disputed claim group membership is one that needs to focus on how group acceptance and community composition operate consistent with customary practice relevant to the groups in question. 'Factual findings' with respect to genealogical descent and self-identity in times past may not be of much assistance to the court since, in this judgment at least, findings of fact did not prevail over findings framed in terms of the *Native Title Act* since this is the determining legislation in the matter.

The *Aplin* case and the politics of social inclusion and exclusion in that native title case have been discussed by David Trigger in an article that examines his role (along with two other anthropologists) in the trial (2015a). Trigger notes that the judge cited him in the judgment in relation to the quantum of community acceptance required (ibid., 203). It was Trigger's view that there has to be 'a reasonable degree of acceptance' or a 'significant proportion', or no longer a 'significant number prepared to argue overtly against' the inclusion or when 'no senior Waanyi person is willing to dispute the claim publicly' (ibid., 203, 205). How this would translate to social practice is unclear, although the implication is that there would need to be some sort of assessment of numbers and opinion. In cases where the claimants hold a common and mostly unified view, 'community acceptance' is not an issue. However, in my experience, claim groups are often characterised by substantial divergences of opinion. How many members of the group would constitute 'substantial'? Given an absence of a customary means to determine this matter, would a simple secret ballot be sufficient to settle the matter? These are legal and administrative matters that lie outside of the anthropology.

---

15   ibid., [250].

Anthropology and group acceptance

The court must decide who holds native title and does so on the basis of the operation of traditional laws and customs. Consequently, the task for the anthropologist is to identify the process that is relevant to acceptance of group membership. The focus of experts' deliberations in relation to disputed membership has to date been very much in terms of genealogical reconstruction and descent. This is because in most native title claims descent from an ancestor, typically identified and accepted as being a member of a particular language group, remains the defining factor in being a member of the claim group. In these cases, descent is determinative. Without it a person cannot be a member of the language group, unless they are adopted. Anthropological research may be able to assist in seeking data that will either support or discredit the identity of an ancestor and whether or not his or her country was within the current application area. However, there are substantial limits to what can be accomplished in this regard. Experts for the different sides in a dispute may simply exhaust to the point of inconclusiveness their inquiries and subsequent opinions on these matters. Given the poverty of some archival materials and the ambiguities implicit in their interpretation, debates between experts employed by the different parties to a dispute may furnish opinions that are, taken as a whole, inconclusive. The extensive debate, material considered and opinions provided by the experts result in a sort of evidentiary cul de sac that is of little or no assistance to the court. Moreover, and significantly as noted above, it appears that in native title 'findings of fact' in relation to prospective claim group membership may not be material to the decision of the court – although subsequent jurisprudence may of course change this.[16]

This does not mean that anthropological inquiry has no place in these disputes. Establishing genealogical facts – if indeed such can be established, may be effected through archival research and the examination of early texts or other records. The provision of an expert view based on these inquiries may be influential in opinion formation within the group and acceptance or rejection of the petitioning party. Indeed, some claimants with whom

---

16   Dowsett J wrote in this judgment that, 'There is, as far as I am aware, no precedent upon which to base a decision as to the availability of judicial relief in the event that persons who, according to traditional laws and customs, are entitled to Native Title rights and interests, are wrongfully excluded from membership of the claim group'. His Honour goes on to list a number of cases that, by analogy, might provide relief. *Aplin* [270] (Dowsett J).

I have worked have suggested that research of this sort may be significant in how they might regard the matter. However, research findings will be only one factor that influences opinion formation within the group and may be disregarded if other considerations prevail. In the absence of an evident ability to establish genealogical facts, anthropologists should turn to two other criteria that claim group members might consider to be important when framing their views about the assertions of a petitioning family or individual. The first relates to knowledge of the country held by the group seeking membership of the claim group; the second to what can be called 'social relatedness'. In this I refer to how dealings with the individuals concerned are accommodated within the kinship relationships that typify the social intercourse of customary interactions.[17]

Country, kin and group membership

Local organisation in Aboriginal Australian has as its fundamental building block the local descent or country group. Aggregations of local groups that share or shared commonalities of language, cultural practices and beliefs and held proximate country together comprised language groups – often referred to in the earlier literature as 'tribes'. Such aggregations depend for their continued operation on social and ritual relationships, as well as mutual obligations and co-dependency. Local groups whose members trace common ancestry are 'local' in the sense that they relate to, have spiritual affiliations with and consequential rights and duties in relation to the country or estate. People without country cannot be situated within the social fabric and network of relationships that are needful for the language group to have vitality, coherence and integrity. Without certainty as to their country there is no way they can be accommodated within the network of relationships that characterise the claimant society. They are, simply stated, *sui generis*.

In many areas of Aboriginal Australia, the manner whereby Indigenous Australians interact in both daily exchanges and ritual dealings is determined by reference to a categorical system often referred to as the 'section' or 'subsection' system (depending on its form) and, more colloquially, as 'skins' or by a term of the claimants' own language. Even in areas where the categorical system is absent (and was so, on the evidence, in earlier times too), classificatory kinship systems articulate and define

---

17   These are considerations also addressed by Trigger (2015a, 204).

a person's place within his or her social universe. Such relationships, whether determined by reference to categorical classification, kinship reckonings or both in complementarity, determine obligations and duties with respect to quotidian interaction, roles in ritual and to the use of country and the benefits that derive from it.

From an anthropological perspective, then, lack of knowledge of the requirements of social relationships and the system that frames them renders the person outside of the language group as they cannot be accommodated within the network of relationships that comprise its visceral quiddity. In some areas where I have worked a person without a 'skin' is classified as a 'stranger', being referred to by a term from the claimants' language that carries this meaning. A 'stranger' in this sense is not just an outsider but is unknown and therefore unpredictable. Consequently, they are to be regarded with suspicion, as potentially inimical to the language group members and beyond the boundaries of ready accommodation. They are intruders to the exclusive command of rights to country that the claimants assert to be theirs. In earlier times they were regarded as being so dangerous that they were killed.

Participation in the sets of relationships that make up the language group requires attributes that must be evidently declared, recognised and accepted by others. These components are the fabric upon which opinions and emotions about relationships and the degree of acceptance or otherwise are based. A family that lacks known and agreed ancestral connection to an estate within the country of the language group cannot be afforded recognition of that group. Similarly, a family whose members lack the wherewithal to effect social accommodation through section term attribution or known kinship relationships is similarly unable to be accommodated within the language group membership. These principles are evidently customary in that they derive from key aspects of cultural practice that are likely to have been in evidence prior to sovereignty. Their application to cases of disputed membership would then equip a claim group to make decisions about membership 'in accordance with traditional laws and customs' (*Aplin* [256] (Dowsett J)).

Methodological and ethical issues

How many anthropologists does it take … ?

The expert's first duty is to the court and not to any party to the proceedings. We should be and should be seen to be independent and non-advocatory. Having two or sometimes more anthropologists as experts is common practice in contested native title claims, reflecting the use of experts by opposing parties in a trial. Where there is a strongly antagonistic environment this may be the only way forward as claimants sometimes consider that having 'their own' anthropologist will be an advantage for them. Moreover, as things often turn out, the anthropologist who commenced the research, working with the initial claim group, may be seen as biased or unreliable by an opposing group. This may be only a perception on the part of the members of the group who are in dispute but it remains an impediment as we can only work with those willing to work with us. The anthropologist should seek to reduce these fears from the outset, but these are matters that are hard to control as a researcher. A difficulty with having an anthropologist for each disputing party is that each gains data from only one group so there is no ability for one researcher to assess the whole of the data, particularly the views of both sets of claimants.

The nature of the legal process as it is currently designed does not readily accommodate the use of a third expert appointed by the court – although this is not unknown.[18] This would appear to provide one means of limiting the possibilities for bias in an account that treats only one side of the data. However, a court appointed expert may have difficulty in gaining unfettered access to claimants and respondents and by my understanding the procedure is not one that is common for the Federal Court. The Land Commissioners appointed under the *Aboriginal Land Rights Act* (NT) invariably had an anthropologist to advise them, but as far as I know those so commissioned did not undertake any primary fieldwork.

To my mind, the use of two anthropologists rather serves to confirm the potentially partisan nature of the expert – at least in the eyes of the claimants. In the practice of our profession we work closely with people in

---

18 See G. Davies 2005. The Federal Court's 'Expert Evidence Practice Note (GPN-EXPT)', October 2016, paragraph 2.1, also recognises this possibility.

order to gain their trust and to establish a relationship that will facilitate discussion of quite personal information and often deeply held beliefs and practices. It is hard to develop such a relationship without also forming friendships or at least sympathetic attitudes. However, native title work requires that we focus on the end game and we have a duty to explain to those with whom we work that our first duty cannot be to them. This raises ethical problems and is contrary to the expectation that was formerly common amongst anthropologists that they would become, over time, advocates for those with whom they worked. Such an approach in the context of native title is not only naive but is untenable. A partisan expert who is an unashamed advocate for one group has no credibility in the legal process and consequently does a substantial disservice to those with whom he or she has worked. What is important is that those with whom we work know from the outset to what purpose the data they provide may be put. This includes the fact that once written as notes'in our field note book and relied on in the formulation of our expert view, it may be discoverable by the court and so to other parties hostile to the application.

The ideally independent position required of the expert facilitates his or her working with those who are on opposite sides of the dispute. In these circumstances where emotions often run high and passions are deep, transparency is all. My personal approach is to explain my role as an independent anthropologist and expert to the court to all those with whom I propose working. The legal representatives of the various parties must be included in this process. I also act on the principle that I do not discuss data provided to me by one group with another, resisting sometimes quite strong demands that I do so. My stock answer to such requests is to explain that should a group or individual wish to know what another group told me, then they should ask them, not me.

The experts should have the opportunity to meet to discuss their findings and to seek to reach agreement on at least some of the issues that lie between them. The legal representatives on both sides of the dispute may wish to agree a set of questions for the experts which can be helpful in giving direction to the conference which is relevant to the legal issues before the court. One drawback of this arrangement I have noted is that our legal colleagues often wish to overload the experts with an impossibly long set of questions (some quite repetitive) and all involved need to be realistic about how many questions the experts can usefully consider in a day. I set the maximum at about six per day – although if there are more than two experts this may be too many. In terms of the practical and realistic allocation of resources, the experts can probably not be asked to meet for more than two days, while in many cases a single day should be sufficient. Such meetings of experts – best termed a 'conference' or 'conclave' of experts although other names are also used[19] – generally feature as a part of the management of the application by the Federal Court and the judge may direct that such a meeting take place usually by a particular date. In my experience in recent years the conference of experts is chaired by a Registrar of the Federal Court who also records the outcomes (points agreed and disagreed and, if the latter, the reasons why). The issues agreed between the experts may be accepted by the parties and the judge as settled and not meriting any further consideration. However, the anthropologist remains only a witness providing a particular sort of evidence and even when experts are agreed their views are not determinative of legal outcomes.

Uncomfortable spaces

Anthropologists who are involved in disputes often find the experience harrowing. This is a research environment often charged with strong emotions marked by acrimony, bitterness and sometimes even physical threats. The expert is almost inevitably drawn to provide a view that will gainsay an Indigenous party's evidence, raising questions or accusations regarding our right to do so and to allegations that as outsiders we should not make comments on cultural matters as in doing so we are appropriating the knowledge that rightly belongs to others. This can, then, be an uncomfortable and challenging environment and is not for the fainthearted. This makes it all the more important that we understand our special role, the limitations of our science and the methodological and ethical standards that we must apply.

Professional anthropologists should be members of the Australian Anthropological Society (AAS) and so bound by its code of ethics.[20] The AAS Code of Ethics states:

> 3.1 Where a conflict of views or interests arises among the parties to research, anthropologists should endeavour to ascertain the views of the various research participants, as independently and impartially as possible.

---

19   See Hughston and Jowett 2014.
20   See www.aas.asn.au/about-aas/code-of-ethics, accessed 21 October 2016.

This is clearly relevant to research conducted in a native title inquiry and supports the proposition that an anthropologist should work across competing parties, rather than with one only. Relevant in this context also is a subsequent portion of the Code of Ethics:

> 3.10 Anthropologists should not knowingly or avoidably allow information gained on a basis of the trust and cooperation of the research participants to be used against their legitimate interests by hostile third parties.

The expert's report (and perhaps, inevitably, this book) is likely to be used in a court of law by a respondent or applicant party that may not seek to use it in the interest of those who provided the information but against them.[21] This raises substantial ethical issues since, as writers of an expert report for the court, we may have no control over how the report or the information within it is used. However, the ethics also instructs:

> 4.2 Anthropologists should maintain integrity in the recording and presentation of anthropological data, and should not discredit the profession of anthropology by knowingly colouring or falsifying observations or interpretations, or making exaggerated or ill-founded assertions, in their professional writings, as expert witnesses, or as authors of any other form of reportage related to their work.

In seeking a balance between objectivity, integrity and the betrayal of trust and cooperation in situations of contestation and conflict, the role to be filled by the researcher and the possible uses to which the material may be put must be explained to the participants at the outset. This is consistent with the requirement to obtain informed consent from those with whom the anthropologist will work (Code of Ethics, 3.4).[22]

The commonsense approach, then, is to ensure that the researcher explains before the research commences the nature of the work, the uses to which it may be put and the possibility of consequences that do not accord with the claimants' wishes. Provision of such advice provides claimants with the

---

21   See Glaskin 2017, 107–111 for a case study relating to the use of field notes in a trial.

22   The principle of informed consent expresses the belief in the need for truthful and respectful exchanges between social researchers and the research participants.

'(a) Negotiating consent entails communicating information likely to be material to a person's willingness to participate, such as: - the purpose(s) of the study, and the anticipated consequences of the research; the identity of funding bodies and sponsors; the anticipated uses of the data; possible benefits of the study and possible harm or discomfort that might affect participants; issues relating to data storage and security; and the degree of anonymity and confidentiality which may be afforded to informants and subjects.'

opportunity to make an informed decision as to whether they wish to be involved in the research process or not. Some potential participants may decline to be involved and we need to accept this with equanimity. Non-participation in the research process by claimants may on at least some occasions be detrimental if a court requires expert evidence based on field data gathered necessarily from the claimants. Understanding this, then, the choice for the claimants as to whether to participate in the research may be an invidious one. Indeed, participation is a natural consequence of the process of making application for the recognition of native title in the first place.

Toward a practice guide

The particular nature of anthropological research conducted in an environment of intra-Indigenous dispute invites application of some guidelines. These are in addition to the more general 'Expert Evidence Practice Note' issued by the Federal Court and updated from time to time.[23] The guidelines I have set out below should not be seen as prescriptive but may provide guidance for those who seek to navigate these difficult waters. Perhaps the most obvious principle to enunciate is that as practising anthropologists we should seek from the outset to avoid the necessity to participate as an expert in situations of contested truth. Solutions like negotiations and mediation arrived at through discussions between the parties are more likely to result in a successful outcome than the application of the research findings of an expert anthropologist to the dispute. Usually, however, by the time the anthropologist is invited on to the scene, the battle lines have been drawn. In such cases the following methodological principles may be of assistance:

- Those approached to participate in the research should understand the process, the consequences of their participation and the likely uses to which their information may be put.
- The expert must be independent, non-partisan and be fearless in expressing sound views. These must be founded upon a reasoned account, based on all available materials, fully referenced and scrupulously researched. There is no room in this process for bias, advocacy or partisanship.

---

23   www.fedcourt.gov.au/law-and-practice/practice-documents/practice-notes/gpn-expt, accessed 3 February 2017.

- The anthropologist should be mindful of the sometimes extreme limitations of the materials with which he/she deals. The anthropologist should ensure that those who commission expert views based on archival materials and early texts understand the likely limitations of such research before it is undertaken.

- Anthropologists should seek clear questions, which it is their task to address. Vagueness and imprecision in the brief provided to the anthropologist has the potential to yield imprecise or ill-focused commentary and will diminish the usefulness of the opinion to the party commissioning the research and so, too, to the court.

- The anthropologist as expert is qualified before the court to provide an opinion on matters that are within his or her expertise. Consequently, the questions that the expert is asked to answer must relate directly to the expertise of the anthropologist. The anthropologist should be consulted first about the questions contemplated and reject any questions that he or she considers to lie outside of their area of specialist knowledge. The list is best developed by agreement between the legal team and the researcher.

Disputes in native title are a notable feature of the legal, administrative and research environments. As more of the difficult (i.e. contested) claims come to the attention of the court and post-native title procedures seek to test membership and jurisdiction, I think that they are likely to increase rather than diminish. Anthropologists are now unlikely to avoid involvement in issues of contested rights. Nor, to my mind, should they seek to do so if the application of their discipline to real-life situations is a part of their understanding of the proper uses of anthropology. In facing these challenges there needs to be a more realistic understanding and declaration of the limits of anthropology in this particular regard – and that in relation to the research I have discussed in this chapter there is no 'God's Truth' out there to which anthropologists have access via the interpretation of archival texts and early ethnographies. Practitioners need to be cognisant of the particular issues that should be the subject of their research that have relevance to disputes over 'right people for country' and claim group membership. These methodological as well as ethical issues need robustly to inform our practice and give direction to the sort of research we undertake.

9

Genealogies

Genealogy as an anthropological tool

At the heart of every good native title claim lies a robust genealogy. I iterate this truism because it is not always evident. Genealogies tend to get left behind in the research process – being regarded as a task that does not merit immediate attention and that might well be left to some more junior person to complete. This is a grievous error and one that will compound difficulties not only during the native title claim itself but, upon its resolution, thereafter as those charged with administering the native title rights recognised by the court seek answers to questions about membership and rights that are likely to lie, in part at least, within the genealogical account. Long after the legal disputes about extinguishment and continuity of laws and customs have been forgotten, the genealogy will remain an important point of reference. As such, it is our duty to make sure that we provide genealogical data that are the best possible given the circumstances, our resources and the problems we will encounter when dealing with genealogical knowledge. Genealogies, whether in analogue or digital form, become 'things' in the sense that they exist in the context of their own creation divorced from the diverse research environment wherein their component parts were created. It is essential, then, that their integrity is able to withstand a lack of attendant exegesis, explanation or excuse. We cannot now ask Tindale what he meant by writing on a genealogy that a person was 'of' such and such a place, which would be handy given such annotations are commonly referred to in native title inquiries. The deficiency now limits the usefulness of the original text and, had Tindale paid greater attention to his meaning, our research task would be all the easier today.

The idea of a genealogy or family tree has a long history dating back well beyond the development of anthropology as a discipline. They feature in the Old Testament and are found in many non-literate societies as formal recitations of lineal descendants passed on from generation to generation as oral tradition. Commentators on the history of genealogical recording have noted that 'genealogical reckoning came to serve as a model of distinction in early European society', and that 'aspects of its visual representation appear in fascinating diffraction in many places' (Bamford and Leach 2009, 4). These authors provide an illustration of a family tree hung in the Royal Palace of Jogjakarta in Central Java (ibid., 5, 20). They continue:

> By the end of the twelfth century, genealogy had become the surest means of preserving the memory of one's ancestors and of enhancing the prestige of an elite family. Demonstrated birth and membership in an aristocratic family became the legitimizing criteria for anyone who wanted to take advantage of the automatic inheritance system for fiefs. By 1500, a 'well born' man thought of his ancestors and descendants as a group of people through whose veins flowed the same noble blood. (ibid., 4)

Barnes (1967, 101) suggests that family membership and family position (presumably meaning social status) are used 'as criteria for membership and position in larger social units'. He shows how genealogical accounts have been a part of many cultures for many centuries in both Europe and elsewhere (ibid., 102–103). Barnes's epigraphic citation to Oswald Barron, contributor to the 1911 *Encyclopaedia Britannica*, confirms the antiquity of genealogical study, but raises an associated difficulty of veracity:

> The medieval baron, knight or squire, although proud of the nobility of his race, was content to let it rest upon legend handed down the generations. The exact line of his descent was sought only when it was demanded for a plea in the king's courts to support his title to his lands. From the first the work of the genealogist in England had that taint of inaccuracy tempered with forgery from which it has not yet been cleansed. (Barron 1911, 575–576)

Genealogies prepared in relation to claims of right or title are not neutral documents existing in some space separate from bias or even, in extreme cases, fabrication. While genealogies purport to set out either as text or as a diagram the lineage of a person, they must also be understood potentially as social constructs.

Barnes distinguished 'pedigrees' from 'genealogies' while accepting that the two terms were often used interchangeably (Barnes 1967, 102–103). The former is a charter of lineal descent that serves to support an asserted social position or status. The latter is a statement 'made by an ethnographer as part of his field record or analysis' (ibid., 103). For the most part in native title research we are likely to be collecting 'pedigrees' (as Daisy Bates also called them). However, the term 'pedigree' has connotations that relate to the animal kingdom and is probably best avoided as this may give offence.

In Australia, Sir George Grey was perhaps the first European observer to make use of genealogies with respect to social inquiry – proving a list 'to show the manner in which a native family becomes divided' (Grey 1841, II, Appendix A, 391–394).[1] He collected these names and relationships from the Perth area, Western Australia,[2] being interested in how obligations developed from family relationships, and used his genealogical data to provide an indication of age (Grey 1841, II, 231, 247). W.H.R. Rivers is generally credited with introducing what he called the 'genealogical method' into anthropological practice (Rivers 1900; Barnes 1967, 104). Rivers had visited the Torres Strait as a part of the Haddon expedition in 1898. Wishing better to understand the relationship between those upon whom he and his expedition colleagues were conducting psychological tests, he commenced collecting genealogies. He found, 'the knowledge possessed by the natives of their families was so extensive, and apparently so accurate' that it spurred him to collect genealogies from a substantial majority of those resident on both Murray and Mabuig islands (ibid., 74). Rivers defined his own fieldwork methodology (ibid., 75–76), noting that issues of confidentiality were a concern on Murray Island and claimed the 'essential accuracy' of his data (ibid., 76). He also raised two additional points to which I return later in this chapter. One related to the difficulty he encountered when trying to ascertain what he termed the 'real' father in a system that classified a number of individuals (typically ego's father's

---

1   Available from gutenberg.net.au/ebooks/e00055.html
2   Grey 1841, II, 324.

brother) as a 'father' (ibid., 75, 77). The other related to the issues of adoption, common in Torres Strait societies (ibid., 76–77) and a frequent feature of native title genealogical accounts.

Rivers saw genealogies as a means to study kinship (ibid., 77–78), marriage choices and customs (ibid., 78–80), totemism, fertility and history (ibid., 81–82). Rivers recognised the potential for genealogical information to provide the means for the analysis of abstract concepts through the provision of 'concrete facts' by those he interviewed – the provision of which he regarded as the product of their 'extraordinary memory for detail' (ibid., 82). Interestingly, Rivers notes that two lawsuits had been tried before the court on Murray Island, both dealing with disputes over title to land that 'turned on the question of adoption and on the real parentage of two men' (ibid., 77). Rivers tells us that his genealogies matched the accounts provided in the trial but he did not appreciate at that time what a seminal role genealogies would later play in native title and intra-Indigenous disputes over land (ibid.).

Pioneering Australian anthropologists including Radcliffe-Brown, Elkin, Kaberry and others (including Daisy Bates) all collected genealogies as a means to better understand the social relationships of those with whom they worked, how different family members were named, their rules for marriage, the descent of totemic affiliation and, at least to some extent, their rights to country through patrifiliation. For good reason the genealogical method became a stock-in-trade for anthropological inquiry and a frequently encountered component of a good ethnography.

Genealogies and native title

The collection of genealogical data and the construction of genealogical charts commonly feature in native title research in two forms. The researcher can use genealogical data to explore with claimants kinship terminology, marriage preferences, totemic affiliations and relatedness and this should provide a basis upon which at least some aspects of the laws and customs and associated normative referents are defined for the community of native title holders. This provides a valuable insight into the likely continuity (or otherwise) of these rules and ways of behaving since the date of effective sovereignty. Such information does not have to be elicited through genealogical research, but this is a task that will most likely have to be undertaken in any event, unless of course it has already been done by a reliable and accurate researcher previously. The second form of genealogical research is the account of descent from an apical ancestor, and this research activity tends, in my experience, rather to overshadow the first-mentioned activity to the former's ultimate detriment.

Native title claims are typically made by those who are described in the application as being the descendants of one or more of those listed as ancestors of the claimants. These forebears are known commonly as 'apical ancestors', which simply means they are at the apex of the genealogical account. It is sometimes the case that research undertaken in relation to the early texts (including the genealogies of pioneering anthropologists) will reveal additional names beyond those listed as apical ancestors on the Form 1 application.[3] Locating the names and country identities of individuals even one generation above the apical listed on the Form 1 extends the compass of knowledge about the descent of rights and is likely to be helpful to the application. Claimants are unlikely to know the names of those more than two or, in some cases, three generations above ego, so it may be useful in any discussion to employ the name of a person who is remembered by the older claimants as a point of reference with the lineal relationship included. Thus, in a fictitious example, apical ancestor John Brown whose father's father is discoverable from an early genealogy as Jinggandari is rendered as 'Jinggandari, FF of John Brown'.

The wording on the Form 1 will vary on a case-by-case basis and it is not unusual for those adopted, perhaps 'according to the laws and customs of the claimants', to be included. In addition the requirement that there be 'community recognition' of claim group membership may also find a place in the Form 1 wording. As I have discussed in the previous chapter, these are important legal qualifications that may require consideration by the anthropologist.

Native title genealogical essentials

In terms of the anthropological inquiry the genealogical account of descent from a named ancestor is, in its essentials, straightforward. Assuming that the system under review is one based on a descent of rights through filiation (that is, through a perceived relationship between ego

---

3   The 'Native Title (Federal Court) Regulations 1998' require that the 'Form 1' be used for an application mentioned in s. 61(1) of the *Native Title Act 1993* by a claimant for a determination of native title in relation to an area for which there is no approved determination of native title. See www.fedcourt.gov.au/forms-and-fees/forms/native-title-regulations, accessed 6 November 2017.

and a forebear), what is required is an account of the genealogy, showing descent through agnatic or cognatic links (as the case may be) with lineal antecedents stretching back to the apical ancestor. Ultimately, what is required is evidence that the ancestor was in command of the claimed land (or a portion of it) at the time of effective sovereignty or before. Data brought to bear on this issue derive either from the claimants themselves as part of their oral account of their ancestral connection or from the early literature and in some cases from more recent prior native title research. While the essentials are disarmingly simple, the reality is indeed much more complex.

W.H.R. Rivers, and the early Australian anthropologists who followed, collected their genealogical data from those with whom they worked. It was, then, strictly an oral account, although Rivers noted that the 'chief' on Mabuiag had himself drawn up genealogies of residents of the island that River found agreed, for the most part, with his own data and augmented them (1900, 76). Anthropologists working in Aboriginal Australia on native title claims are unlikely to have such a clear run. Genealogical accounts collected by previous researchers may serve to confirm, correct or contradict the oral account. This can lead to disputes between groups and a variance of opinion between the claimants and the anthropologist should the genealogical record not accord with that now espoused by the claimants. In my experience claimants sometimes turn up to native title meetings with their own independently researched genealogies, which they may or may not wish to hand over to the anthropologist who is researching the claim. The provision of a number of genealogical sources seldom results in unambiguous concurrence, or the material available may be uncertain, unclear or incomplete. All the difficulties I have already discussed in preceding chapters relating to the use of early texts apply. The potential for disagreement and conflict is, then, high, particularly as claimants usually see the genealogical materials as the pass to claim group membership, which indeed in part at least, it may be.

Given that this is an important and often contested field, it is important that genealogical research be undertaken with due respect for method, the time required and resources needed. It is a task that requires careful, methodical and professional application. In what follows I set out just some of the guiding principles that may assist, noting that others have written at length on the genealogical method, including Barnes (1967) and, with respect to native title, Sutton (see, in particular, 2003, 179–205).

Some methodological and procedural issues

Despite the shallowness of the genealogical record (Barnes 1967, 119; Sansom 2006), the claimants' own knowledge of their family and antecedents remains an important basis for preparing the research documentation required for a native title claim. The court generally regards genealogical accounts provided by claimants as 'evidence' but of course has to allocate them weight according to the credibility of the witness, consistency and other factors including whether it is likely that the data have been derived from books, papers or lawyers during the native title process. For the anthropologists, in terms of field research, collecting genealogical data means sitting down with senior claimants to gather genealogical information. A necessary precursor to this process (as with all field research) will be an explanation of the process to be followed and the reason why genealogical data are so important, what will happen to the data once collected and the uses to which they will be put. For each individual, names should be recorded, place and date of birth noted and country affiliation and language group identity sought. Other data that might be helpful include section or subsection terms and totemic affiliation, but the data to be collected will depend on both availability and relevance to the native title arguments. Each item of information should be explored as thoroughly as possible. A person may have several names and multiple language identities. If the knowledge is absent, make a note that this is the case. Different cultural conventions govern the use of names, particularly of the deceased, so it is probably best to discuss this first before attempting to collect a genealogy as it is next to impossible to do so accurately without using the names of deceased ancestors. As with all field data, the resulting chart and accompanying notes should be dated and the persons from whom the information was gathered set down. Genealogies should be checked with the claimants that supplied them as well as with members of other branches of the family that share the same ancestors. Generally, however, I have found it a sound rule not to discuss genealogical details belonging to one family with another as this is usually seen as a betrayal of confidential information and should be avoided.

The systematic methods required to collect these genealogical data in the field have been set out elsewhere (Barnes 1967, 105–112). The researcher should decide on the symbols to be used in the charts, typically ○ for a woman and △ for a man and perhaps a □ or ◇ if the sex is not known. A deceased person can be marked by a solid infill of the symbol or a / through it. The person from whom the genealogy is collected should be identified as 'ego' and his or her ascending generations are shown by vertical lines, collaterals by horizontal lines. Marriage is shown by the use of =; alternatively and sometimes more convenient if there are multiple wives, by a horizontal line with short terminal vertical lines above linking marriage partners. Names should be included where they are known. There is some preference for distinguishing males from females by the use of capitals for the former and lowercase for the latter, particularly if the symbols noted above are not used (Rivers 1900, 74). Some researchers have reversed this arrangement including Daisy Bates who often has her women in capitals and her men in lower case, as did Norman Tindale. Whatever convention is adopted, it should be explained in the text or along with the genealogical charts so the reader can be clear as to the data the genealogical chart presents. The date, place of collection and identity of the ego of the chart should be noted on the chart or genealogical account.

Discussion of relationships is best done by reference to conventional abbreviations. Thus F = father, MF = mother's father, mm = mother's mother, z = sister, S = son and so on. Males are distinguished from females by the use of the upper case for the former and the lower case for the latter. A fuller account of these conventions is provided by Sutton (2003, 181–182), which date back to Murdock's writing on genealogical method in 1947 (cited in Barnes 1967, 122–123).

Genealogical accounts required for a native title claim, which provide explanatory text as to how claimants are descended from a named ancestor, are necessarily complex and sometimes tortured affairs. They should be kept as simple as possible while ensuring that there is no ambiguity resulting from the loose use of pronouns. Thus statements like 'Molly had a daughter Jessie and her mother's sister was called Jane' leave the reader uncertain as to whether Jane is Jessie's mz (aunt) or Jessie's mmz (great aunt). It is better to repeat a name than risk such misunderstandings. Thus, 'Molly had a daughter Jessie. Molly's sister was called Jane'. Or, 'Molly had a daughter Jessie. Molly's mother [name] had a sister who was called Jane'.

Genealogical accounts as text should be properly referenced to the source in the researcher's field notes. In this way material collected from the claimants about their knowledge of an ancestor can be sourced to a particular claimant and consequently the bases for any resultant expert view is evident to the reader or those who seek to adjudicate the matter.

Reliance will also have to be placed on archival and earlier anthropological work, particularly genealogies collected in the past. The limitations of these data, if apparent, should be considered, and such deficiencies as are considered to qualify opinions made clear. Conclusions must be founded on these data as a whole and, in the event that there is insufficient materials available from all sources, the anthropologist should simply state that there is insufficient data available to form a concluded view.

A critical task is to provide an opinion on whether each apical ancestor was in command of portions of the application area at or before the date of effective sovereignty. This requires the provision of a likely birth date for the ancestor in order to show whether the individual was born prior to the date of effective sovereignty. If these data are not a part of the archival record (which in the majority of cases it is not), then the researcher has to provide reasonable grounds for estimating one. When seeking to posit dates of birth of those in the higher generations beyond oral recall it is my practice to work backwards from the oldest person whose birth date is known with some certainty – perhaps from a Tindale reference, a birth, death or marriage certificate or other document. This may not take us back very far but from then on the application of calculated birth dates is one way to proceed, provided the method and its assumptions are clearly set down for the reader and the limitations of the system accepted. In computing possible birth dates, where these are not known from the archival or other records, I allow 20 years between generations for a woman and 25 years for a man. This is a rough estimate given that women may be younger and men often older than this when their first child is born and other researchers have adopted different inter-generational time periods (e.g. Sutton 2003, 162, 168). However, what I suggest provides a helpful guide as to possible birth dates of ancestors when no other information is available in this regard while the bases for ensuing conclusions in this regard are set out for the reader to evaluate.

The identity of the ancestor's country is also seldom readily available from the evidence so, again, the researcher must provide reasonable grounds for the provision of an opinion with respect to this and some reliance will have to be placed in this regard on the archival record, if such is available.

Tindale's genealogies

Tindale collected many hundreds of genealogies from all round Aboriginal Australia. As I discussed in Chapter 7, parcels of Tindale's gargantuan corpus frequently figure in native title claims and his genealogies are no exception. Consequently, given the widespread use of Tindale's genealogical data in native title claims, these materials merit commentary here. While other early researchers have also collected genealogical accounts, including charts which are used in native title claims, an evaluation of the use of Tindale's genealogical materials also provides lessons applicable to the materials collected by others.

Understanding Tindale's genealogies is first about developing an appreciation of their original purpose. Keen, in an article he titled 'Norman Tindale and me' (1999), pointed out that the genealogies prepared by Tindale now provide a 'wonderful resource for many Aboriginal people … in the preparation of native title claims'. However, they were also the work of a man who was 'a strong advocate of assimilation and the dispersal of Aboriginal communities in the southeast, at the time of the White Australia policy' (ibid., 99). Tindale was of the view that mixed race Aboriginal people should be absorbed as rapidly as possible into the mainstream population (white, Anglo-European). He was interested to discover which of the many racially mixed groups would best adapt to assimilation (ibid., 102; Tindale 1941, 68). He identified mixed race individuals in his genealogies by the use of the annotations F1 (typically a European father and Aboriginal mother) and F2 (the child of two F1 individuals). He also used the then popular terms like 'quadroon' and 'octroon' or by the fraction value of the 'mixed blood' he calculated from the genealogical information available to him (Keen 1999, 100). This 'racial reductionism' as Keen called it (ibid., 103) is both striking and disturbing to a modern reader but it explains Tindale's apparent preoccupation with collecting genealogies, which he often coupled with his anthropomorphic measurements, mental ability tests and photographs, undertaken at times with his long-term colleague Joseph Birdsell (Tindale 1940b).

A good example of Tindale's research interests in this regard is found in a page of his journal, written in 1939 while visiting the Aboriginal settlement of Koonibba on the west coast of South Australia (1938–1939,

1020[4]). Tindale made a copy of a 'Work Classification' evidently drawn up by Pastor Traeger who became the superintendent of Koonibba Mission in 1936. Traeger's list was, in turn, based on a 'similar list used by Pastor Mueller' (ibid.), the previous superintendent of the mission. Tindale's entry takes the form of a table and comprises a list of men employed at the mission and a ranking of their ability to undertake employment. The table has four columns with the headings, 'Men able to undertake contract work successfully', 'Men reliable when left to work alone', 'Men who give best results if white man works with them' and 'Unreliable'. Against each name is a measure of the individual's 'blood' – that is, F1, F2, ¾ and so on with a cross reference to the genealogical chart he had drawn up as part of his research program. All the names in column 1 are classified as F1; of the nine names in column 4, six are classified as 'fb', two as ¾ and one as F1. Elsewhere Tindale reported that F1 individuals showed 'apparently greater adjustment to white life' than did F2 individuals, but he was unable to explain why this was so (1940b, 282). Tindale commented in his journal, 'when fully analysed this list should be very instructive as an independent assessment of the high place taken by F1s as compared with F2s and others' (1938–1939, 1021).

The quality and legibility of Tindale's genealogies vary enormously. Some are quite sparse in terms of their details, while others appear to have been the product of a number of sessions, with copious information squeezed in to a corner, with lines showing family connections that could not otherwise be accommodated in the space available. Tindale generally wrote the European names of the people he recorded, using upper case for women and lower case for men. Tindale also annotated some of the names he recorded, but there is no consistency in this regard. He sometimes wrote 'tribal' names alongside the name of individuals where these were known or collected as well as a geographic location. The significance of these locations is unclear. Tindale sometimes wrote that a person was 'of' such and such a place, or 'at', the implication being that the former preposition indicated that the place was their traditional country, the latter that they were living at the place mentioned. However, this apparent differentiation is not explained by Tindale and can only be drawn by inference. It is important to remember that Tindale did not generally record details of the country wherein a person held customary rights but rather used

4   The copy of the journal I have accessed has two sets of page numbers. The one cited here appears to have been Tindale's original. A portion of the original journal has been renumbered, commencing as page 2 for the 24 March 1939 entry.

a 'tribal' identity to situate them within a social setting. Tindale also sometimes gave approximate ages and other comments or annotations that can sometimes yield helpful ethnographic information he obviously collected at the time he took the genealogy.

Tindale did not identify his 'ego' (that is, the person from whom he collected the genealogy) although this, too, may sometimes be inferred by his cross reference to a record card (e.g. 'R726'). These cards were prepared by Tindale or by his co-researchers and contain additional data collected on such things as social history, 'tribal affiliation' or anthropometric data, depending on the expedition and his style of research at the time. The cards sometimes provide additional data and are worth consulting, if they are available. Tindale also took portrait photographs of his subjects

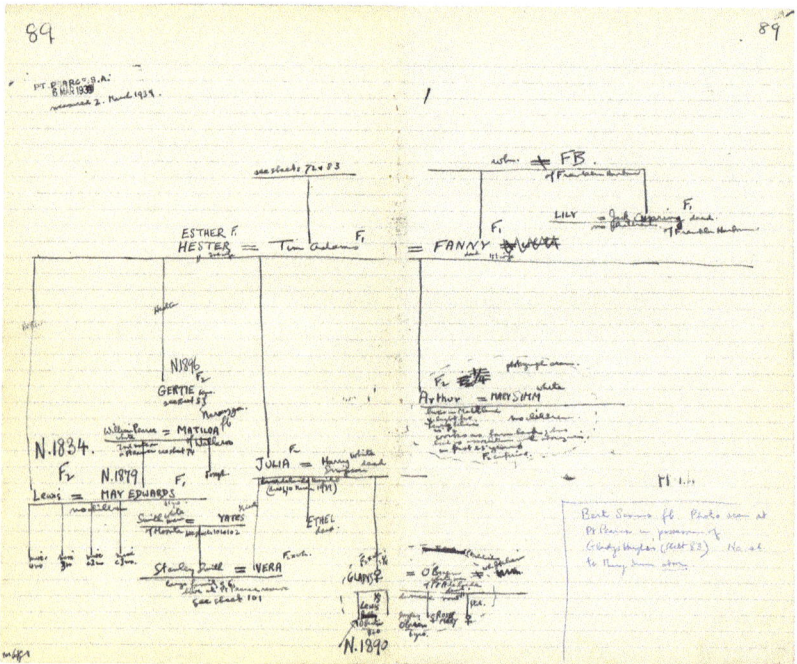

Figure 9.1: Tindale sheet 89 collected from Point Pearce, SA, in 1939

Source: Genealogy reproduced by kind permission of the Board for Anthropological Research Collection, South Australian Museum. Courtesy of Lewis Yerloburka O'Brien, South Australian Museum collection AA346/5/3/6_Point Pearce_89.

I have provided a copy of one of Tindale's 1939 genealogies as Figure 9.1. Tindale collected this genealogy from Point Pearce on 6 March in that year. He generally wrote the place of collection at the head of the chart, along with the date, while the numbering of the genealogies makes referencing unambiguous.

Genealogies such as the one shown above provide useful information in native title research, provided of course that they can be directly linked to the claimants. Difficulties arise when names are uncertain or when names very common at the time they were collected by Tindale may result in misidentification. So, for example, if a family know they had a forebear whose name was Daisy it is possible to erroneously assume that a woman in a Tindale genealogy with this name was that woman. Consequently, it is important to cross-check other details like date of birth, place of residence or 'caste' (which Tindale often included in his annotations) to provide greater certainty as to the applicability of the genealogy. Tindale sometimes collected the name of the same person on more than one genealogy and appears to have been quite thorough in providing cross-references to these names. It is important, then, to check these cross-referenced sheets to see what other information might be available there relating to the family. Tindale's annotations are sometimes hard to read and copies provided through Native Title Representative Bodies are always photocopies of the originals (which are held at the South Australian Museum in Adelaide), while some are clearly copies of copies with resultant deterioration. I have even come across copies that have been amended by an unknown hand, and in one case some names were actually crossed out and rendered illegible – presumably because someone disagreed with Tindale's record of the family. Perhaps the greatest and most frequent point of dispute relates to the 'tribal' identity, which may be the subject of subsequent debate particularly in areas where group names were variable or inconsistently applied.

Working with Tindale's genealogies requires practice and patience, extensive cross-checking where this is possible and sound contemporary fieldwork to ensure that the genealogy considered is indeed relevant to the family being researched. At their best Tindale's genealogies may provide evidence of an ancestor's links to the application area. By calculating birth dates backwards from those Tindale supplies, individuals represented in Tindale's oldest generation level may be shown to have been in possession of the claim area at the time of effective sovereignty. At their worst, Tindale's genealogies provide data that is inconsistent with other materials and contrary to the evidence of the claimants. In any event, if there is a Tindale genealogy relevant to a forebear of a claimant, it must be properly and comprehensively assessed, taking into account the circumstances of its collection, Tindale's purpose in making it and any other data that may be relevant to the conclusions and opinions that may be drawn from it.

Genealogies and adoption

Adoptive relationships are common in native title genealogical accounts. Some are asserted to be of some antiquity (that is, said to have occurred three or more ascending generations above ego) but others may be comparatively recent. The former may be subject to some differences of opinion amongst claimants when relied upon to assert membership of the claimant group. Since both the adoptee and adopting parent or parents are now long dead, it is not possible to gain first-hand field data about the adoptive relationship, its qualities and characteristics. Consequently, forming a view about the nature of the adoptive relationship must rely on the memory of the claimants or, most likely, on an oral tradition of unknown pedigree. The reliability of such conclusions is readily open to negative scrutiny.

At the heart of the difficulty is the concept of filiation. Anthropologists distinguish between descent and filiation (Sutton 2003, 188–191; Meyer Fortes 1959, 203). Filiation can be understood as the relationship between a child and his or her parents and grandparents, as recognised by peers and relations. Filiation in this context is the social, emotional and practical aspects of a family relationship between parent and child.[5] The substance of these relationships is the flux that quickens the descent of rights through genealogical connection. 'One-step filiation', 'two-step filiation' and 'serial filiation' are terms used to accommodate relationships between ego and their parent, grandparent and through successive ascending generations, respectively (Sutton 2003, 188). Descent is somewhat different and has been defined as 'a genealogical connexion recognised between a person and any of his ancestors or ancestresses. It is established by tracing a pedigree' (Meyer Fortes 1959, 206).

---

5   Oxford English Dictionary, *filiation*: 'the fact of being the child of a specified parent. Also a person's parentage; "Whose son one is"'.

It is commonly the case in native title claims that claimants cite serial filiative links with known forebears as the basis for their claims to country. Sutton observes, 'members of a descent group share a common, identifiable individual ancestor, or sometimes a set of ancestors such as two or three siblings, or a married couple, from whom they reckon their group membership' (2003, 189). Consequently, the normative system that is relied upon to determine rights to country is one based on descent from a named ancestor and the filiative links to ego's parents and grandparents. These filiative links generally rely on consanguineal ties. But in some cases they must rely on other forms of filiation, such as adoption. Transforming adoption into descent with recognition of filiation requires the transformation of a baby (or child) into a son or daughter. That such a transformation has taken place requires community acceptance in order to have validity within the country group membership. Social recognition and non-recognition are creatures of social relationships, local politics, personal preferences, antagonisms and even grudges. The question that generally excites debate is whether an adopted child, who is not a member of a country group lineage by birth, can acquire filiation through adoption. It is the anthropologist's job to show that the recognition of descent within an adoptive relationship is neither arbitrary nor contingent but rather based upon a system of customary principles.

A useful first step is to determine whether the *idea* of adoption is recognised in the Indigenous language of the claimants and is the subject of laws and customs. In some areas where I have worked, I have been able to collect a term from the claimants' language that translates as 'adopted'. In some cases the term is glossed as 'growing up' which may be understood to carry the meaning that the child is 'just like' a natural child in terms of gaining rights to country. However, the ethnography is the determining factor when deciding how to represent an adopted child on a genealogical chart and how they should be described in the explanatory text. Generally, in my experience, it is often accepted that if a man or woman 'grew up' a baby, then it would be accepted as his or her natural child. By amalgamating field data in relation to such principles that can be understood to endorse the view that an adoptive relationship has become equal to and indistinguishable from a relationship based on descent, implied filiation can be understood to provide a relationship that bears graphic representation as a child on a native title genealogy.

The difficulties that develop from complete reliance on an oral tradition with respect to adoptive relationships that are asserted to have occurred in times prior to the claimants' recollection finds no simple resolution. Sometimes it is possible to locate independent archival references that support the fact of an asserted adoption. For example, I once found a reference in a Native Welfare File that a man had paid all the education expenses of a child who was not his natural daughter, which lent weight to the assertion that he was the child's adopted father. In other cases I have canvassed a range of views from numerous claimants and found a clear consensus that an adoptive relationship was 'the same as' one based on biological descent. However, I have also come across many cases where an asserted adoption was subject to dispute amongst claimants. In these cases the best that can be done is to provide an account of the competing views and any relevant laws and customs and set out such independent archival accounts as might be available. In this way an expert view can be provided if there is sufficient data available – otherwise, the anthropologist must simply state that there is insufficient data available to form a concluded view as the claimant testimony is contested. In such cases it may be a matter to be determined by the court.

Genealogical truth

W.H.R. Rivers was sanguine about the accuracy of the genealogies he collected on Murray and Mabuiag islands. He described his 'extensive genealogies' as possessing 'a high degree of accuracy' (Rivers 1900, 76). On Murray he obtained genealogies 'from two or more independent sources, with the result that different accounts corroborated one another to an extent which forms the best guarantee of the truthfulness and accuracy of memory of the natives' (ibid., 76). On Mabuiag Island, Rivers:

> often compiled [his] genealogies sitting in the huts, or on the sand, with a crowd of women and children sitting round listening to the information which the men were giving me. In some cases, even the women were consulted. Often I was able to get several of the older men together, who consulted about points of detail, and it was obvious that some were looked up to by the rest as authorities on the subject. (ibid., 76)

Cross-checking and collaboration were the tools Rivers used to bring some certainty to the oral genealogical account. I stated above in the section 'Methodological and procedural issues' that, in the contested field of native title genealogical research, discussing family history with anyone other than the members of the family in question can be controversial. However, checking genealogical details before a jural public can provide confirmation of a general acceptance of the account as rendered – or, alternatively, alert the researcher to potential disputed ground. The availability of genealogies collected by earlier researchers, particularly those produced in the pre–native title area, provides a useful corrective to and confirmation of the contemporary account, although there is no certainty that genealogies collected by Elkin, Kaberry, Radcliffe-Brown or Tindale (and others) were without error. Rivers sought to establish that his data 'possessed a high degree of accuracy' (ibid., 77). In native title inquiries the anthropologist can strive for the best genealogical account available. However, there should be a clear qualification to any genealogical account that it is founded on data that reflect a social construction of the past. Orally transmitted genealogies are best understood as one account of family relationships and a representation of the way people understand themselves to be related to others, both living and dead. This means that oral genealogical accounts derived from different claimants may exhibit differences in detail or even in how relationships are calculated. In an oral genealogical tradition, the nature of relationships in the third and higher ascending generation level is sometimes assumed, imprecise or not remembered. Additionally, some relationships in lower generation levels may not be accurately recalled, particularly in the case of an extended family with numerous affinal relationships and many children. The larger the genealogy, the greater is the likelihood of errors or variations being identified. Genealogies will need to be subject to correction and emendation as new information comes to light. It is best to set out these qualifications as to the accuracy of the oral account at the beginning of any discussion of the genealogical data.

In some cases the oral account can be corroborated by historical or other documentary sources, as I have discussed above. The accuracy of archival records should not be taken for granted. Government officials were susceptible to error and prone to misunderstandings, particularly in cross-cultural encounters. The use of historical sources provides an adjunct to an oral account, enabling the construction of genealogies, in some cases, beyond that which relies on the comparatively shallow oral account.

Managing genealogical data

Anyone who has attempted to assemble genealogical accounts will know all too well that data are multitudinous and their representation poses some formidable challenges. In times past it was usual for anthropologists to draw up their genealogies by hand on long sheets of paper, glued end on end such that the total length of the genealogy was measured in many yards. There was, I recall, a certain pride that characterised some PhD research, occasioned by citing the length of the accompanying genealogy. These mute memorials to the genealogical method were inaccessible, impractical and had little to recommend them. Fortunately, the digital age has rendered them redundant and provided a range of alternatives that are now important tools for native title research.

Genealogical programs are widely available on the internet for download or obtainable in some stores. Prices are generally well below $100 and most provide updates, web support and tutorials. The principal problem with this software is its evident ephemeral nature, its sustainability over different operating platforms over time and the compatibility of different programs. At the time of writing (early 2018), two formerly popular programs (Family Tree Maker and The Master Genealogist) used by many Land Councils and Native Title Representative Bodies were no longer available as stand-alone programs, although many of us continued to use our existing software successfully. Despite the apparent demise of these programs, a search on the internet revealed 10 other programs that were readily available for purchase that appeared to perform in a very similar manner to those with which I am familiar. The choice of the software program is a matter for the commissioning organisation, which needs to consider suitability, cost, reliability and ease of use as well as security. Consultants undertaking genealogical research should be asked to use the same software or ensure that they can readily generate the common genealogical transfer data file (known as a GEDCOM file).[6] Organisations

---

6   'GEDCOM (an acronym standing for *Genealogical Data Communication*) is an open *de facto* specification for exchanging genealogical data between different genealogy software. GEDCOM was developed by The Church of Jesus Christ of Latter-day Saints (LDS Church) as an aid to genealogical research. A GEDCOM file is plain text (usually either ANSEL or ASCII) containing genealogical information about individuals, and meta data linking these records together. Most genealogy software supports importing from and exporting to GEDCOM format. However, some genealogy software programs incorporate the use of proprietary extensions to the format, which are not always recognized by other genealogy programs, such as the GEDCOM 5.5 EL (Extended Locations) specification. While GEDCOM X and several other files have been suggested as replacements, the current 1996 version remains the industry standard 20 years on.' www.en.wikipedia.org/wiki/GEDCOM accessed 28 November 2016.

will need to ensure that they maintain and update their genealogical files on a regular basis and that this is undertaken by a person who has had proper training and is equipped to manage the system and generate the data required. Genealogical databases are vulnerable to mis-entries, duplication and even erasure, so they need to be managed according to the same standards that apply to accounting software and digital archives. This is no simple or cheap task. However, genealogical databases will be required in the post-determination administration and will be of fundamental importance to the management of any benefits that develop from the recognition of native title. It is, then, essential to get this aspect of data management right from the outset.

Genealogical databases have significant advantages over hand-drawn charts. First, they can be easily updated should new or corrective material come to light. Second, they are easily accessible. Any named individual in the database can be readily found and details of his or her relationships, children, partners and personal particulars recovered. Third, they are easily used by the researcher in the field (on laptop or tablet), obviating the necessity to do battle with yards (metres) of paper. Fourth, they allow easy input of additional data including all important authorities for information, scanned copies of archival materials including genealogies, certificates and photographs. A single entry is, then, a gateway to a whole volume of supportive data, readily available to the researcher. Finally, they are easily transmissible *in toto* and relatively flexible and adaptive to other formats.

Some of these evident advantages also bring with them incipient dangers. Genealogical databases are vulnerable and like any digital content can be easily erased or corrupted. The research, then, needs to ensure that the database is properly managed and that it is subject to regular backups. The generation of digital charts (most programs have a choice of several different ones) is no substitute for publishing paper charts for safekeeping. Generally the charts produced by genealogical software do not provide for the symbols common to anthropological genealogical charts (as noted above) but rather produce names in boxes, with males distinguished from female by the nature of the box border – choice being afforded to the user in this regard. In some cases a hand drawn chart may be a better option for a native title report if some details or particulars are required to be shown. However, in terms of time and resources the production of digital charts by a genealogical program (whether printed out or not) is a far better option than attempting to draw extensive genealogies by hand – as was the case in times past.

The wealth of data that can be included in a genealogical database has significant implications for security and the protection of personal information. This is a matter that the researcher will need to discuss with the commissioning organisation, prior to the development of the database. Organisations holding genealogical databases will also need to consider the security of their genealogical materials in the same way as they seek to protect legal, accounting or written documents that are confidential to their organisation.

A genealogical database, like any digital compilation, is only as good as the data entered into it. I have inherited numerous genealogical databases, initiated by unknown researchers in times past with varying degrees of skill and accuracy. Sometimes it has taken me many hours to correct errors in the database, eliminate duplicate names and fix up wrong relationships. Genealogical databases are an essential tool of native title research. Like other aspects of this very practical enterprise, their use, maintenance and data input needs to be undertaken by those properly qualified and equipped for the complex task at hand. Genealogical research should never be seen as a secondary and lesser research task. It requires careful thought, adequate resources and experienced and trained researchers.

10

Compensation

Compensation and native title

The *Native Title Act* contemplated that the recognition of Indigenous rights to land might also require the payment of compensation where actions that occurred after the introduction of the *Racial Discrimination Act 1975* (Cth) on 31 October 1975 by the Commonwealth, states or territories had either impaired or extinguished native title. Consequently, the *Native Title Act* 'provides for the Federal Court to make determinations of native title and compensation' (*Native Title Act* 4(7)(a)). The term 'compensation' occurs in the 'Preamble' to the Act several times, being presented in association with the 'claims to native title'.[1] Listed as one of the topics covered by the Act is 'compensation for acts affecting native title' (*Native Title Act* 4(2)(b)), while a whole Division of the Act (Division 5) is dedicated to this matter. The compensation is to be calculated according to 'just terms for any loss, diminution, impairment or other effect of the act on their native title rights and interests' (section 51(1)). The payment of compensation is subject to qualifications relating to compulsory acquisitions (*Compulsory Acquisition Act* (defined in section 253)), partial extinguishment (sections 51(3), 240) and single payments (section 49). This is complex legislation and well beyond my expertise to

---

1   'It is important that appropriate bodies be recognised and funded to represent Aboriginal peoples and Torres Strait Islanders and to assist them to pursue their claims to native title *or compensation*' (*Native Title Act 1993*, Preamble, 3. Emphasis added).

discuss further, although reviews of this aspect of the *Native Title Act*, as well as how the compensation issue might be addressed by the Federal Court, are not hard to find in the available literature.[2]

Given the relative prominence that compensation receives in the *Native Title Act* it is perhaps surprising that the issue of compensation has received little public or scholarly attention. After an initial period during which the matter was considered in an abstract and largely theoretical manner,[3] the subject subsequently received scant attention while the scholarly debate and commentary focused on the principal business of the Federal Court in relation to the *Native Title Act*: the determination of applications for the recognition of native title. Compensation could only be awarded if there was evidence of an impairment or extinguishment of native title as a result of post-1975 acts. Claims for compensation are, then, post-native title actions so applications can only be made where native title can be shown to exist, a factor likely to limit the claims for compensation. The Yulara claim was a case in point where a failure to gain recognition of native title meant that the claim for compensation was dismissed.[4] At the time of writing (March 2018), claims for compensation were thin on the ground. The National Native Title Tribunal (NNTT) website, 'Native Title Applications, Registration Decisions and Determinations', revealed there to have been only 41 compensation applications[5] dating from February 1994, of which all but six had either been withdrawn, dismissed or discontinued and four determined.[6] For both the Tjayuwara Unmuru Compensation Application and the Barkandji (Paakantyi) People #11, it was determined that native title did not exist, rendering the applicants ineligible for compensation. The terms of the De Rose Hill settlement were agreed in mediation and have not been publicly disclosed. However, the case set the precedent for the awarding of compensation under the terms of the *Native Title Act*.[7] A recent attempt to gain compensation

---

2   See, for example, C. Humphry 1998, 'Compensation for native title: the theory and the reality', *E Law*, 5.1 (March 1998). www.murdoch.edu.au/elaw/indices/issue/v5n1.html accessed 23 December 2016. A short annotated reference list on 'native title compensation' was prepared by L. Wiseman in 2009, which contains some helpful references and comments (see L. Wiseman 2009, 'Native title compensation annotated reference list', Native Title Research Unit, AIATSIS 2009).

3   See, for example, Burke 2002.

4   *Jango v Northern Territory of Australia* [2006] FCA 318; 152 (31 March 2006) (Sackville J). Summary, 11 and 12.

5   www.nntt.gov.au/searchRegApps/NativeTitleClaims/Pages/default.aspx, accessed 15 March 2018.

6   Tjayuwara Unmuru Compensation Application, De Rose Hill Compensation Application, Town of Timber Creek and the Barkandji (Paakantyi) People #11.

7   See Whittaker and Bunker 2013, for a brief review.

in relation to the Gibson Desert Nature Reserve (WAD86/2012) was discontinued when the Federal Court found that petroleum tenures from the 1920s had extinguished exclusive possession rights. This significantly affected the state's compensation liability, and the claim group decided to discontinue the application in May 2016.[8]

Timber Creek, NT

In August 2016, the Federal Court handed down the first assessment of compensation in *Griffiths v Northern Territory of Australia* (Timber Creek).[9] Mansfield J ordered payment of $3.3 million to the native title holders (the Ngaliwurru and Nungali peoples). Of this some $512,000 was awarded for economic loss, $1.488 million was paid for interest that would otherwise have accrued and $1.3 million was paid for non-economic loss. The payment of $1.3 million for non-economic loss was in response to the claim for compensation for 'the diminution or disruption in traditional attachment to country and the loss of rights to live on, and gain spiritual and material sustenance from, the land' (Timber Creek [46]). In his judgment the trial judge, Mansfield J, identified the non-economic loss by the legal term 'solatium' following 'the term used by the Territory' (Timber Creek [59]).[10] The decision was appealed to the Full Federal Court which handed down its decision in July 2017. The appeal court dismissed most grounds of appeal (*Northern Territory of Australia v Griffiths*).[11] However, the Full Bench did find that the discount on compensation for economic loss should have been 65 per cent of the freehold value (rather than the 80 per cent provided by Justice Mansfield). The court also did not uphold some damages awarded for invalid future acts. Significantly, however, the Full Federal Court endorsed Mansfield's decision to award compensation for non-economic loss and his 'intuitive' approach for determining the amount to be paid reflecting 'just terms'

8   See www.centraldesert.org.au/native-title-item/gibson-desert/, accessed 24 December 2016.

9   *Griffiths v Northern Territory of Australia* (No. 3) [2016] FCA 900 (Mansfield J). See McGrath 2017 for a discussion of this case.

10   His Honour was of the view that, 'It is also appropriate to adopt the description "solatium" to describe the compensation component which represents the loss or diminution of connection or traditional attachment to the land. To the extent to which the LAA [*Lands Acquisition Act* (NT)] principles apply, both the Territory and the Commonwealth accepted that adaptation of that principle would accommodate an appropriate allowance for solatium. The Applicant was also content with using that expression. In my view, it provides a suitable focus for ensuring also that there is no overlap of the compensation awarded for the economic loss discussed above, and for this element of the compensation to which the Claim Group is entitled.' Timber Creek [300].

11   *Northern Territory of Australia v Griffiths* [2017] FCAFC 106 (Timber Creek appeal).

(Timber Creek appeal [394–396] and [420]). The judgements, as cited, are in the public domain at the time of writing. In February 2018, the High Court of Australia granted leave to the Commonwealth of Australia, the Northern Territory of Australia and the Northern Land Council (on behalf of the native title holders) to appeal the decision of the Full Court of the Federal Court of Australia ([2017] FCAFC 106). The appeal was expected to be heard in June or August 2018. Despite the appeal, the compensation claim and the ensuing legal process provide some useful indication of the role that anthropology might have in applications made to the Federal Court of this sort. That stated, it is important to bear in mind that this is an evolving and largely unresolved area of legal action, so the comments that follow may need to be revised in the light of the developing jurisprudence.

An initial but important observation that can be made in relation to the Timber Creek claim is that the majority of actions for which compensation might be sought are likely not to be the province of the anthropologist. Principal amongst these is the calculation of the value (in dollar terms) of land lost to native title. This seems clearly to be the province of land valuers and the trial judge devoted some time to a consideration of the experts and their opinions provided to the court in this regard (Timber Creek [393–434]). The applicant did employ an economic anthropologist (Professor Jon Altman) but his Honour stated that it was his 'intention to exclude from this category ['Consideration: non-economic loss'] of damages any element of economic loss'. Consequently, his Honour 'preferred to place no particular weight on [Professor Altman's] evidence for this purpose' (Timber Creek [367]).

It is possible that economic anthropology might be brought to bear on the question as to whether customary activity (such as hunting and gathering) should be factored in to calculated land values. However, in this case it would seem his Honour decided that such value (should it be material) was factored in to the 'less tangible cultural losses' and was understood to be a part of the claimants' 'attachment to country' rather than having any economic value ascribed to it (e.g. Timber Creek [364]).

With respect to compensation, economic loss is understood to include the quantum of interest that would have accrued on the sum had it been paid at the time the loss was suffered. An important issue here is whether the interest that might be paid is to be calculated according to simple or compound bases, the former being favoured by his Honour (Timber Creek [279]). This, again, is not a matter for social anthropology, although it was a matter that substantially occupied the attention of the court and the judgment.[12] In these considerations I observe that case law seems to have informed the judgment rather than expert opinion (cf. Timber Creek [285]).

'Intangible loss'

In the Timber Creek decision, Mansfield J sets out some legal principles for an entitlement to compensation paid as money despite the fact that there is no market value for what has been lost or diminished. His Honour wrote:

> 313. Nevertheless, it is important to recognise, as the parties accept, that the law provides an entitlement to compensation in money value even where there is no market for what is lost and where the value to the dispossessed holder rests on non-financial considerations: see e.g. Wurridjal at [337] per Heydon J. In Crampton v Nugawela (1996) 41 NSWLR 176, Mahoney A-CJ observed that:

> 'There is no yardstick for measuring these matters. Value may be determined by a market: there is no market for this. There is no generally accepted or perceptible level of awards, made by juries or by judges, which can be isolated and which can indicate the "ongoing rate" or judicial consensus on these matters. And there is, of course, no statutory or other basis. In the end, damages for distress and anguish are the result of a social judgment, made by the jury and monitored by appellate courts, of what, in the given community at the given time, is an appropriate award or, perhaps, solatium for what has been done.'

> 314. Albeit in the context of an appeal from a significant award of damages in a defamation claim, those observations are nevertheless apt to the present circumstances.[13]

His Honour was of the view that the court needed to consider a number of issues that might be relevant to assessing the quantum of the amount to be awarded. These included questions of causation and the nature of the claimed loss. This claimed loss might include the spiritual significance of places within traditional country, the effects of the compensable acts, the nature and extent of intangible loss and the extent of traditional country

---

12   Timber Creek [246–289].
13   ibid., [313–314].

affected (Timber Creek [315]). Also identified were such things as '"loss of amenities" or "pain and suffering" or reputational damage' (Timber Creek [318]). In this regard there appears to have been common ground between the parties. Payment of compensation for non-economic loss had been agreed in principle (Timber Creek [316]), as was the view that it should be assessed according to 'traditional laws and customs acknowledged and observed by the Claim Group'. There was also agreement that it be paid to the group as a whole[14] (Timber Creek [317]). In terms of making an assessment of compensation to be based on these and related issues, his Honour was of the view that 'evidence about the relationship with country and the effect of acts on that will be paramount' (Timber Creek [318]).

In this regard, his Honour was strongly of the view that it was the totality of the land that had to be considered, not specific parcels within it as dissociated entities. He wrote:

> The direct evidence of Alan Griffiths,[15] and the anthropological opinion evidence, does not depend on any proposition that some parts of Aboriginal landscape are more important than others. As Dr Palmer[16] observed, the 2002 paper of Professor Sansom[17] is in relation to the damage of loss, and 'the hurt feelings of a hunting ground, of a generalised area, a resource lost.' The broad expanse of the *kulungra* area[18] is a similar example in this case. As Professor Sansom accepted, the kind of contention advanced by the Territory and the Commonwealth that there can be a significant area of landscape that is unimportant to Aboriginal people, or that there could be an area that is devoid of spirituality, defies logic in the Aboriginal tradition.[19]

The trial judge listed three 'particular considerations' that he regarded as being of significance to the assessment of 'the appropriate amount of compensation' (Timber Creek [378]). The first was the construction of water tanks servicing the town water supply ('the *kulungra* area'). They were built on the path of a Dreaming track, action which his Honour found had 'caused clearly identified distress and concern' (Timber Creek

---

14   With the qualification in parenthesis, 'with the apportionment or distribution as between members being an intramural matter'. Timber Creek [316].

15   Footnote added: A senior claimant and native title holder of the area of the Timber Creek town site.

16   Footnote added: Expert anthropologist commissioned by the applicant.

17   Footnote added: Expert anthropologist commissioned by the first respondent. The article is Sansom 2002.

18   Footnote added: The area of Timber Creek where water tanks had been built, so damaging the track of the Dingo Dreaming (Timber Creek [352]).

19   Timber Creek [370].

[378]). The second were acts that had affected the claimants' ability to 'conduct ceremonial and spiritual activities' not solely in relation to parcels of land that had been alienated but on adjoining areas as well (Timber Creek [380]). Such a view is consistent with the finding that 'native title is a feature of a wider area of country than any of the particular and individual acts now under consideration' (Timber Creek [380]). Thirdly, his Honour found that compensable acts had 'to some degree' reduced the area over which the claimants could exercise their native title rights:

> each in an imprecise way has adversely affected the spiritual connection with the particular allotments, and more generally, which the Claim Group have with their country. Again, the point should be made that that connection is not divisible geographically, but each chipping away of the geographical area necessarily must have some incremental detriment to the enjoyment of the native title rights over the entire area. Associated with that collective diminution of the cultural and spiritual connection with land, is the sense of failed responsibility for the obligation, under the traditional laws and customs, to have cared for and looked after that land. Again, that is not geographic specific, save for the more important sites, but it is a sentiment which was quite obvious from the evidence led from the members of the Claim Group. That evidence, understandably, was more focused on the area of the town water tanks, as that is clearly a more significant area, and in other areas in the vicinity of Timber Creek which were also of significant importance.[20]

Accepting that the jurisprudence is still developing, these 'particular considerations' may be helpful when thinking about the sort of anthropology that might be embarked upon in future research that seeks to assist the court in determinations of native title compensation. His Honour's assessment of these specific considerations in terms of the quantum of the compensation for non-economic loss was founded on the evidence of the case as well as on the adoption of findings of prior native title judgments (Timber Creek [328] to [367]). The detail is beyond the scope of this review but is available for further analysis in the judgment, which is a matter of public record. The evidence to the court comprised complex ethnographic data. It was the product of claimant testimony as well as of the expert views of the anthropologists for the applicant (Palmer and Asche) and that of Sansom for the Territory. In summary, his Honour had regard to the particular and deeply spiritual relationship between the claimants and their countryside, understanding the latter comprised a totality of country rather than component parcels

---

20 ibid., [381].

of land that were the subject of compensable acts. This relationship and concomitant rights to the country also involved the exercise of a duty to protect and safeguard the integrity of that country, including through the conduct of (in this instance) restricted male ritual. Land alienated through European settlement and development rendered this duty impossible to acquit, resulting in guilt, pain, suffering and emotional distress. It also resulted in social opprobrium and even negative spiritual repercussions (Timber Creek [328–367]).

It was in the context of these understandings that the special spiritual relationship between Aboriginal people and their country had to be evaluated. This is the determinant of the anguish, emotional pain and suffering as well as the alienation of spiritually significant places that are relevant to the assessment of compensation (Timber Creek [376–377]). His Honour conceded that, given these considerations, 'the assessment of the appropriate compensation is a most complex one' (Timber Creek [374]).

Anthropological research and compensation claims

The research undertaken should always respond to the brief issued to the anthropologist. As the jurisprudence changes, the issues that the lawyers may consider will be helpful to the prosecution of their application will undoubtedly change. However, reviewing the judgment delivered in relation to non-economic compensation discussed above, I think it likely that some elements may remain constant. Compensation for non-economic loss is about emotional pain and suffering ('damages for distress and anguish'). The anthropologist's job is to provide understandings of how the pain and suffering might be manifest as well as how such emotional distress develops from the alienation of land – that is, the past acts post-1975 in the native title context. An understanding of emotional distress will depend upon a thorough appreciation of how the claimants relate to their country in terms of spiritual attachment. A concomitant of this relationship are the tenets of the system of proprietary rights to country and the duties in this regard that were required (under traditional law and custom) of the native title holders. It is the failure (or inability) to acquit these duties and responsibilities that lie at the heart of the emotional distress that is the basis for the calculation of the solatium. This analysis yields three research questions that are fundamental to the case law as it now stands. The first relates to the spiritual relationship between the native title holders and their country. The second relates to what might be termed broadly the management of country, including the exercise of duties and responsibilities. The third relates to emotional distress and suffering. In what follows I consider each of these in reverse order, commencing with sentiment and suffering and ending with spiritual attachment.

Sentiment

It is helpful when developing an understanding of another culture to explore concepts expressed in the language of that culture. This may provide an insight as to how those with whom we work think and feel. Given the importance of emotions to the assessment of compensation, such research into 'emic' categorisation can be considered as fundamental, which is why I have considered it first. When I commenced research on the Timber Creek compensation application in 2012 with Wendy Asche, I identified words in the local language (Ngaliwuru) that captured what we considered might be key concepts relevant to loss or alienation of country and damage to it. In Ngaliwuru *paark* expresses the idea that something is 'broken', and can be used of a pencil or a human leg or of the countryside itself. Generally, *paark* conveys the idea that the damage is not remediable – that is, something that is *paark* could probably not be fixed. *Maring* was used of something that was damaged or 'buggered up', having the sense of being 'spoilt', and can be used in conjunction with the word for country (*yakpali*) to mean 'spoiling the country'. Intense personal feelings that accompany an act of spoiling are termed *puru maring*. The word *puru* means 'insides', 'guts' but not specifically the stomach. The phrase then carries the general meaning of 'broken up or spoiled inside', which is presumably rather like English 'broken hearted' or perhaps better 'churned up inside' or 'gut wrenching'.[21] Similar phrases are found in other languages: *tuni kura*, for example, in Western Desert languages literally translates to 'bad stomach' but is a term used to express deep-felt emotional distress and upset, even anger. We were then able to explore and explain how the claimants' responses to the loss of land in the determination area had adversely affected their feelings and their emotions. This gave the necessary background and explanation as to why claimants were distressed as a result of those actions for which they sought compensation. This included concepts of pain, suffering and reputational

---

21 See Timber Creek [350] for evidence adduced on this.

damage, particularly as a result of an inability to perform a duty. In this way we sought to comprehend how the claimants experienced these emotions in terms of their own language and culture.

Not all research relating to claims for compensation will be conducted in areas where the native title holders have fluency in their own language. In such cases terms from Aboriginal English or even standard English will need to be explored. In my experience words common to standard English may be used by native title holders in a very particular way. Moreover, the relationship between certain actions taken with respect to country and those who regard it as their ancestral country is quite distinct and should be explored fully, elaborated and thoroughly comprehended. There should be no diminishment simply because the words used to express the emotions are (apparently) words of standard English.

Duty and the management of country

This should be more familiar ground and, given that a claim for compensation follows the native title application, data relating to these issues should have been included in the expert anthropological report. If the application went to trial (as had been the case at Timber Creek) these matters should have been addressed in evidence and the judgments of the court. While these are the obvious sources for these data, good fieldwork should build on these materials and so affirm the vitality of the system in the context of the compensation claim. I have discussed the presentation of materials relating to the exercise of duty and the management of country elsewhere in this book (see Chapter 3). At Timber Creek and elsewhere where I have worked the collection of words from the local language are keen aids to exegesis. Thus words for 'countryman' or 'traditional owner' (*yakpalimululu*), 'stranger' (*miyakari*), speaking to the spirits of the country ('calling out to country' or *pampaya*), the concept of dangerous country (*mutkiyan yakpali*) are helpful to the ensuing analysis. The ritual of introducing strangers to country to ensure the safety and proper conduct of visitors may also have a place here. In the Timber Creek area the ritual is known as 'head wetting' or *mulyarp* in the local language.

What is, then, needed are data that show that, according to traditional laws and customs, those with proprietary rights to country are considered to hold not only rights to their country, but to be required to exercise a duty to others with respect to that country. Inability to perform that duty is a breach of customary law and brings with it sanctions, social opprobrium, reproach and fear of supernatural consequences both for the visitor and owner. The Timber Creek judgment would also appear to indicate that the size of the country lost, the extent of the damage or impairment and the degree to which 'amenities' had been lost were relevant to the assessment of compensation. This probably means that the research should be undertaken with at least some basic knowledge of the location and extent of the potentially compensable land – information that was not made available to us during the Timber Creek research.[22]

Generally in Aboriginal Australia, duties to be exercised in relation to country include looking after the countryside to ensure its physical safety and so its spiritual integrity. Good research in relation to this aspect of customary land management will reveal that this duty extends well beyond the actual physical policing of the countryside and attempts to prevent unauthorised access and subsequent damage that is deemed to be contrary to what is acceptable, according to customary law. Much ritual activity, including the spiritual maintenance of certain objects through performance and song, is believed to sustain and enliven the countryside and so is an important part of a countryperson's duty to their land. An inability to perform these rituals could, then, be understood to result in emotional stress to those who feel it their duty to do so. These are matters that can rightly be examined in anthropological research undertaken with respect to a claim for compensation.

Spiritual assonance and total country

The third topic that can be identified from the Timber Creek judgment is also one that should find plenty of support from the prior anthropological native title literature, court transcripts and judgments. It is also a subject that I have discussed in terms of research approaches in an earlier chapter of this book (see Chapter 5). Although the actual areas of land that may be subject to claims for compensation will vary on a case by case basis, I think it likely that other applications will, like Timber Creek, include 'parcels' of land. In this case portions of the native title application area were excluded from the determination because they had been alienated. This raised the legal issue as to whether compensation should only be accorded in relation to the specific bounded parcels – an approach which Mansfield J rejected, as I have noted above.[23] It will,

---

22 Timber Creek [349].
23 His Honour found that 'a parcel-by-parcel approach to the assessment of those consequences is not appropriate, having regard to the fact that many of the acts in issue occurred some 30 or so years ago. They were incremental and cumulative' (Timber Creek [324]).

then, be an important consideration for the anthropological research to provide a full and comprehensive account of the relationship to country in terms of spiritual correspondence to the entirety of country. Mansfield J commented that the idea that land could be segmented and that parts were 'devoid of spirituality, defies logic in the Aboriginal tradition' (Timber Creek [370]). This finding was based on the evidence provided to the court. It is a matter that requires close attention in any anthropological research conducted in relation to a claim for compensation in the native title context.

Understanding our role

The awarding of an amount as compensation for the loss of native title rights and the emotional as well as financial consequences of this loss is a function of the *Native Title Act*. There is no necessity that it be shown to have parallels or correspondence with customary dealings within Australian Aboriginal or Torres Strait Islander societies. While the trial judge in Timber Creek made his assessment of compensation payable for non-economic loss according to customary considerations, straight economic loss (the value of the alienated blocks and loss of simple interest) are not matters that require any understanding of customary systems, beliefs, practices and normative systems. This necessarily means that there is much activity in making a compensation claim that is of no concern to the anthropologist and he or she will have no role to play in the legal agitation of these matters. It also means that the process of laying claim to compensation is even more centrally situated within the mainstream legal process than an application for recognition of native title.

These things admitted, the court has, to date at least, shown itself ready to accept that customary values and principles are central to an assessment of the compensation that should be paid as solatium for non-economic loss. Understanding this loss in terms that reflect the thoughts and feelings, hopes and fears of the claimants is very much the job of the anthropologist. The compass of the inquiry should, however, be constrained by the relevance the ethnographic data and accompanying exegeses can have to the legal matters likely to be of assistance to the court. As the jurisprudence develops further these issues may expand or contract. This is very much a question then of 'watch this space'.

11

The art of the possible

And in the end?

The native title era in Australian is necessarily ephemeral. Applications for the recognition of native title will not continue indefinitely. The time will come when no new claims are lodged and those made will be determined or will have been discontinued, for whatever reason. Looking back in the future, the native title era will be seen as a comparatively short period of time marked by the confluences of a postcolonial desire to right past wrongs, to bring certainty following the Mabo decision and as yet another component in the complex rubric of Indigenous–state relationships. And how will it be judged? The deficiencies and limitations of native title will be apparent from a reading of this book. Applications for the recognition of native title require complex and often expensive legal process over which the claimants have little or no control. Outcomes are uncertain as claimants cannot know beforehand how the court will respond to their application or how it will judge their claims. Proof of continuity is not only a problem in terms of the evidence required, but seems an especially unfair requirement for those so thoroughly dispossessed and who were the subject of multiple policies that worked to eradicate the very laws and customs now demanded of them by the native title law. For those Indigenous Australians who were hardest hit by the European settlement of their country and their cultural dispossession most marked, the requirements of the proof of native title are unlikely to be within reach. Generally, recognition of native title favours those in remote areas of Aboriginal Australia and disadvantages those in urban and rural parts

– particularly in the south. This seems hardly fair or equitable. Claims are giving rise to considerable disagreements between Indigenous groups that have split some communities. Redress is often sought through the courts thus furthering the entrenchment of the legal process in the determination of proprietary interests in land for Australian Indigenous minorities. While recognition of prior rights to country is undoubtedly of value to many Aboriginal people, the tangible and economic benefits of native title may prove elusive in some cases at least.

There will, then, be some harsh judgments. Some I expect will say that it was 'too little too late'. Others, better understanding the necessity of the native title legislation, may see it as compromised legislation vainly designed to fix a problem that started with the declaration of sovereignty by the British Crown in 1788 which had no simple or single solution.

I commenced this book with some recent history and outlined a number of the events, political thinking and idealism that led to the enactment of the *Native Title Act*. So, did the Act furnish the opportunities Paul Keating promised it would? Did it provide for certainty where only uncertainty had existed? Did it mark an historical turning point and the basis of a new relationship between Indigenous and other Australians? The fact is that after the Mabo High Court decisions there was a new relationship between Indigenous and other Australians; the *Native Title Act* can take no credit for that. The European settlers had not possessed vacant land. It belonged to someone else under a system of laws and customs that the settlers' law belatedly recognised. After Mabo, then, nothing was quite the same again, including the relationship between Indigenous Australians and the state. For the majority of the Australian landmass, legal certainty was achieved by the passage of the Act. While the process required to settle native title claims was for many protracted and expensive, the Act provided the framework for an orderly settlement of claims as well as for the negotiation of just terms for future acts over claimed land. As for the 'opportunities', some at least could have been embraced without native title or Mabo. The Keating government's response to Mabo was a trinity of measures. The first was the *Native Title Act*, validating past grants of land to the new settlers and setting up a process for the recognition of rights that had survived the colonisation of the continent. The second was the establishment of the Indigenous Land Fund managed by the Indigenous Land Corporation (ILC) that acquired, by purchase, alienated land for Indigenous groups (Sullivan 2009, 8). The third, a social justice package, was never implemented, prompting some to observe that the *Native Title Act* was never designed to provide the full remedy to Indigenous disadvantage.

> 3.75 Stakeholders have pointed out that the Native Title Act was never intended to be the sole response to Mabo v Queensland [No. 2] and to Indigenous demands for land justice, or to the economic and social disadvantage that is a consequence of dispossession. It was to be accompanied by a land fund and social justice package, thus providing a comprehensive response.
>
> 3.76 In 2008, the then Social Justice Commissioner, Dr Tom Calma, commented that 'the other two limbs did not eventuate in the form intended, and this abyss is one of the underlying reasons why the native title system is under the strain it is under today'.[1]

The functions and policies of the ILC are not my concern here, although they have received attention by other scholars (see, for example, Sullivan 2009). The *Native Title Act* has operated in a policy vacuum that has undoubtedly rendered it more imperfect than it otherwise might have been. That accepted, the *Native Title Act* has accomplished a number of things that had never been afforded to Indigenous Australians before. First, it gave recognition that Indigenous Australians were the first Australians and that their rights to country not only existed in a manner capable of recognition by the invaders but that some of these rights had endured to this day despite repeated acts of aggression, dispossession and ignorance. Second, the *Native Title Act* secured the rights of Indigenous Australians to have a say about any future acts planned for country subjected to a registered claim. Third, it provided a means whereby rights to country could be determined by the Federal Court to have validity, in the same way as other Australians enjoyed property rights. Native title applications provide one way (and perhaps now the only way) to gain recognition of rights within terms legitimated by the conquerors. Finally, it made provision for the payment of compensation (in some circumstances) for the loss of native title rights. These are no mean achievements.

---

1 Australian Law Reform Commission (ALRC) 2014, 63–64. (Original referencing footnotes excluded.)

The Single Noongar Claim

There are many examples of successful claims in Australia and I could, no doubt, have chosen others to illustrate my point. The native title process is one that requires an appreciation of the limitations of the *Native Title Act* as well as what is possible given the standards of proof required. But it is also one that needs an inspired appreciation of the possibilities. I was privileged to undertake the research for the Single Noongar Claim.[2] The report I wrote in this regard is published elsewhere and, as is therein noted, much transpired after the initial case was heard in 2005 (Palmer 2016, vii). While the final outcome was not a determination of native title by the Federal Court, protracted negotiations undertaken by the South West Aboriginal Land and Sea Council resulted in a number of Indigenous Land Use Agreements (ILUAs) approved by Noongar people at six authorisation meetings held across Noongar country between January and March 2015 (ibid.). This result was not without controversy and some members of the Noongar community strenuously opposed the settlement. One principal sticking point was that the claimants were required to exchange their native title rights for the rights and benefits contained in the ILUAs.

The agreement met a legal obstacle in early 2017 in the form of a court challenge to the Tribunal's registration of ILUAs that were to effect the arrangement. In short, it was asserted that not all applicants had signed the necessary documents. The majority of the Full Bench of the Federal Court found:

> 244 … if, in relation to any proposed area agreement, one of the persons who, jointly with others, has been authorised by the claim group to be the applicant, refuses, fails or neglects, or is unable to sign a negotiated, proposed written indigenous land use agreement, for whatever reason, then the document will lack the quality of being an agreement recognised for the purposes of the NTA [*Native Title Act*].[3]

---

2   Single Noongar Native Title Claim (W6006 of 2003 & W6012 of 2003); *Bennell v Western Australia* [2006] FCA 1243; *Bodney v Bennell* (2008) 167 FCR 84.
3   *McGlade v Native Title Registrar* [2017] FCAFC 10.

The decision had implications for many existing ILUAs that had not been signed by all named applicants, some of which involved substantial development projects.[4] The Turnbull government introduced the Native Title Amendment (Indigenous Land Use Agreements) Bill 2017 on 15 February 2017. The bill was referred to the Senate Legal and Constitutional Affairs Legislation Committee and was eventually passed into law on 22 June 2017. It confirmed the legal status of existing agreements and ensured that ILUAs could be registered without requiring the signature of every named applicant.[5]

There can be little doubt that from the outset there was much scepticism about the possibility of winning a combined claim to the whole of Australia's southwest. There was substantial opposition to such a claim from respondent groups; the more traditional anthropology available was, at least in part, not supportive of the proposition that there could be shown to be a continuity of laws and customs. The size of the claim, the disparate groups and internal wrangling all made this seem like a challenge of unprecedented proportions. However, the claimant evidence was strong, the legal case painstakingly and adroitly put together and the field data collected substantial. The trial judge found in favour of the applicant although the case was sent back to the court on appeal and reassigned to a new hearing, though no finding was made that rejected the claim. Out of this seemingly unpromising odyssey came recognition and benefits that merit more attention than they appear to have received. As a part of the agreement reached between the parties, the Western Australia Government passed the *Noongar (Koorah, Nitja, Boordahwan) (Past, Present, Future) Recognition Act 2016*. This is 'An Act for the recognition of the Noongar people as the traditional owners of lands in the south-west of the State'. The Preamble to the short Act, which provides recognition of the Noongar people and their lands, runs as follows:

> A. Since time immemorial, the Noongar people have inhabited lands in the south-west of the State; these lands the Noongar people call Noongar boodja (Noongar earth).

> B. Under Noongar law and custom, the Noongar people are the traditional owners of, and have cultural responsibilities and rights in relation to, Noongar boodja.

---

4   See, for example www.theaustralian.com.au/national-affairs/indigenous/george-brandis-failed-to-act-on-land-rights-warning/news-story/b9e1fe24cd744fdaadfa4250cb7a4906, accessed 9 March 2017.
5   www.aph.gov.au/Parliamentary_Business/Bills_Legislation/Bills_Search_Results/Result?bId=r5821, accessed 9 March 2017. *Native Title Amendment (Indigenous Land Use Agreements) Act 2017*.

C. The Noongar people continue to have a living cultural, spiritual, familial and social relationship with Noongar boodja.

D. The Noongar people have made, are making, and will continue to make, a significant and unique contribution to the heritage, cultural identity, community and economy of the State.

E. The Noongar people describe in Schedule 1 their relationship to Noongar boodja and the benefits that all Western Australians derive from that relationship.

F. So it is appropriate, as part of a package of measures in full and final settlement of all claims by the Noongar people in pending and future applications under the *Native Title Act 1993* (Commonwealth) for the determination of native title and for compensation payable for acts affecting that native title, to recognise the Noongar people as the traditional owners of the lands described in this Act.

[Assented to 16 May 2016]

The website of the WA Department of the Premier and Cabinet describes the settlement as:[6]

The South West Native Title Settlement (the Settlement) is the most comprehensive native title agreement proposed in Australian history, comprising the full and final resolution of all native title claims in the South West of Western Australia, in exchange for a package of benefits. The historic agreement involves around 30,000 Noongar people and covers approximately 200,000 square kilometres. The Settlement represents a significant investment in both the Noongar community and the shared future of the Western Australian community as a whole.

The Settlement will provide the Noongar people with long-term benefits and opportunities for developing Noongar interests. The Settlement will also provide an opportunity for the WA Government to work in partnership with the Noongar people to improve economic, social and cultural outcomes for the Noongar community. In addition the Settlement will deliver long term cost benefits to the WA Government and land users through the resolution of native title and the removal of all 'future act' obligations across the south west.

---

6   www.dpc.wa.gov.au/lantu/south-west-native-title-settlement/Pages/default.aspx, accessed 5 January 2017.

The settlement package included the establishment of a perpetual trust funded at $60 million per annum over 12 years, the establishment of regional corporations, and the creation of a Noongar land estate comprising a minimum of 320,000 hectares of Crown land into the Noongar Boodja Trust over five years. Other benefits included joint management programs, heritage agreements and economic development.[7]

The settlement package will always attract its critics and it will remain a matter for judgment as to whether the deal was a good one. The alternative would have been to go back to the court, fight the claim anew and await the uncertain outcome of the trial and the inevitable subsequent appeals. It stands as a good example of an alternative settlement and, on the facts as they are presented in the public domain, has much to recommend it. In considering this outcome, it is pertinent to remember that the settlement is the product of an application for the recognition of native title. Without the forthright engagement in that process by Noongar claimants, their lawyers and anthropologists, this end point is unlikely to have been reached. The reality of the native title legislation and the court findings provided the leverage that effected the final result.

And anthropologists?

Otto von Bismarck is credited with saying that politics was the art of the possible.[8] In coming to an understanding of what Bismarck may have meant by this saying, it is enough to note that Bismarck was a man who liked to get things done, generally in difficult circumstances and against the odds. The saying is apposite to native title, not because Bismarck can be understood to have any correspondence or likely sympathy with native title principles (in fact, the opposite is likely to be the case), but because it encapsulates a relevant principle. Like politics, native title is an art that seeks positive outcomes through an appreciation of what is practically obtainable. Anthropologists who participate in the native title process need to appreciate this fact and employ that comprehension when they become involved in a native title process. What is possible and

---

7   www.dpc.wa.gov.au/lantu/south-west-native-title-settlement/Pages/default.aspx, accessed 5 January 2017.
8   'Politics is the art of the possible, the attainable …the art of the next best'. (In German: Die Politik ist die Lehre vom Möglichen.) This sentence was printed in the newspaper *St. Petersburgische Zeitung*, on 11 August 1867. Reprinted in, *Fürst Bismarck: neue Tischgespräche und Interviews*, Vol. 1, p. 248 (1895). www.shmoop.com/quotes/politics-art-of-impossible.html, accessed 9 January 2017.

attainable is circumscribed by three factors. These I distil from the native title processes in which I have been involved. They are not, of themselves, particularly complex or mentally challenging. However, I am frequently surprised by the lack of attention to them by some of my anthropological colleagues.

Finding your role in the legal performance

Seeking recognition of native title is a legal process. It is a matter filed with the court, mediated by the court and ultimately determined by the court. Accordingly, it is a business for lawyers. It will be members of the legal profession that decide how cases are to be run, how time and resources are to be apportioned and, ultimately, how evidence will be presented to the court – including the evidence of experts. The legal process allocates a quite specific responsibility to anthropologists – usually as an expert and potentially as a witness. It is, then, essential to understand the dynamics of the process and the sort of role allocated to the researcher. In this anthropologists are unlikely to have, and indeed should not have, an executive or directing role. When it comes to the actual prosecution of the application an anthropologist in a native title claim occupies a back seat. This does not mean that we should be inattentive to the process or to the substance of what transpires, particularly if the matter goes to trial. Part of the job of the anthropologist is likely to be the provision of expert testimony to the court. In this the evidence of the claimants will provide an essential part of how we develop our opinions.

Anthropologists do, then, have a substantial and significant role to play in native title claims. This contribution is one that must be understood in the context of all other players. In this regard I have long advocated for a genuine, inclusive team approach to native title work involving the claimants, their lawyers, staff of the Representative Body as well as the anthropologist. The dynamic observable between lawyers and anthropologists has been subject to a degree of exploration and self-analysis – a matter I have reviewed elsewhere (Palmer 2007). So, part of the art of the possible is getting the balance right between those who run the claim (the lawyers) and those whose expertise is essential to the success of the application. This demands respect and patience on both sides but, above all, an appreciation of the true topography of the native title process which is governed by legal contours.

The role allotted to anthropologists in the native title process may not sit comfortably with all members of the profession. Some, perhaps as a result of long-term relationships formed through fieldwork or, to my mind, the erroneous belief that they have a privileged appreciation of those whom they study that is denied to others, consider they merit a role and status beyond that which is likely to be afforded to them. Anthropologists can all too easily become precious about their role and unrealistic about their importance. Anthropologists have been reluctant to let go of the special access they have enjoyed to social policy development and governance as well as input to the drafting of legislation relevant to Australia's Indigenous peoples. Anthropologists have, in my mind rightly, been replaced by advice from Indigenous individuals and groups who command now greater legitimacy.

Understanding our role as anthropologists should also instruct us to avoid straying too far into the legal domain of analysis and opinion. While it is important that we understand what is required of us in a native title claim, both in terms of the original legislation and subsequent case law, this does not equip us to present views and opinions that should more properly be furnished by trained lawyers.

Knowing what is required

Native title is elemental in the sense that its recognition is determined by specific elements identified in the originating legislation and subsequent case law. Aspects of the conditions necessary for the recognition of native title will be subject to substantial legal argument (if the matter goes to trial) and different lawyers will take different approaches – some wiser than others. This accepted, there remain some basic factors that are important to the proof of native title (or its disproof), all of which (I hope) I have covered in this book. For example, native title recognition requires that there be shown to be a continuity of laws and customs of the claimant group, including those laws and customs that relate to the holding of rights to land. These laws and customs must be shown to have substantial continuity since the acquisition of sovereignty by the British Crown. The laws and customs observable are the creation of a society. Consequently, that society (or societies) needs to be shown to have had continuity since the date of sovereignty in order that the laws and customs of that society are also understood to have remained, more or less, intact. If the system of gaining rights to country is via descent, then accounts of how the claimants trace descent from those who might properly be regarded as being in possession of the country of the claim at the time of sovereignty must be provided. The court or evaluating respondent groups (particularly the state or territory) will be interested to know to what degree the laws and customs of the claimant group have remained intact. They may be interested to know some detail about how the claimants relate to the country of the claim, how it holds special significance for them as well as how they visit and use the country today. There are many additional strands to what might be included in the anthropologist's account. However, these represent some of the more important ones.

What is not included and what needs to be excluded are data and expert opinion on matters that have no relevance to a native title application. There is sometimes a danger that a researcher has a favoured topic – a bone to pick or pet obsession – and sees the native title report as a means of expiation. If this is not eradicated in good time by counsel this can be quite damaging to the case: at worst eroding the credibility of the expert and at best wasting time and resources by the provision of distracting and irrelevant materials. Native title research is not an indulgence but should be a focused exercise in applied anthropology.

Understanding what is possible

Anthropologists work from their field data, which must provide a sound basis for the opinions and expert views advanced. Field data or the researcher's ethnography are the fundamental building blocks upon which the opinions are founded. Should the data not support positive responses to fundamental native title questions, then it is imperative to state that this is so. Whether commissioned by the applicant or the respondent, transparency, honesty and total absence of advocacy are all critical elements. The work of the anthropologist is to bring his or her expertise to bear on the issues identified for them openly, veraciously and with scholarship and proper study.

Forays into the battleground that is the contested realm of Australia's relationship with its Indigenous peoples readily evokes emotion, idealism, aspiration and demands for social justice. Native title activity readily affords a portal into this beleaguered world. Useful work may only be performed by anthropologists in this domain by understanding that their participation cannot allow for the distractions of partisan participation. Rather, it is a matter of appreciating what can be accomplished with what is available: the native title law, the reality of the claimant testimony and their ethnography, the archival evidence, and the role assigned to the expert. Those directly involved in the realising of native title aspiration need to accept that some claims will never gain the recognition the claimants seek. The onus of proof rests with the applicant and the bar is set high. Alternatives to recognition of native title rights should never be discounted.

Native title is a practice for lawyers and anthropologist that seeks to utilise federal legislation that sought to bring certainty in the face of apparent uncertainty. This developed from the acceptance by the High Court that Indigenous rights had not been wholly extinguished and that *terra nullius* was a convenient legal fiction without basis or foundation. It was legislation born of political necessity and tempered by a desire to engineer social advantage in the face of persistent and historical disadvantage. It was but one of three measures to remedy past wrongs – one of which never saw the light of day. This provides for an imperfect and potentially unsatisfactory means whereby prior rights can be recognised. In this, given the circumstances, the legal context and the imperfections, a sound appreciation of what is possible is paramount. A necessary part of the pursuit of native title must be a proper and realistic understanding of what it is capable of achieving and, most importantly, what it is unlikely to achieve. This is the exercise of the art of the possible. It is an art and a practice that must be based on both a comprehensive understanding of what can be accomplished by application of compromised legislation as well as the scholarly representation of the ethnography that it is the anthropologist's task to comprehend and explain to others. Australian anthropology pursued in the context of native title claims is a specialised endeavour in that it requires a thorough understanding of the parameters that circumscribe the hoped-for outcomes and their interrelationships. This book has sought to explore some of these.

References

Altman, J. 1983. *Aborigines and mining royalties in the Northern Territory.* Australian Institute of Aboriginal Studies, Canberra.

Australian Law Reform Commission (ALRC). 2014. *Review of the Native Title Act 1993.* Discussion Paper 82. Australian Law Reform Commission, Sydney.

Australian Law Reform Commission (ALRC). 2015. *Connection to country: Review of the Native Title Act 1993 (Cth).* ALRC Report 126. Australian Law Reform Commission, Sydney.

Bamford, S. and Leach, J. 2009. 'Pedigrees of knowledge: Anthropology and the genealogical method.' In *Kinship and beyond: The genealogical model reconsidered.* S. Bamford and J. Leach (eds). Berghahn Books, New York, pp. 1–23.

Barnes, J.A. 1967. 'Genealogies.' In *The craft of social anthropology.* L. Epstein (ed.). Tavistock, London, pp. 101–127.

Barron, O. 1911. 'Genealogy.' In *Encyclopædia Britannica* (11th ed.). Cambridge University Press, Cambridge.

Barwick, L. 1999. Transcript of archival field tape No. 9 A 13360–A1 3361 (side 1). Record of interview by Tindale with Don and Nuna Roundhead, recorded, Kalgoorlie 1966. Australian Institute of Aboriginal and Torres Strait Islander Studies, Canberra.

Bastin, R. and Morris B. 2004. 'Introduction.' In *Expert knowledge: First world peoples, consultancy and anthropology.* B. Morris and R. Bastin (eds.). Berghahn Books, New York, pp. 1–11. doi.org/10.3167/ 015597703782353041

Bates, D. 1913. 'Social organisation of some WA tribes by Mrs D.M. Bates 1913.' Typescript ms. Acc 1212A, Battye Library, Perth.

Bates, D. 1985. *The native tribes of Western Australia*. I. White (ed.). National Library of Australia, Canberra.

Bates, D. n.d. Folio 9/31. Ms 365. National Library of Australia, Canberra.

Bates, D. n.d. Folio 68/23. National Library of Australia, Canberra.

Bates, D. n.d. Typescript from notebook 15. National Library of Australia, Canberra.

Bates, D. various dates. Unpublished manuscripts. Ms 365. National Library of Australia, Canberra.

Beals, R.L. and Hoijer, H. 1971. *An introduction to anthropology*. Macmillan, New York and London.

Beattie, J. 1964. *Other cultures: Aims, methods and achievements in social anthropology*. Routledge and Kegan Paul, London.

Bell, D. 1983. *Daughters of the Dreaming*. McPhee Gribble/George Allen and Unwin, Melbourne and North Sydney.

Bell, D. 2005. '"Women's business": What is it?' In *Aboriginal religions in Australia: An anthology of recent writings*. M. Charlesworth, F. Dussart and H. Morphy (eds). Ashgate, Burlington, Vermont, pp. 81–92.

Berndt, R.M. 1951. *Kunapipi: A study of an Australian Aboriginal religious cult*. Cheshire, Melbourne.

Berndt, R.M. 1952. *Djanggawul: An Aboriginal religious cult of north-eastern Arnhem Land*. Routledge and Kegan Paul, London.

Berndt, R.M. 1959. 'The concept of the "tribe" in the Western Desert of Australia.' *Oceania*, 30, pp. 81–107. doi.org/10.1002/j.1834-4461.1959.tb00213.x

Berndt, R.M. 1965. 'Law and order in Aboriginal Australia.' In *Aboriginal man in Australia*. R.M. Berndt and C.H. Berndt (eds). Angus and Robertson, Sydney, pp. 167–206.

Berndt, R.M. 1970. *The sacred site: The western Arnhem Land example*. Australian Institute of Aboriginal Studies, Canberra.

Berndt, R.M. 1976. 'Territoriality and the problem of demarcating sociocultural space.' In *Tribes and boundaries in Australia*. N. Peterson (ed.). Australian Institute of Aboriginal Studies, Canberra, pp. 133–161.

Berndt, R.M and Berndt, C.H. 1964. *The world of the first Australians*. Ure Smith, Sydney (first edition).

Berndt, R.M and Berndt, C.H. 1988. *The world of the first Australians*. Australian Institute of Aboriginal and Torres Strait Islander Studies, Canberra.

Berndt, R.M and Berndt, C.H. 1993. *A world that was: The Yaraldi of the Murray River and the Lakes, South Australia*. Melbourne University Press, Melbourne.

Biernoff, D. 1978. 'Safe and dangerous places.' In *Australian Aboriginal concepts*. L.R. Hiatt (ed.). Australian Institute of Aboriginal Studies, Canberra, pp. 93–105.

Birdsell, J.B. 1970. 'Local group composition among the Australian Aborigines: A critique of the evidence from field work conducted since 1930.' *Current Anthropology*, 11, pp. 115–141. doi.org/10.1086/201114

Blackshield, S., Sackett, L. and Hughston, V. 2011. 'Good, bad and ugly connection reports: A panel discussion at the "Turning the Tide: Anthropology for native title in South-East Australia" workshop, Sydney 2010.' In *Unsettling anthropology: The demands of Native Title on worn concepts and changing lives*. T. Bauman and G. Macdonald (eds). Australian Institute of Aboriginal and Torres Strait Islander Studies, Canberra, pp. 102–121.

Brandenstein, C.G. von. 1973. 'Place names of the North-west.' *The Western Australian Naturalist*, 12.5, pp. 97–107.

Burke, P. 2002. 'How can judges calculate native title compensation?' AIATSIS Native Title Research Unit, Australian Institute of Aboriginal and Torres Strait Islander Studies, Canberra.

Burke, P. 2007. 'The problem when flexibility is the system.' *Anthropological Forum*, 17.2, pp. 163–165.

Burnside, S. 2012. 'Outcomes for all? Overlapping claims and intra-indigenous conflict under the *Native Title Act.' Australian Indigenous Law Review*, 16.1, pp. 2–14.

Cane, S. 2002. *Pila Nguru*. Fremantle Arts Centre Press, Fremantle, WA.

Christensen, W.J.K. 1981. 'The Wangkayi way: Tradition and change in a reserve setting.' PhD thesis, University of Western Australia, Perth.

Cowlishaw, G. 2003. 'Euphemism, banality, propaganda: Anthropology, public debate and Indigenous communities.' *Australian Aboriginal Studies*, 1, pp. 2–18.

Cowlishaw, G. 2010. 'Helping anthropologists, still.' In *Culture crisis: Anthropology and politics in Aboriginal Australia*. J. Altman and M. Hinkson (eds). University of New South Wales Press, Sydney, pp. 45–60.

Curr, E. 1883. *Recollections of squatting in Victoria, then called the Port Phillip District (from 1841 to 1851)*. George Robertson, Melbourne.

Curr, E.M. 1886. *The Australian race: Its origin, languages, customs, places of landing in Australia, and the routes by which it spread itself over that continent*. (Vol. I). Government Printer, Melbourne.

Davidson, D.S. 1938. *An ethnic map of Australia*. American Philosophical Society, Philadelphia.

Davies, G. 2005. 'Court appointed experts.' *Queensland University of Technology Law and Justice Journal*, 89, 5.1. Available at www.austlii.edu.au/au/journals/QUTLawJJl/2005/5.html

Dawson, J. 1881. *Australian Aborigines: The languages and customs of several tribes of Aborigines in the western district of Victoria*. George Robertson, Melbourne.

Dowsett, J.A. 2009. 'Beyond Mabo: Understanding native title litigation through the decisions of the Federal Court.' Paper presented to the LexisNexis National Native Title Law Summit, Federal Court of Australia. Available at www.fedcourt.gov.au/digital-law-library/judges-speeches/justice-dowsett/dowsett-j-20090715

Durkheim, E. 1915. *The elementary forms of the religious life*. Allen and Unwin, London.

Edmunds, M. 1995. 'Conflict in native title claims.' Land, Rights, Laws: Issues of Native Title, Issues Paper No. 7, Australian Institute of Aboriginal and Torres Strait Islander Studies, Canberra.

Elkin, A.P. 1932. 'Nyul Nyul social organisation.' Unpublished manuscript. Elkin papers, University of Sydney, Sydney.

Elkin, A.P. 1933. 'Totemism in north-western Australia (the Kimberley Division).' *Oceania*, 3, pp. 257–296. doi.org/10.1002/j.1834-4461. 1933.tb00074.x

Elkin, A.P. 1934. 'Cult-totemism and mythology in northern South Australia.' *Oceania*, 5.2, pp. 171–192.

Elkin, A.P. 1939. 'Introduction' to Kaberry, P. *Aboriginal woman: Sacred and profane*. Routledge, London and New York, pp. xxvii–xli.

Elkin, A.P. 1945. *The Australian Aborigines: How to understand them*. Angus and Robertson, Sydney.

Fortes, M. 1959. 'Descent, filiation and affinity: A rejoinder to Dr Leach (Parts I and II).' *Man*, 59, pp. 193–197, 206–212, 301, 309. doi.org/ 10.2307/2798060

French, R. 2003. 'A moment of change – personal reflections on the National Native Title Tribunal 1994–98.' *Melbourne University Law Review*, 18, 27(2). Available at www.austlii.edu.au/au/journals/ MelbULawRw/2003/18.html

Gennep, A. van 1960. *The rites of passage*. Routledge and Kegan Paul, London.

Glaskin, K. 2007. 'Manifesting the latent in native title litigation.' *Anthropological Forum*, 17.2, p. 167.

Glaskin, K. 2017. *Crosscurrents: Law and society in a native title claim to land and sea*. University of Western Australia Press, Crawley, Western Australia.

Gluckman, M. 1943. *Essays on Lozi land and royal property*. The Rhodes-Livingstone Institute Papers, No. 10. Livingstone, Northern Rhodesia.

Gluckman, M. 1977. *Politics, law and ritual in tribal society*. Basil Blackwell, Oxford.

Gray, P. 2000. 'Do the walls have ears? Indigenous title and courts in Australia.' *Australian Indigenous Law Reporter*, 1, 5(1).

Grey, G. 1841. *Journals of two expeditions of discovery in North-West and Western Australia, during the years 1837, 1838, and 1839*, Vol. 2. T. and W. Boone, London.

Haddon, A.C. 1890. 'The ethnography of the western tribe of Torres Straits.' *Journal of the Anthropological Institute of Great Britain and Ireland*, 19, pp. 297–442. doi.org/10.2307/2842024

Haddon, A.C. (ed.). 1901–1935. *Reports of the Cambridge anthropological expedition to Torres Strait*, Vols 1–6. Cambridge University Press, Cambridge.

Hamilton, A. 1982. 'Descended from father, belonging to country: Rights to land in the Australian Western Desert.' In *Politics and history in band societies*. E. Leacock and R. Lee (eds). Cambridge University Press, Cambridge, pp. 85–108.

Hawke, S. and Gallagher, M. 1989. *Noonkanbah: Whose land, whose law?* Fremantle Arts Centre Press, Fremantle.

Herzfeld, M. 2001. *Anthropology: Theoretical practice in culture and society*. Blackwell, Oxford.

Hiatt, L.R. 1962. 'Local organisation among the Australian Aborigines.' *Oceania*, 32, pp. 267–286. doi.org/10.1002/j.1834-4461.1962.tb01782.x

Hiatt, L.R. 1965. *Kinship and conflict: A study of an aboriginal community in northern Arnhem Land*. The Australian National University, Canberra.

Hiatt, L.R. 1966. *Arguments about Aborigines*. Cambridge University Press, Cambridge.

Hiatt, L.R. 1984. 'Aboriginal landowners: Contemporary issues in the determination of traditional aboriginal land ownership.' Oceania Monograph No. 27, University of Sydney, Sydney.

Hiley, G. 2008. 'What is the relevant "society" for the purposes of native title? Will any society do?' *Native Title News*, 8, pp.143–147.

Hiley, G. and Levy, K. 2006. 'Native title claims resolution review.' (Report, Attorney-General's Department, 31 March 2006.) Australian Attorney-General's Department, Canberra.

Holcombe, S. 2004. 'The sentimental community: A site of belonging. A case study from Central Australia.' *The Australian Journal of Anthropology*, 15.2, pp. 163–184. doi.org/10.1111/j.1835-9310.2004. tb00250.x

Horton, D. 1994 (ed.). 'Aboriginal Australia.' Map accompanying *The encyclopaedia of Aboriginal Australia*. Australian Institute of Aboriginal and Torres Strait Islander Studies, Canberra.

Howard, M.C. 1976. 'Nyoongah politics: Aboriginal politics in the south-west of Western Australia.' PhD thesis, University of Western Australia.

Howard, M.C. 1979. 'Aboriginal Society in south-western Australia.' In *Aborigines of the West*. R.M. and C.H. Berndt (eds). UWA Press, Nedlands, pp. 90–99.

Howitt, A.W. 1904. *The native tribes of south-east Australia*. Macmillan, London. (Facsimile edition 1996, Australian Institute of Aboriginal and Torres Strait Islander Studies, Canberra.)

Hughston, V. and Jowett, T. 2014. 'In the native title "hot tub": Expert conferences and concurrent expert evidence in native title.' *Land, rights, laws: Issues of Native Title*. 6.1. Australian Institute of Aboriginal and Torres Strait Islander Studies, Canberra.

Humphry, C. 1998. 'Compensation for native title: The theory and the reality.' *Murdoch University Electronic Journal of Law*, 5.1 (March 1998). Available at www.austlii.edu.au/au/journals/MurUEJL/1998/2.html

Jones, P. 1995. 'Norman B. Tindale. 12th October 1900 – 19 November 1993. An obituary.' *Records of the South Australian Museum*, 28.2, pp. 159–176.

Kaberry, P. 1935. Correspondence to A.P. Elkin. University of Sydney Archives, Ms 739 2, item 14.

Kaberry, P. 1936. 'Spirit-children and spirit-centres of the north Kimberley division, Western Australia.' *Oceania*, 6.4, pp. 392–400.

Kaberry, P. 1937. 'Notes on the languages of East Kimberley, north-west Australia.' *Oceania*, 8.1, pp. 90–103. doi.org/10.1002/j.1834-4461. 1937.tb00407.x

Kaberry, P. 1938. 'Totemism in east and south Kimberley, north-west Australia.' *Oceania*, 8.3, pp. 265–288. doi.org/10.1002/j.1834-4461. 1938.tb00422.x

Kaberry, P.M. 1939. *Aboriginal woman: Sacred and profane*. Routledge, London.

Kapferer, B. 2000. 'Star wars: About anthropology, culture and globalisation.' *The Australian Journal of Anthropology*, 11.3, pp. 174–198. doi.org/10.1111/j.1835-9310.2000.tb00055.x

Keen, I. 1997. 'The Western Desert vs. the rest: Rethinking the contrast.' In *Scholar and sceptic: Australian Aboriginal studies in honour of L.R. Hiatt*. F. Merlan, J. Morton and A. Rumsey (eds). Aboriginal Studies Press, Canberra, pp. 65–94.

Keen, I. 1999. 'Norman Tindale and me: Anthropology, genealogy, authenticity.' In *Connections in native title: Genealogies, kinship and groups*. J.D. Finlayson, B. Rigsby and H.J. Beck (eds). Centre for Aboriginal Economic Policy Research, The Australian National University, Canberra, pp. 99–105.

Keen, I. 2004. *Aboriginal economy and society. Australia at the threshold of colonisation*. Oxford University Press, South Melbourne.

Kolig, E. 1972. '*Bi:n* and *Gadeja*: An Australian Aboriginal model of the European society as a guide in social change.' *Oceania*, 43.1, pp. 1–22.

Kolig, E. 1977. 'From tribesman to citizen: Change and continuity in social identities among Kimberley Aborigines.' In *Aborigines and change*. R.M. Berndt (ed.). Australian Institute of Aboriginal Studies, Canberra, pp. 33–53. doi.org/10.1002/j.1834-4461.1972.tb01193.x

Kolig, E. 1978. 'Dialectics of Aboriginal life-space.' In *'Whitefella Business': Aborigines in Australian politics*. M.C. Howard (ed.). Institute for the Study of Human Issues, Philadelphia, 1978, pp. 49–79.

Kolig, E. 1980a. 'Noah's Ark revisited: On the myth–land connection in traditional Aboriginal thought.' *Oceania*, 51, pp. 118–132. doi.org/10.1002/j.1834-4461.1980.tb01962.x

Kolig, E. 1980b. 'Report on Aboriginal relationships to land centred on the pastoral properties of Liveringa and Blina in the West Kimberley.' Report for Whitestone Petroleum Australia Ltd, Perth.

Kolig, Erich 1980c. 'Captain Cook in the Western Kimberleys'. In *Aborigines of the West, their past and their present*. R.M and C.H. Berndt (eds). University of Western Australia Press, Perth. pp. 274–282.

Kolig, E. 1981. *The silent revolution. The effects of modernisation on Australian Aboriginal religion*. Institute for the Study of Human Issues, Philadelphia.

Kolig, E. 1982. 'An obituary for ritual power.' In *Aboriginal power in Australian society*. M.C. Howard (ed.). University of Queensland Press, St Lucia, pp. 14–31.

Kolig, E. 1987. 'Post-contact religious movements in Australian Aboriginal society.' *Anthropos*, 82, pp. 251–259.

Kolig, E. 1988. *The Noonkanbah Story*. University of Otago Press, Dunedin.

Kolig, E. 1989. *Dreamtime politics: Religion, world view and utopian thought in Australian Aboriginal society*. Dietrich Reimer Verlag, Frankfurt.

Land Tribunal, Queensland, 1994. 'Aboriginal Land Claim to Simpson Desert National Park. Report of the Land Tribunal established under the Aboriginal Land Act 1991 to the Hon the Minister for Lands.' Land Tribunal, Brisbane.

Lattas, A. and Morris, B. 2010a. 'The politics of suffering and the politics of anthropology.' In *Culture crisis: Anthropology and politics in Aboriginal Australia*. J. Altman and M. Hinkson (eds). University of New South Wales Press, Sydney, pp. 61–87.

Lattas, A. and Morris, B. 2010b. 'Embedded anthropology and the Intervention.' *Arena*, September. Available at arena.org.au/embedded-anthropology-and-the-intervention/

Layton, R. 1983. 'Ambilineal and traditional Pitjantjatjara rights to land.' In *Aborigines, land and land rights*. N. Peterson and M. Langton (eds). Australian Institute of Aboriginal Studies, Canberra, pp. 15–32.

Maddock, K. 1974. *The Australian Aborigines: A portrait of their society*. Penguin, Harmondsworth.

Maddock, K. 1981. 'Warlpiri land tenure: A test case in legal anthropology.' *Oceania*, 52.2, pp. 85–102.

Martin, D. 2004. 'Capacity of anthropologists in native title practice.' Report to the National Native Title Tribunal. Anthropos Consulting Services, Canberra.

Mathew, J. 1910. *Two representative tribes of Queensland: With an inquiry concerning the origin of the Australian race.* T. Fisher Unwin, London.

Mathews, R.H. 1898a. 'Australian divisional systems.' *Journal of the Royal Society of New South Wales*, 32, pp. 66–87.

Mathews, R.H. 1898b. 'The group divisions and initiation ceremonies of the Barkunjee tribes.' *Journal of the Royal Society of New South Wales*, 32, pp. 241–255.

Mathews, R.H. 1898c. 'The Victorian Aborigines: Their initiation ceremonies and divisional systems.' *American Anthropologist*, 11, pp. 325–343. doi.org/10.1525/aa.1898.11.11.02a00000

Mathews, R.H. 1898d. 'Initiation ceremonies of Australian tribes.' *Proceedings of the American Philosophical Society*, 37, pp. 55–73.

Mathews, R.H. 1898e. 'Divisions of Queensland Aborigines.' *Proceedings of the American Philosophical Society*, 37, pp. 327–335.

Mathews, R.H. 1900. 'The origin, organization and ceremonies of the Australian Aborigines.' *Proceedings of the American Philosophical Society*, 39, pp. 556–578 and map (plate VIII) facing page 574.

McGrath, P. 2017. 'Native title anthropology after the Timber Creek decision.' *Land, rights, laws: Issues of Native Title.* 6.5, January 2017. Australian Institute of Aboriginal and Torres Strait Islander Studies, Canberra.

McGrath, P. and Acciaioli, G. 2016a. 'Preliminary results from the AAS National Survey of Anthropological Practice 2015.' Unpublished report provided by the authors, Australian Anthropological Society.

McGrath, P. and Acciaioli, G. 2016b. 'Blurred boundaries in anthropological practice in Australia: What the AAS survey tells us about what we are doing.' Paper presented at Anthropocene Transitions, AAS 2016 Annual Conference, Sydney, 12–16 December 2016.

McGregor, W. 1988. 'A survey of the languages of the Kimberley region – report from the Kimberley Language Resource Centre.' *Australian Aboriginal Studies*, 1988.2, pp. 90–102.

Meggitt, M. 1962. *Desert people*. Angus and Robertson, Sydney.

Meggitt, M. 1966. *Gadjari among the Walbiri Aborigines of Central Australia*. Oceania Monograph No. 14, Sydney.

Monaghan, P. 2003. 'Laying down the country: Norman B. Tindale and the linguistic construction in the north-west of South Australia.' PhD thesis, University of Adelaide.

Morphy, H. 1993. 'Colonialism, history and the construction of place: The politics of landscape in Northern Australia.' In *Landscape, politics and perspectives*. B. Benders (ed.). Berg, Providence, pp. 312–338.

Morphy, H. 1995. 'Landscape and the reproduction of the ancestral past.' In *The anthropology of landscape: Perspectives on place and space*. E. Hirsch and M. O'Hanlon (eds). Oxford University Press, Oxford, pp. 184–209.

Morphy, H. 2006. 'The practice of an expert: Anthropology in native title.' *Anthropological Forum*, 16.2, pp. 135–151. doi.org/10.1080/00664670600768342

Morris, B. 2004. 'Anthropology and the state: The ties that bind.' In *Expert knowledge: First world peoples, consultancy and anthropology*. B. Morris and R. Bastin (eds). Berghahn Books, New York, pp. 102–15.

Morton, J. 1988. 'Introduction.' In *Children of the desert II. Myths and dreams of the Aborigines of Central Australia by Geza Roheim*. J. Morton (ed.). Oceania Publications, Sydney, pp. vii–xxx.

Morton, J. 2007. 'Sansom, Sutton and Sackville: Three expert anthropologists?' *Anthropological Forum*, 17.2, pp. 70–73.

Mulvaney, D.J. 1975. *The prehistory of Australia*. Penguin Books, Harmondsworth.

Myers, F.R. 1986. *Pintupi country, Pintupi self: Sentiment, place, and politics among Western Desert Aborigines*. Smithsonian Institute Press, Washington and London and Australian Institute of Aboriginal Studies, Canberra.

Neate, G 2010. 'Achieving real outcomes from native title claims.' In *Dialogue about land justice.* L. Strelein (ed.). Aboriginal Studies Press, Canberra, pp. 198–252.

O'Farrell, P. 1979. 'Oral history: Facts and fiction.' *Quadrant,* November 1979, pp. 3–9.

Palmer, K. 1981. 'Aboriginal religion and the ordering of social relations.' PhD thesis, University of Western Australia.

Palmer, K. 2007. 'Anthropology and applications for the recognition of Native Title.' *Land, Rights, Laws: Issues of Native Title.* Issues paper 3.7. Australian Institute of Aboriginal and Torres Strait Islander Studies, Canberra.

Palmer, K. 2009. 'Societies, communities and Native Title.' *Land, rights, laws: Issues of Native Title.* Issues paper 4.1. Native Title Unit, Australian Institute of Aboriginal and Torres Strait Islander Studies, Canberra.

Palmer, K. 2010a. 'Understanding another ethnography: The use of early texts in native title inquiries.' In *Dilemmas in applied native title anthropology in Australia.* T. Bauman (ed.). Australian Institute of Aboriginal and Torres Strait Islander Studies, Canberra, pp. 72–96.

Palmer, K. 2010b. 'Societies, communities and native title.' In *Dialogue about land justice: Papers from the National Native Title Conference.* L. Strelein (ed.). Aboriginal Studies Press, Canberra, pp. 139–158.

Palmer, K. 2011a. 'Piety, fact and the oral account in native title claims.' *Anthropological Forum,* 21.3, pp. 269–286.

Palmer, K. 2011b. 'Anthropologist as expert in native title cases in Australia.' AIATSIS Native Title Research Unit, Australian Institute of Aboriginal and Torres Strait Islander Studies, Canberra. Available at aiatsis.gov.au/publications/products/anthropologist-expert-native-title-cases-australia

Palmer, K. 2016. *Noongar people, Noongar land.* Aboriginal Studies Press, Canberra.

Peterson, N. 1976. 'The natural and cultural areas of Aboriginal Australia.' In *Tribes and boundaries in Australia.* N. Peterson (ed.). Australian Institute of Aboriginal Studies, Canberra, pp. 50–71.

Peterson, N. 1983. 'Rights, residence and process in Australian territorial organisation.' In *Aborigines, land and land rights.* N. Peterson and M. Langton (eds). Australian Institute of Aboriginal Studies, Canberra, pp. 134–145.

Peterson, N. 2006. '"I can't follow you on this horde-clan business at all": Donald Thomson, Radcliffe-Brown and a final note on the horde.' *Oceania*, 76, pp. 16–26. doi.org/10.1002/j.1834-4461.2006. tb03030.x

Peterson, N. 2008. 'Too sociological'? Revisiting "Aboriginal territorial organization".' In *An appreciation of difference: W.E.H. Stanner and Aboriginal Australia.* M. Hinkson and J. Beckett (eds). Aboriginal Studies Press, Canberra, pp. 185–197.

Peterson, N., Keen I., and Sansom B. 1977. 'Succession to land: Primary and secondary rights to Aboriginal estates.' Submission to the Ranger Uranium Environmental Inquiry, in, Joint Select Committee on Aboriginal Land Rights in the Northern Territory. *Official Hansard Report*, pp. 1002–1014.

Peterson N. and J. Long. 1986. *Australian territorial organisation*. Oceania Monograph, University of Sydney, Sydney.

Piddington, M.O. and R.E. 1932. 'Report on fieldwork in northwestern Australia.' *Oceania*, 2.3, pp. 342–358.

Piddington, R. 1932. 'Totemic system of the Karadjeri tribe.' *Oceania*, 2.4, pp. 373–400. doi.org/10.1002/j.1834-4461.1932.tb00041.x

Piddington, R. 1950. *An Introduction to Social Anthropology*. Volume 1. Oliver and Boyd, Edinburgh and London.

Queensland Government. 2003. *Guide to compiling a connection report for native title claims in Queensland.* Brisbane: Native Title and Indigenous Land Services. Department of Natural Resources and Mines.

Radcliffe-Brown, A.R. 1913. 'Three tribes of Western Australia.' *Journal of the Royal Anthropological Institute*, 48, pp. 143–194.

Radcliffe-Brown, A.R. 1930–31. 'The social organisation of Australian tribes.' *Oceania*, 1.1–4. (Oceania Monograph No. 1). University of Sydney, Sydney.

Radcliffe-Brown, A.R. 1945. 'Religion and society.' *Journal of the Royal Anthropological Institute*, LXXV, parts I and II.

Radcliffe-Brown, A.R. 1952. *Structure and function in primitive society.* Cohen and West, London.

Ritter, D. 2009. *Contesting native title.* Allen and Unwin, Crows Nest, NSW.

Rivers, W.H.R. 1900. 'A genealogical method of collecting social and vital statistics.' *The Journal of the Anthropological Institute of Great Britain and Ireland*, 30, pp. 74–82. doi.org/10.2307/2842619

Rose, D. 1991. *Hidden histories: Black stories from Victoria River Downs, Humbert River and Wave Hill stations.* Australian Institute of Aboriginal and Torres Strait Islander Studies, Canberra.

Rose, D. 1992. *Dingo makes us human. Life and land in an Australian Aboriginal culture.* Cambridge University Press, Cambridge.

Rose, D. 2002. 'Reflections on the use of historical evidence in the Yorta Yorta case.' In *Through a smoky mirror: History and native title.* M. Paul and G. Gray (eds). Aboriginal Studies Press, Canberra, pp. 35–47.

Roth, W.E. 1897. *Ethnological studies among the North-West-Central Queensland Aborigines.* Government Printer, Brisbane. Facsimile edition 1984, *The Queensland Aborigines,* Vol. 1. Hesperian Press, Perth.

Roth, W.E. 1906. 'Notes on government, morals and crime.' *North Queensland Ethnography*, Bulletin No. 8. Government Printer, Brisbane.

Roth, W.E. 1907. 'Burial ceremonies and disposal of the dead.' *North Queensland Ethnography*, Bulletin No. 9. Government Printer, Brisbane.

Rowley, C.D. 1980. *The destruction of Aboriginal society.* Penguin, Harmondsworth (first published 1970).

Rumsey, A. 1993. 'Language and territoriality.' In *Language and culture in Aboriginal Australia.* M. Walsh and C. Yallop (eds). Aboriginal Studies Press, Canberra, pp. 191–206.

Sackett, L. 2006. 'Anthropology purely applied.' Paper presented at the 50 year anniversary of Anthropology, University of Western Australia.

Sackett, L. 2007. 'A potential pathway.' *Anthropological Forum*, 17.2, pp. 173–175.

Salmond, J. 1920. *Jurisprudence*. Sweet and Maxwell, London.

Sansom, B. 2001. 'Irruptions of the Dreamings in post-colonial Australia.' *Oceania*, 72, pp. 1–32. doi.org/10.1002/j.1834-4461.2001.tb02762.x

Sansom, B. 2002. 'A frightened hunting ground: Epic emotions and landholding in the western reaches of Australia's Top End.' *Oceania*, 72, pp. 156–194. doi.org/10.1002/j.1834-4461.2002.tb02785.x

Sansom, B. 2006. 'The brief reach of history and the limitation of recall in traditional Aboriginal societies and cultures.' *Oceania*, 76, pp. 150–172. doi.org/10.1002/j.1834-4461.2006.tb03042.x

Sansom, B. 2007. 'Yulara and future expert reports in native title cases.' *Anthropological Forum*, 17.1, pp. 71–92. doi.org/10.1080/00664670601168575

Spencer, B. and Gillen, F.J. 1899. *The native tribes of Central Australia*. Macmillan and Co., London.

Stanner, W.E.H. 1958. 'The Dreaming.' In *Reader in comparative religion: The anthropological approach*. W.A. Lessa and E.Z. Vogt (eds). Row, Peterson, Evanston, Illinois.

Stanner, W.E.H. 1959–61. 'On Aboriginal religion.' *Oceania*, 30.2 and 4; 31.2 and 4; 32.2; 33.4 and 34.1.

Stanner, W.E.H. 1965. 'Aboriginal territorial organization: Estate, range, domain and regime.' *Oceania*, 36, pp. 1–26. doi.org/10.1002/j.1834-4461.1965.tb00275.x

Stanner, W.E.H. 2001. 'Some general principles of Aboriginal land holding.' In *People from the dawn*. W.E.H. Stanner and J.H. Martin (eds.), Solas Press, Antioch, pp. 103–118.

Stanton, J. 1984. 'Conflict, change and stability at Mt Margaret: An Aboriginal community in transition.' PhD thesis, University of Western Australia, Perth.

Strehlow, T.G.H. 1947. *Aranda traditions*. Melbourne University Press, Melbourne.

Strehlow, T.G.H. 1965. 'Culture, social structure and environment in Aboriginal Central Australia.' In *Aboriginal man in Australia. Essays in honour of Emeritus Professor A.P. Elkin.* R.M. and C.H. Berndt (eds). Angus and Robertson, Sydney, pp. 121–145.

Strelein, L. 2009. *Compromised jurisprudence: Native title cases since Mabo.* Australian Institute of Aboriginal and Torres Strait Islander Studies, Canberra.

Strelein, L. 2010. *Dialogue about land justice.* Aboriginal Studies Press, Canberra.

Sullivan, P. 2009. 'Policy change and the Indigenous Land Corporation.' AIATSIS Research Discussion Paper No. 25, Australian Institute of Aboriginal and Torres Strait Islander Studies, Canberra.

Sutton, P. 2003. *Native title in Australia: An ethnographic perspective.* Cambridge University Press, Cambridge. doi.org/10.1017/CBO 9780511481635

Sutton, P. 2007. 'Norms, statistics, and the Jango case at Yulara.' *Anthropological Forum*, 17, pp. 175–192.

Sutton, P. 2015. 'Norman Tindale and native title: His late appearance in the Jango case.' *Journal of the Anthropological Society of South Australia*, 39, pp. 26–72.

Sutton, P. 2017. 'Remembering Roxby Downs: Mythology, mining and the latent power of archives.' *Griffith Review*, 55, pp. 135–159.

Sutton, P. and Palmer, A. 1980. 'Daly River (Malak Malak) claim.' Northern Land Council, Darwin.

Tindale, N.B. 1938–1939. 'Harvard and Adelaide Universities anthropological expedition, Australia, 1938–1939. Journal and notes by Norman B. Tindale.' Ms, SA Museum, Adelaide, AA338/1/15/2.

Tindale, N.B. 1939. 'Genealogical data on the Aborigines of Australia gathered during the Harvard and Adelaide universities anthropological expedition 1938–39'. Vol. VII, including sociological cards and miscellaneous notes. South Australian Museum, Adelaide.

Tindale, N.B. 1940a. 'Distribution of Australian tribes: A field survey.' *Royal Society of South Australia*, 64.1.

Tindale, N.B. 1940b. 'Expeditions: Summary of a lecture delivered before the Society by Mr. N.B. Tindale on 23 October 1939.' *Mankind*, 2.8, pp. 281–283.

Tindale, N.B. 1941. 'A survey of the half-caste problem in South Australia.' *Proceedings of the Royal Geographical Society of Australasia (South Australian Branch)*, 42, pp. 66–161.

Tindale, N.B. 1953a. 'N.W. Australia journal.' Mss AA338-1-19-1 and 2. Unpublished manuscripts. South Australian Museum, Adelaide.

Tindale, N.B. 1953b. Genealogical sheets collected from Western Australia. Unpublished manuscripts. South Australian Museum, Adelaide.

Tindale, N.B. 1966. 'Journal of a trip to Western Australia in search of tribal data.' Unpublished manuscript. South Australian Museum, Adelaide.

Tindale, N.B. 1974. *Aboriginal tribes of Australia*. Australian National University Press, Canberra.

Tindale, N.B. 1976. 'Some ecological bases for Australian tribal boundaries.' In *Tribes and boundaries in Australia*. N. Peterson (ed.). Australian Institute of Aboriginal Studies, Canberra, pp. 12–29.

Tindale, N.B. Various dates. Genealogical sheets, unpublished manuscripts. South Australian Museum, Adelaide.

Toussaint, S. 2004. *Crossing boundaries: Cultural, legal, historical and practice issues in native title*. Melbourne University Press, Carlton, Victoria.

Trigger, D. 2011. 'Anthropology pure and profane: The politics of applied research in Aboriginal Australia.' *Anthropological Forum*, 21.3, pp. 233–255. doi.org/10.1080/00664677.2011.617675

Trigger, D. 2015a. 'The politics of social inclusion in native title negotiations.' In *Native title from Mabo to Akiba: A vehicle for change and empowerment?* S. Brennan, M. Davis, B. Edgeworth and L. Terrill (eds). Federation Press, Leichhardt, NSW, pp. 199–212.

Trigger, D. 2015b. 'Change and succession in Australian Aboriginal claims to land.' In *Strings of connectedness*. P. Toner (ed.). ANU Press, Canberra, pp. 53–73. doi.org/10.22459/SC.09.2015.03

Turner, V. 1968. *The drums of affliction*. Oxford, Clarendon Press.

Turner, V. 1974. *The ritual process*. Pelican Books, Harmondsworth.

Walker, D.M. 1980. *The Oxford companion to law*. Clarendon Press, Oxford.

Walsh, M. 2002. 'Language ownership: A key issue for native title.' In *Language and native title*. J. Henderson and D. Nash (eds). Aboriginal Studies Press, Canberra, pp. 231–244.

Warner, L. 1937. *A black civilization: A social study of an Australian tribe*. Harper Row, New York.

Weiner, J. 2007. 'Anthropology vs. Ethnography in native title: A review article in the context of Peter Sutton's *Native Title in Australia*.' *The Australian Journal of Anthropology*, 8.2.

Whittaker, J. and Bunker, T. 2013. '*De Rose v. South Australia* – the first approved native title compensation determination.' Corrs, Chambers, Westgarth, Lawyers. Available at www.corrs.com.au/publications/corrs-in-brief/de-rose-v-south-australia-the-first-approved-native-title-compensation-determination/

Williams, N. 1982. 'A boundary is to cross: Observations on Yolngu boundaries and permission.' In *Resource managers: North American and Australian hunter-gatherers*. N. Williams and E. Hunn (eds). American Association for the Advancement of Science, Boulder, Colorado, pp. 131–154.

Williams, N. 1986. *The Yolngu and their land. A system of land tenure and the fight for its recognition*. Australian Institute of Aboriginal Studies, Canberra.

Williams, N. 1999. 'The nature of "permission".' In *Land rights at risk?* J.C. Altman, F. Morphy, and T. Rowse (eds). Centre for Aboriginal Economic Policy Research, The Australian National University, pp. 53–64.

Williams, R. and McGrath, P. 2014. *Native title and Indigenous cultural heritage management. Bibliography.* AIATSIS Native Title Research Unit, Australian Institute of Aboriginal and Torres Strait Islander Studies, Canberra. Available at aiatsis.gov.au/sites/default/files/products/research_outputs_web_publication/native-title-cultural-heritage-bibliography.pdf

Wiseman, L. 2009. 'Native title compensation annotated reference list.' AIATSIS Native Title Research Unit, Australian Institute of Aboriginal and Torres Strait Islander Studies, Canberra.

Case law

Akiba on behalf of the Torres Strait Islanders of the Regional Seas Claim Group v State of Queensland (No. 2) [2010] FCA 643.

Aplin on behalf of the Waanyi Peoples v State of Queensland [2010] FCA 625.

Aplin on behalf of the Waanyi Peoples v State of Queensland (No. 3) [2010] FCA 1515.

Bennell v State of Western Australia [2006] FCA 1243.

Bodney v Bennell (2008) 167 FCR 84.

Daniel v State of Western Australia [2003] FCA 666.

Dempsey on behalf of the Bularnu, Waluwarra and Wangkayujuru People v State of Queensland (No. 2) [2014] FCA 528.

Gawirrin Gumana v Northern Territory of Australia (No. 2) [2005] FCA 1425.

Graham on behalf of the Ngadju People v State of Western Australia [2012] FCA 1455.

Griffiths v Northern Territory of Australia (No. 3) [2016] FCA 900.

Griffiths v Northern Territory of Australia [2006] FCA 903.

Harrington-Smith on behalf of the Wongatha People v State of Western Australia (No. 9) [2007] FCA 31.

Hunter v State of Western Australia [2009] FCA 654.

Jango v Northern Territory of Australia (2006) 152 FCR 150.

Jango v Northern Territory of Australia [2006] FCA 318.

Lampton on behalf of the Juru People v State of Queensland [2015] FCA 609 (Juru People Part B).

Lovett on behalf of the Gunditjmara People v State of Victoria [2007] FCA 474.

Mabo v Queensland [No. 2] (1992) 175 CLR 1.

Mabo v Queensland [1992] 1 Qd R 78.

McGlade v Native Title Registrar [2017] FCAFC.

Members of the Yorta Yorta Aboriginal Community v Victoria (2002) 214 CLR 422.

Members of the Yorta Yorta Aboriginal Community v Victoria [2002] HCA 58.

Milirrpum v Nabalco Pty Ltd (1971) 17 FLR 141.

Neowarra v State of Western Australia [2003] FCA 1402.

Northern Territory of Australia v Alyawarr, Kaytetye, Warumungu, Wakaya Native Title Claim Group [2005] 145 FCAFC 135.

Northern Territory of Australia v Griffiths) [2017] FCAFC 106.

Prior on behalf of the Juru (Cape Upstart) People v State of Queensland (No 2) [2011] FCA 819.

Rubibi Community v State of Western Australia (No. 5) [2005] FCA 1025.

Sampi on behalf of the Bardi and Jawi People v State of Western Australia [2010] FCAFC 26.

Sampi v State of Western Australia [2005] FCA 777.

The Lardil Peoples v State of Queensland [2004] FCA 298.

Ward on behalf of the Miriuwung and Gajerrong People v Western Australia (1998) 159 ALR 483.

Ward v Western Australia (Miriuwung Gajerrong #4 Determination) [2006] FCA 1848.

Watson on behalf of the Nyikina Mangala People v State of Western Australia [2015] FCA 1132.

Index

Note: page numbers in **bold** indicate tables, figures or other illustrative material. Footnotes are indicated by page numbers in the form '96n14', this example meaning footnote 14 on page 96.

early texts
archival documents and disputes, 195
and comparative ethnography, 161
debate regarding age, 162–3, 164
limitations of, 161–2, 164, 190, 198, 206
use of in native title, 8, 160–3, 164, 190, 194
effective sovereignty *see* sovereignty
Elkin, A.P., 75, 79, 115, 116, 148, 163, 164, 194, 210, 223
estate (of country group), 59, 80, 88, 89, 103, 104, 194
choice, exercise in relation to, 91–2, 97
deceased *see* succession
early view of, 82
loss of, 89, 89n8, 199–200
movement between, 72, 74, 82
and range, 80
rights in several, 75, 80, 81, 82, 87, 90–1
size of, 72, 75
totemic affiliation with, 79
see also local organisation; local organisation—clan; country group
ethics *see* anthropologist
ethnography *see* early texts
Eucla, 163
evidence, 30, 48, 51, 53, 60, 68, 88, 89, 95, 100, 104, 112, 138, 139, 153, 154, 155, 188–9, 232, 246
of claimants, 1, 2, 7, 22, 34, 135, 136, 136n3, 137, 140, 149, 150, 152, 157, 220, 233, 243
see also anthropologists—as expert witness; *Evidence Act*; hearsay
Evidence Act, 136n4, 136n5, 139
expert evidence practice note, 201n18, 205

expert witness
see anthropologists; anthropology
extinguishment and native title, 17, 20–1, 65, 227, 228

family history *see* genealogies
family tree *see* genealogies
Family Tree Maker, 224
Federal Court of Australia, 1, 17, 20–1, 22, 112, 185, 186–7, 188, 201, 203, 205, 227, 228, 229, 230, 241, 242
field data, 7, 29, 43, 50, 59, 61, 70, 79, 81, 83, 98–9, 108, 119–21, 124, 129, 134, 151–2, 156, 163–4, 166, 172, 174, 176–7, 180, 182, 182n21, 205, 213, 220–1, 143, 248
field notes, 121, 131, 174, 202, 204n21, 214
see also field data
fieldwork *see* anthropology
filiation, 8, 118, 211, 220–1
matrifiliation, 64, 74, 81, 90, 94
patrifiliation, 72, 75, 79, 81, 90, 94, 210
see also adoption; descent—patrilineal and matrilineal
Finniss River, 69
Form 1, 211, 211n3
Forrest River, 165, 168, 169
foundation ethnography, 160, 163–4, 166, 172, 183, 189
importance in disputes, 189–90, 194
see also early texts
Fraser Range, 179
'future acts', 17, 229, 240, 241, 244

Gallagher, M., 13n4
Ganggalida, 64, 66, 67
Gawirrin Gumana v Northern Territory of Australia, 138
GEDCOM files, 224, 224n6

www.ingramcontent.com/pod-product-compliance
Lightning Source LLC
Chambersburg PA
CBHW050807270326
41926CB00026B/4608